THE IMPACT OF SUPREME COURT DECISIONS ON US INSTITUTIONS

This book bridges the disciplines of legal studies and sociology in its engaging introduction to the history, purpose, function, and influence of the Supreme Court, demonstrating through ten landmark decisions the Court's impact on the five key sociological institutions in the United States: family, education, religion, government, and economy. It gives an insightful picture of how these major decisions have additionally affected other sociological categories such as gender, sexual orientation, race, class/inequality, and deviance. The reader not only gains familiarity with foundational concepts in both sociology and constitutional law, but is given tools to decipher the legal language of Supreme Court decisions through non-intimidating abridgments of those decisions, enhancing their critical literacy. This book demonstrates the direct applicability of the Supreme Court to the lives of Americans and how landmark decisions have far-reaching repercussions that affect all of us.

The Impact of Supreme Court Decisions on US Institutions is essential reading for undergraduate students in social science courses as well as others interested in the workings of the justice system.

Robert Costello, JD., EdD., is Chair and Professor of Criminal Justice at SUNY Nassau Community College and Adjunct Professor of Sociology at Hofstra University. He earned a Doctor of Education from Dowling College, a Master of Arts in Criminal Justice from SUNY Albany, a Master of Arts in Sociology and a Juris Doctorate both from St. John's University and a Bachelor of Arts in Social Sciences from Hofstra University. An author of over 75 publications, he received a Fulbright Scholar's Award in Law to lecture at the University of Malta Faculty of Law. Other honors include serving as a Visiting Scholar at the University of Cambridge's Institute of Criminology/Socio-Legal Group, Associate Faculty Member at Columbia University's Faculty Seminar Series/Drugs & Society, and Research Associate at Hofstra University's Maurice A. Deane School of Law/Center for Children, Families and the Law. His prior books include *New York's Criminal Justice System* (2019) and *New Jersey's Criminal Justice System* (2020). He also writes a column for *Criminal Justice*, a quarterly periodical of the American Bar Association. A dedicated classroom educator, his work and commitment to students has been recognized with various honors including a SUNY Chancellor's Award for Excellence in Teaching, Faculty Appreciation Awards from the NCC Center for Students with Disabilities and the NCC Student Organization of Latinos.

Admitted to practice law in New York State, he is a Certified Impartial Hearing Officer and adjudicates disputes between parents and public schools over special education matters within the New York City region. He is also admitted to the United States Federal District Court for the Southern District of New York and the United States Federal District Court for the Eastern District of New York. His community work includes serving as a board member for several non-profits and on editorial boards for academic journals.

Colleen Eren, PhD., is Program Director of Criminology and Criminal Justice and an Associate Professor at William Paterson University. A member of the Criminal Justice Research Alliance, her first book, *Bernie Madoff and the Crisis: The Public Trial of Capitalism* (2017) examined how the Ponzi scheme became a vehicle through which to discuss socio-economic issues behind the financial crisis of 2008. Her upcoming book, *Reform Nation: The Movement Against Mass Incarceration*, with Stanford University Press explores the unlikely confluence of stakeholders uniting around criminal justice reform for the past 20 years. She has been published in numerous academic journals and media outlets, including *The Journal of White Collar and Corporate Crime*, the *Journal of Criminal Justice Education*, *New Politics*, as well as in *the New York Times*. She previously served as Director of Organizing at New Yorkers Against the Death Penalty, helping to successfully lead a statewide campaign, and was a steering committee member of Amnesty's Program to Abolish the Death Penalty. She is an executive committee board member of New Hour for Women and Children.

THE IMPACT OF SUPREME COURT DECISIONS ON US INSTITUTIONS

A Sociology of Law Primer

Robert Costello and Colleen Eren

Routledge
Taylor & Francis Group
NEW YORK AND LONDON

First published 2022
by Routledge
605 Third Avenue, New York, NY 10158

and by Routledge
2 Park Square, Milton Park, Abingdon, Oxon, OX14 4RN

Routledge is an imprint of the Taylor & Francis Group, an informa business

Library of Congress Cataloging-in-Publication Data
Names: Eren, Colleen P., author. | Costello, Robert G., author.
Title: The impact of Supreme Court decisions on U.S. institutions : a sociology of law primer / Colleen Eren & Robert Costello.
Description: New York, NY ; Abingdon, Oxon : Routledge, 2022. | Includes bibliographical references and index.
Identifiers: LCCN 2021016506 (print) | LCCN 2021016507 (ebook) | ISBN 9780367898496 (hardback) | ISBN 9780367898489 (paperback) | ISBN 9781003021438 (ebook)
Subjects: LCSH: United States. Supreme Court. | Sociological jurisprudence—United States—Cases. | Constitutional law—United States—Cases. | LCGFT: Textbooks.
Classification: LCC KF8742 .E74 2022 (print) | LCC KF8742 (ebook) | DDC 347.7326/0264—dc23
LC record available at https://lccn.loc.gov/2021016506
LC ebook record available at https://lccn.loc.gov/2021016507

ISBN: 9780367898496 (hbk)
ISBN: 9780367898489 (pbk)
ISBN: 9781003021438 (ebk)

DOI: 10.4324/9781003021438

Typeset in Bembo
by Apex CoVantage, LLC

All royalties from this book will be donated directly to Gideon's Promise, a public defender organization whose mission is to transform the criminal justice system by building a movement of public defenders who provide equal justice for marginalized communities. website: Additional information about Gideon's Promise is available by visiting their website: gideonspromise.org

RC: *For Martha & James Costello: thank you, Mom and Dad, for everything!*

CE: *For my undergraduate professors, now life-long friends, who took me under their wing: Silvia Federici, Arthur Dobrin, and Conrad Herold*

CONTENTS

INTRODUCTION

The United States is home to over 300 million people from different socioeconomic backgrounds, racial and ethnic groups, cultural heritages, gender identities, and religious beliefs. With such a diverse population, it is pivotal to have a judicial system in place that recognizes the country's differences but that also sustains its unity by binding together so many communities and creeds. The main component of that system is the Supreme Court.

Established on September 24, 1789, after President George Washington signed the Judiciary Act, the Supreme Court comprised six justices—the Jay Court—who had to commit to serving the court until their retirement or death. Article III of the US Constitution gave the Supreme Court its power and authority, granting the highest court jurisdiction over the constitutionality of laws. Once the Supreme Court has made a decision, it is final and can only be changed by another Supreme Court decision or by adding a constitutional amendment. Although the structure of the court underwent several modifications over time—including the number of justices allowed on the court, which was eventually settled on nine with the Judiciary Act of 1869—its authority and scope remained intact.

The Supreme Court justices have decided cases, referred to as landmark cases, that have had far-reaching legal, but also social and political implications. These decisions do not take place absent a socio-historical context. As such, over the years, the Supreme Court rulings have reflected and also have been reflected in evolving norms and standards. These decisions have had a direct impact (and not always positive, by contemporary sensibilities) on those living in the US and the major social institutions that envelop their everyday lives—education, family, religion, politics/government, and economy—especially as they relate to the rights and privileges of people based on their gender, sexual orientation, race/ethnicity, and class status within these institutions. The Justices, for instance, desegregated schools, prohibited gender-based stereotyping in hiring decisions, upheld the minimum wage, defended voting rights, prohibited laws that restricted or undermined the constitutional right to privacy, declared interracial marriage—and later on, same-sex marriage—to be constitutional, and much more.

Given the interdisciplinary importance of the Supreme Court, we noticed the lack of texts that have used these crucial landmark decisions as a way of exploring foundational concepts, theories, and trends in the social sciences. The purpose of this volume is therefore twofold. First, it provides an approachable and engaging introduction for readers to a socio-legal perspective, in other words, looking at the relationship between law and society. We do this by examining the

DOI: 10.4324/9781003021438-1

background context in which ten carefully selected landmark decisions were situated, as well as those decisions' influence on five key sociological institutions over time. How did they influence US history, society, and affect individual Americans' lives? Second, it provides a primer in both constitutional law, giving the reader a clear understanding of the role of the Supreme Court, how decisions are reached, a familiarity with the actual text of decisions and legal concepts, as well as a thorough grounding in fundamental concepts in the discipline of sociology. In doing so, we attempt to provide an essential framework for readers to further explore Supreme Court decisions and the law more broadly through a sociological and historical lens. As such, we hope this volume will be an asset to students and instructors across disciplines such as sociology, legal studies, and political science, as well as the interested general reader.

Organization and Contents of the Book

This book is divided into seven chapters. Chapter 1 covers a thorough history of the US Supreme Court, connecting the US Constitution to the US Supreme Court, explains how Justices are selected, and instructs the reader on how to read a Supreme Court decision. It also highlights a few landmark cases argued by the court. Chapter 2 presents an introduction to the major sociological institutions that will be referenced throughout the book: family, education, religion, politics/government, and economy. It provides sociological definitions for these institutions, introducing readers to foundational concepts and theorists within sociology such as Max Weber, Karl Marx, and Erving Goffman. The chapter sketches these institutions' essential characteristics, and gives an overview of historical and current trends in the United States for each of them.

Chapters 3–7 each center around two landmark decisions and their impact over time on one key societal institution in the US—family, education, religion, government, and economy, respectively. These chapters begin with the background history of the plaintiff or defendant—aiming at providing readers with enough context to understand why and how the case eventually reached the highest court. The chapters proceed to an abridged text of the decision itself, allowing the reader to become familiar with the language and argumentation used. They move on and conclude with a comprehensive examination of how the decision has impacted that institution, tying in key sociological concepts, theories, and empirical data. The book also presents four short legal boxes that focus on the history of the Fourteenth Amendment, the due process clause, the equal protection clause, and Title VII of the Civil Rights Act of 1964, as well as sociology boxes that focus on tightly connected topics such as inequality in the US, and the healthcare system. To better focus the reader, reinforce the material, and provide for discussion, learning objectives, key terms, and review questions are provided.

Focusing on the institution of education, Chapter 3 covers the landmark case of *Brown v. Board of Education of Topeka* of 1954. In a unanimous decision, the Supreme Court ruled in favor of Brown and stated that racial segregation in public schools violated the Equal Protection Clause of the Fourteenth Amendment. This decision's impact on the institution of education is explored by looking at the effects of integration in K-12 schools, the failed promise of the decision as evidenced by persisting segregation, and its legacy in higher education. This chapter also explores the *Rodriguez v. San Antonio School District* decision, which the Supreme Court heard and argued in 1972. Demetrio Rodriguez and other concerned parents formed the Edgewood District Concerned Parents Association and sued the State of Texas for its unequal public-school funding. The nine Justices voted 5–4 for the San Antonio School District. After presenting the case decision, we look at the influence of sociological variables such as class, socioeconomic status, wealth inequality, and income inequality on both formal and informal educational settings since *Rodriguez*.

Moving on to the institution of family, Chapter 4 highlights two pivotal cases. First, it focuses on the 1967 Supreme Court case of *Loving v. Virginia*. Richard Loving and his wife Mildred were arrested for violating Virginia's Racial Integrity Act of 1924, which positioned interracial marriage as a crime. This case resulted in a unanimous decision for the plaintiff. We probe how this landmark decision has left its imprint on US society, looking at interracial marriages and pre and post *Loving*, interracial marriage stability, children in such multiracial families, and attitudes towards interracial relationships in the United States. Second, the chapter presents the 2015 *Obergefell v. Hodges* case, where the appellants sued their state agencies for banning same-sex marriages or for failing to recognize as legal same-sex marriages that occurred in states that allowed them. In a 5–4 decision, the Roberts Court sided with Obergefell. Among the sociological impacts of this decision, we look at how *Obergefell* affected the institution of family in terms of marriage, the growth of same-sex families, and changes to American attitudes toward same-sex unions.

The institution of religion is the focus of the next chapter. Chapter 5 covers the *Engel v. Vitale* decision of 1962, where the Supreme Court, in a 6–1 ruling, decided that holding non-mandatory and non-denominational prayers in public schools violated the establishment of religion clause of the First Amendment of the US Constitution. In this section, we investigate the decision's impact on the institution of religion by looking at both Robert Bellah's concept of civil religion in the United States, and well as traditional institutionalized religion. We show how attitudes about religion generally as well as in schools in the US have changed, and provide a brief history of the role of religion in US schools prior to *Engels*. Chapter 5 also focuses on one of the most controversial cases of the 20th century, which although it did not deal directly with religion, has become inextricably meshed with the issue: *Roe v. Wade*. In 1973, the Supreme Court, in a 7–2 ruling, stated that the Due Process Clause of the Fourteenth Amendment protects a woman's right to privacy and, as such, her right to choose whether or not to terminate her pregnancy. In this section, we show how this case has affected religion in the US, particularly through the involvement of religious institutions in the healthcare system, the politicization of religion, and personal religious beliefs.

Chapter 6 explores the institution of government through the controversial case of *Citizens United v. Federal Election Commission* of 2010, in which the Justices sided with Citizens United in a 5–4 ruling, regulating financial support of political campaigns. This decision had a large impact on government, as we present an investigation of how it altered the balance of power among individuals and groups to have their interests represented and policies benefiting them enacted. Specifically, we look at Americans' attitudes to money in politics, how *Citizens United* affected the financing of campaigns, and the link between money, organizations, and winning elections. The chapter concludes the focus on government with the 1857 case of *Dred Scott v. Sandford*, in which the Supreme Court ruled 7–2 that Dred Scott, born enslaved in Missouri and later becoming a free man in Illinois and the Louisiana Territory, could be excluded from the rights of US citizenship. We show the impact of the case sociologically by looking at the connection between race, power, and citizenship, with a focus on the way in which the *Scott* decision's disenfranchisement of people partially on the basis of race continues de facto through the criminal justice system.

The final chapter covers two cases that affected the institution of economy in the United States. Chapter 7 offers insight into the *West Coast Hotel v. Parrish* decision of 1937, in which the Supreme Court ruled 5–4 in favor of Elsie Parrish and agreed that the establishment of a minimum wage for women was indeed constitutional, as well as into the 1971 case of *Philipps v. Martin Marietta*. In a decision in favor of Ida Philipps, the Supreme Court ruled that refusing to hire women because of their school-aged children violated the Civil Rights Act of 1964. Among the sociological implications covered in this chapter are the socio-economic effect of minimum wage laws more broadly, the persistence of the wage gap in spite of a minimum wage for women, current minimum wage laws and attitudes about these in the US, the rise of dual-income households and changes to divisions of labor, and changes in the workplace and society in response to the need for work/life balance.

Taken as a whole, these seven chapters offer a foundational understanding of the history of the US Supreme Court and the most important cases ever argued by the Justices that have had a direct impact on the very fabric of American society, while at the same time giving the reader the sociological vocabulary, theory, and insight with which to understand these changes.

Robert Costello and Colleen Eren
March 2021

1

THE US SUPREME COURT

A Brief Overview

Learning Objectives

After reading this chapter, students should be able to:

- Describe the United States Supreme Court
- Explain why, when, and how the Supreme Court was established
- Discuss a few of the most important cases ever presented to the Supreme Court
- Define the process in which Supreme Court Justices are selected
- Understand how to read a Supreme Court opinion
- Explain how the Supreme Court decides which cases to hear
- Discuss what happened during the Constitutional Convention
- Evaluate how important the US Constitution is to the Supreme Court

Key Terms

Associate Justice
Certiorari
Chief Justice
Constitutional Convention
Court of Appeals
Framers of the Constitution
Judicial Review
Judiciary Act of 1789
Main Opinion
Per Curiam Opinion
Plaintiff
Preamble
Provision
Respondent
Supreme Court
Supreme Court Opinion
Syllabus

Introduction: History of the United States Supreme Court

In 1787, the **Framers of the Constitution** gathered in Philadelphia. Over 50 Framers—the youngest of them being Jonathan Dayton, who was in his mid-20s, and the oldest being Benjamin Franklin, who was in his 80s—discussed the need to create a third branch of the US Government, one that would accompany the executive and the legislative branches: the judicial

DOI: 10.4324/9781003021438-2

FIGURE 1.1 US Supreme Court

branch. With memories of the revolution against the British monarchy still fresh, the Framers' main goal was to create an independent federal judiciary, a desire brought on by their certainty that the new national political branches could not go unchecked.

Two years later, the First United States Congress adopted the federal statute of the Judiciary Act, which represented the establishment of the federal judiciary of the United States. The **Judiciary Act of 1789** was originally titled *An Act to Establish the Judicial Courts of the United States.* The Act, which President George Washington signed on September 1789, made the creation of the Supreme Court official, but it did specify that Congress had the authority

> to create lower federal courts as needed. Principally authored by Senator Oliver Ellsworth of Connecticut, the Judiciary Act of 1789 established the structure and jurisdiction of the federal court system and created the position of attorney general. Although amended throughout the years by Congress, the basic outline of the federal court system established by the First Congress remains largely intact today.
>
> *(Library of Congress, n.d.a)*

According to Article III, Section 1 of the US Constitution, the Act originally declared that the number of justices on the Supreme Court should be six—one Chief Justice and five Assembly Justices:

> Be it enacted by the Senate and House of Representatives of the United States of America in Congress assembled, That the Supreme Court of the United States shall consist of a chief justice and five associate justices, any four of whom shall be a quorum, and shall hold annually at the seat of government two sessions, the one commencing the first Monday of February, and the other the first Monday of August.
>
> *(Yale Law School Lillian Goldman Law Library, n.d.)*

With the Judiciary Act of 1869, the number of Justices rose from six to nine—one Chief Justice and eight Associate Justices, all having a lifetime tenure unless they resign, are removed from office, or die.

In 1789, the first assembly of the Supreme Court of the United States of America was officially appointed by President George Washington, who chose John Jay as the Chief Justice and John Rutledge, William Cushing, James Iredell, James Wilson, and John Blair as Associate Justices. Washington appointed these men because he considered them faithful supporters of the US Constitution as well as the Federalist cause. Many of them had also honorably served in the American Revolution and were actively involved in the political life of their own states and that had, over time, gained the invaluable support of prominent Federalists—meaning they had the blessing of those who favored a strong national government.

The Supreme Court Justices met for the first time in the Royal Exchange Building in New York City—then, the nation's capital—in 1790. When Philadelphia became the capital, the Supreme Court met there from 1791 to 1800 and, once Washington D.C. was built, the Court moved to the Capitol building in 1801. However, when the British burned the building down in 1814, the Justices were forced to meet elsewhere—sometimes even in private homes. It wasn't until 1929 that the Supreme Court was finally granted its own building in Washington, D.C. after Chief Justice William Taft—who was also President of the United States of America from 1909 to 1913—urged Congress to establish a budget for the project—which ended up costing almost $10 million (around $154 million in 2021). Construction for the US Supreme Court building ended in 1935. Today, the building—which is made with marble imported from Italy—features many amenities, including a gym on the third floor with a basketball court named The Highest Court in the Land. However, people are not allowed to play basketball while the Court is in session.

Under the presidency of George Washington, 11 Supreme Court Justices were appointed, and the record-setting number still holds to this day. In fact, the only other President who ever came close to matching Washington's record was Franklin D. Roosevelt with nine Justices, while William Harrison, Zachary Taylor, Andrew Johnson, and Jimmy Carter did not appoint any new Justice during their presidential terms. The political ideology of each Justice on the Supreme Court certainly matters when it comes to choosing a new Justice. However, even though Justices appointed by a Republican President currently tend to lean more toward conservative values while those appointed by a Democratic President tend to lean more toward liberal values, it does not mean that their political party affiliations determine the outcome of a specific case. For example, even though President Ronald Reagan appointed Associate Justice Anthony Kennedy, a Republican whose tenure on the Supreme Court began in 1988 and lasted until his retirement in 2018, Kennedy was considered the swing vote during the Roberts

Court—especially after Associate Justice Sandra O'Connor retired—as he tended to take a more liberal approach rather than the more obvious conservative one.

But what criteria are taken into account when Supreme Court Justices are selected and appointed? As we've already seen, it is the President of the United States of America who nominates a Justice, who is then approved by the Senate by simply voting for the candidate—the majority wins. Although all Justices must have been trained in the law, it might come as a surprise that the job requirements to be considered a potential candidate for the role of Supreme Court Justice do *not* include being a native-born citizen of the United States of America, being of a certain age, being a lawyer, or having graduated from law school. For example, James F. Byrnes, who was Associate Justice on the Stone Court from 1941 to 1942, not only did not graduate from law school; he never graduated from high school. Instead, he was self-taught and passed the Bar at the age of 23 after studying law on his own. Robert Jackson, who was an Associate Justice on two different courts—the Stone Court (1941–1946) and the Vinson Court (1946–1953)—studied law at the Albany Law School in New York. However, he only received a graduation diploma from the university because he was only 20 years old at the time he graduated and, as such, did not meet the age requirement that stated a student had to be at least 21 to graduate from law school. Eventually—30 years later—he was presented with the actual law degree.

When a new Justice is nominated by the President and approved by the Senate, he or she must take the constitutional oath of office. Over the years, there have been many occasions in which the new candidate has made history with his or her constitutional oath of office, but none of them can perhaps be compared to the one that Thurgood Marshall took.

Born in 1908 in Maryland, Thurgood—whose original name was Thoroughgood until he shortened it to the one he's remembered by—descended from enslaved people from both sides of his family. His parents instilled in him a love and respect for the United States Constitution and his father made sure to take him to hear court cases so he could witness the art of debating, which is why he wrote that his father, although never told him to become a lawyer, eventually turned him into one by constantly challenging him to prove every statement he ever made.

Hugo Black was born 22 years before Marshall, in 1886. The youngest of eight children, Black originally wanted to become a doctor like his older brother, who however recommended that young Black attend law school instead—which he did, even though he had never finished high school. After serving in the army during World War I, Black joined the Ku Klux Klan, which granted him membership for life, information revealed once he became Associate Justice to the US Supreme Court in 1937. After the uproar caused by this revelation—which President Roosevelt, who had nominated him for the Supreme Court role, stated he was unaware of—Black admitted that, although he did join the Klan, he had also resigned and had absolutely no intention of ever joining the Klan ever again.

Marshall's and Black's paths would eventually cross when Marshall asked Black—who was once an Alabama Klansman—to administer him the oath when Marshall was voted by the Senate to the Supreme Court, a decision that was rather symbolic and spoke volumes as to how committed Marshall was to making an overture to the South. Hugo Black's acceptance of Marshall's proposal was also rather significant as he had also proven his liberal bona fides on the Supreme Court.

After making history also for becoming the first African American Supreme Court Justice—one of two to date, the other one being Clarence Thomas who actually replaced Marshall himself—Marshall voted on the *Brown v. Board of Education* case, among many others.

Demographics of the United States Supreme Court Justices

Of the 115 Justices that have served on the Supreme Court since its establishment, there have been:

- One hundred and eight white men Justices
- Five women Justices (Sandra Day O'Connor, Ruth Ginsburg, Sonia Sotomayor, Elena Kagan, and Amy Coney Barrett)
- One Latina Justice (Sonia Sotomayor)
- Two African American men Justices (Thurgood Marshall and Clarence Thomas)
- One Italian American Justice (Antonin Scalia)
- Eight Jewish Justices
- None have identified as members of the LGBTQ+ community

The Supreme Court has changed significantly since its establishment in 1790, especially in its everyday operations and customs. For example, during the Marshall Court only had a few cases to deal with and, for this reason, didn't need to meet for longer than six weeks. However, during the more recent Roberts Court, the Justices meet for nine months—beginning in October of each year and ending in June the following year. Even though in the early days of the Supreme Court, the Justices only met for a short period of time, they were assigned other duties that exhausted them to the point that Chief Justice Jay was close to resigning. In fact,

> The Judiciary Act of 1789 required them to journey twice a year to distant parts of the country and preside over circuit courts. For decades they would grumble, and hope Congress would change this system; but Congress meant to keep them aware of local opinion and state law.

Therefore,

> Stagecoaches jolted the Justices from city to city. Sometimes they spent 19 hours a day on the road. North of Boston and in the South, roads turned into trails. Justice Iredell, struggling around the Carolinas and Georgia on circuit, and hurrying to Philadelphia twice a year as well, led the life of a traveling postboy.
>
> *(The Supreme Court Historical Society, n.d.)*

Finally, in 1793, Congress decided that one circuit trip a year for the Supreme Court Justices would suffice.

Something else that has changed since 1790 is the attire that Supreme Court Justices wear. In fact, even though business was lacking for the Justices at the beginning, the courtrooms were full, and spectators admired the robes worn by Justices for their class, elegance, and the way they carried themselves. However, one day, while Associate Justice Cushing was walking down the streets of New York City, wearing the typical full-bottom professional wig of British judges, and little boys were running after him. Suddenly, a sailor looked at him and shouted, "My eye! What a wig!" That reaction prompted Justice Cushing to never wear the wig again (The Supreme Court Historical Society, n.d.).

Periods Within the Supreme Court's History

Since the establishment of the Supreme Court, there have been 17 courts, each one named after the Chief Justice's last name. After the Jay Court, which only lasted five years given the Chief Justice's resignation, the Rutledge Court began. However, the Rutledge Court ended after only 138 days because the Chief Justice was denied confirmation by the Senate—the Chief Justice is nominated by the President and confirmed by the US Senate.

- The Ellsworth Court (1796–1800)
- The Marshall Court (1801–1835)
- The Taney Court (1836–1864)
- The Chase Court (1864–1873)
- The Waite Court (1874–1888)
- The Fuller Court (1888–1910)
- The White Court (1910–1921)
- The Taft Court (1921–1930)
- The Hughes Court (1930–1941)
- The Stone Court (1941–1946)
- The Vinson Court (1946–1953)
- The Warren Court (1953–1969)
- The Burger Court (1969–1986)
- The Rehnquist Court (1986–2005)
- The Roberts Court (2005–present)

The first case ever presented to the Supreme Court did not even require the then-six Justices to discuss the case at all, as it ended in a settlement. The case, called *Van Staphorst v. Maryland*, was brought to the attention of the Court in 1791 because, during the Revolutionary War, the State of Maryland had been loaned money by the Van Staphorst brothers. However, once the War was over, the State of Maryland had not paid the loan back and—to make matters worse—had allegedly refused to return the money that the brothers had temporarily given them. This obviously went against the terms and conditions that had been set in place by the Van Staphorst brothers, who were determined to get their money back, even if it meant going all the way to the Supreme Court. After being threatened with the very real possibility of having to face a litigation, the State of Maryland reached a settlement with the brothers and managed to keep the case outside of the Court.

The first important case presented to the Jay Court—one of four presented to this specific court—that had a significant impact was *Chisholm v. Georgia* and it came two years after *Van Staphorst v. Maryland*. The case focused on a dispute that occurred in South Carolina the year prior, in 1792, when

> Alexander Chisholm, who was the executor of the Robert Farquhar's estate, tried to sue Georgia State in the Supreme Court regarding payments for goods that were owned by Farquhar from the American Revolutionary War. General Edmund Randolph, the US Attorney, argued on behalf of the plaintiff. Meanwhile, Georgia refused to appear as the defendant, claiming that it could not be sued as a sovereign state without granting consent to the suit.

The Court decided in favor of the plaintiff.

> The justices argued that Article III, Section II, of the Constitution rescinded the sovereign immunity of the states and gave federal courts the power to hear disputes between States and private citizens. Because of the case, the Eleventh Amendment of the Constitution was ratified in 1795. Doing so removed federal jurisdiction in situations where citizens of a specific state tried to sue another state. However, a citizen of one state still had the power to sue the Federal courts if the state consented to the suit or if Congress abrogated the immunity of the state under the Fourteenth Amendment.
>
> *(Laws, n.d.)*

In the 230 years of the Supreme Court ruling, there have been many more important cases that have shaped the course of history for the United States of America, only a sample of which will be covered in the chapters to follow as we explore their impact on US institutions. We briefly mention a few other examples here. *Marbury v. Madison* was one of those cases:

> At the end of President John Adams' term, his Secretary of State failed to deliver documents commissioning William Marbury as Justice of the Peace in the District of Columbia. Once President Thomas Jefferson was sworn in, in order to keep members of the opposing political party from taking office, he told James Madison, his Secretary of State, to not deliver the documents to Marbury. Marbury then sued James Madison asking the Supreme Court to issue a writ requiring him to deliver the documents necessary to officially make Marbury Justice of the Peace.
>
> *(Landmark Cases of the US Supreme Court, n.d.)*

Presented to the Marshall Court, it established the **judicial review**, meaning the power that the Court has to strike down a law the Justices determine to be against the Constitution of the United States of America. However, many argue that this case might as well have been called *Marshall v. Jefferson*. Chief Justice Marshall and President Thomas Jefferson were second cousins with a strenuous relationship to say the least and their well-documented—yet not that well-mannered—exchanges eventually led to a heated confrontation regarding what the actual role of the judiciary branch should have been in comparison to the other two branches of the government.

The two high-profile individuals complained about each other and questioned each other's authority. Jefferson tried to impeach Marshall, and Marshall declared that his second cousin was completely unfit to be President. However, aside from their personal animosity, they also strongly disagreed on the "proper role of government and the appropriate balance between the judicial and the executive branches." After Marshall declared that "courts, as well as other departments are bound by [the Constitution]," and that " 'it is emphatically the province and duty of the judicial department' what the Constitution means," he established one of the main principles of the US Supreme Court that still stands today—which is why the portraits of Marbury and Madison are showcased in the Justices' dining room in the Supreme Court (O'Connor, 2014, pp. 5–6).

In recent years, one of the most important cases that the Supreme Court argued was *Whole Woman's Health v. Hellerstedt*, which focused on "Two **provisions** [bold added] in a Texas law—requiring physicians who perform abortions to have admitting privileges at a nearby hospital and requiring abortion clinics in the state to have facilities comparable to an ambulatory surgical center," that "place a substantial obstacle in the path of women seeking an abortion, constitute an undue burden on abortion access, and therefore violate the Constitution" (SCOTUSblog, n.d.).

In 2016, the Roberts Court, through Associate Justice Breyer, delivered the decision stating that,

> We agree with the District Court that the surgical center requirement, like the admitting privileges requirement, provides few, if any, health benefits for women, poses a substantial obstacle to women seeking abortion, and constitutes an "undue burden" on their constitutional right to do so.
>
> *(Texas Department of State Health Services, "Syllabus", n.d.)*

The verbiage used to deliver the decision is a direct reference to two important cases that came before this one: *Roe v. Wade* (1973) and *Planned Parenthood of Southeastern Pa v. Casey* (1992).

The first case, *Roe v. Wade* (see Chapter 5) which was argued in the Burger Court, resulted in the Supreme Court decision that a woman's right to take control of her body by deciding whether or not she is pregnant, was more important than the state's desire to control the unborn child's life—highlighting that this decision would be valid until the child was born, at which point the state had the authority to protect the child's life by ruling over the mother's choice to have an abortion.

The second case, discussed once again by the Roberts Court, declared that

> there "exists" an "undue burden" on a woman's right to decide to have an abortion, and consequently a provision of law is constitutionally invalid, if the "purpose or effect" of the provision "is to place a substantial obstacle in the path of a woman seeking an abortion before the fetus attains viability".
>
> *(SCOTUS Syllabus, n.d.)*

Therefore, the Supreme Court decision in 2016, which had a domino-effect on other states that had tried to place restrictions on abortion—including Wisconsin, Alabama, and Mississippi where these attempts failed—stood on solid foundations set by these two strong precedents that were clearly referenced in the Supreme Court decision.

Reading a Supreme Court Decision

Reading a Supreme Court decision—which is known as **opinion**—can be an overwhelming task, especially considering that, on average, the Supreme Court issues 75 opinions a year and each opinion has roughly 5,000 words. However, each opinion follows a similar structure, which makes the reading process easier to handle. In chapters 3–7, we provide abbreviated decisions so the reader can gain experience with this process. Before even digging into the document itself, it is important to notice that the heading contains some of the most important information of the opinion: Case name—which states the parties involved, the first being the **plaintiff**, meaning the person or group who initiated the lawsuit, against the **respondent**, meaning the person or party that will have to defend themselves against the lawsuit filed by the plaintiff, which is why every case follows the typical *Plaintiff v. Respondent* structure; court term in which the opinion was announced; case docket number; dates when the case was discussed and the decision was taken. It is important to know that

> there might be an explanation of where the case came from before reaching the Court. Often, there is a note about certiorari, an order by which a higher court reviews the

decision of a lower court. For example, an opinion may reference "**Certiorari** [bold added] for the United States Court of Appeals for the Ninth Circuit." That means the Court reviewed the case from the lower court, the US Court of Appeals of the Ninth Circuit.

Each case is usually introduced with the answer to the common questions of who, what, when, and where—which is why the case usually begins with a person, thing, place, and time, so it's easy to establish the most important details right away. Given how detailed the document that explains the decision of the Supreme Court is—as it usually includes cases that were presented years prior but whose decisions have set a precedent for the case in question—it is important to keep focused on the proverbial bigger picture and understand its takeaways. A Supreme Court opinion is usually comprised of the following two main components:

- **Syllabus**: it comes before the Main Opinion and it is "a summary added by the Court to help the reader better understand the case and the decision. The syllabus outlines the facts of the case and the path that the case has taken to get to the Supreme Court. The last portion of the syllabus sometimes summarizes which justice authored the main opinion, which justices joined in the main opinion, and which justices might have issued concurring or dissenting opinions."
- **Main Opinion**: this is the official decision that the Supreme Court has reached on a specific case and it can "take different forms, depending on how the justices decide certain issues. Sometimes decisions are unanimous—all of the justices agree and offer one rationale for their decision, so the Court issues one *unanimous opinion*. When more than half of the justices agree, the Court issues a *majority opinion*. Other times, there is no majority, but a plurality, so the Court issues a *plurality opinion*. Typically, one justice is identified as the author of the main opinion. ***Per curiam*** opinions, however, do not identify any authors, and are simply, opinions of the Court" (American Bar Association, n.d.).

Process and Procedure

Even though every year thousands of cases are filed with the Supreme Court—around 8,000 in recent years, which is a significant increase when considering the cases were roughly 1,200 in the 1950s—roughly only 75 of them are actually heard by the Court. That is because the Supreme Court "will consider only cases for which at least four of the nine justices vote to grant a '**writ of certiorari**,' [bold added] a decision by the Supreme Court to hear an appeal from a lower court." The Latin word *certiorari* means "to inform," thus meaning that the writ of certiorari is tasked with informing a lower court that the Supreme Court is considering taking on a specific case, for which a group of people has filed a petition for writ of certiorari against the lower court's ruling.

However, the most common way for cases to reach the Supreme Court is by appealing a decision that had been issued by one of the **Courts of Appeal**. "The 94 federal judicial districts are divided into 12 regional circuits, each of which has a court of appeals. The appeals courts decide whether lower trial courts had applied the law correctly in their decisions." During appeal cases, there are three judges but no jury (Longley, 2019).

Overview of the United States Constitution

> We the People of the United States, in Order to form a more perfect Union, establish Justice, insure domestic Tranquility, provide for the common defense, promote the

> general Welfare, and secure the Blessings of Liberty to ourselves and our Posterity, do ordain and establish this Constitution for the United States of America.
>
> *(Library of Congress, n.d.b)*

This is the **Preamble of the Constitution** of the United States of America. It was during a summer day in August 1787 that the first draft of the Constitution was presented and accepted. It would take five weeks for the final version to be ready.

However, it all began few months prior, in the spring of 1787, when at the Pennsylvania State House—Independence Hall, as it is known today—an important vote took place. The meeting was so important that guards stood outside the State House making sure curious onlookers would be kept at a safe distance. Inside, Robert Morris, a merchant from England who had distinguished himself during the Revolution and had been recognized as one of the Founding Fathers of the United States, initiated the vote that would unanimously recognize General George Washington as the President of the historical event that was taking place at that moment. This event is known as the **Constitutional Convention**. Washington didn't even feel like attending the Convention and he had thought long about just staying home for the day—he wouldn't have been the only one declining the invitation either, since 74 people had been asked to attend but only 55 did, especially because Rhode Island refused to send its delegates since they believed the Convention to be a conspiracy to overthrow the existing government. It was because of his uncertainty of attending the event that it took many more months for the Convention to take place. He was advanced in age and suffering from all the classical ailments that people over 70 years old go through—although perhaps his rheumatism was a bit worse than most. He also doubted the efficiency of the Convention and didn't really believe they would accomplish much during the event, even though he certainly hoped so. Either way, he finally decided to attend, a decision that resulted in him being bestowed upon the title of President of the Convention, which other younger attendees, such as 36-year-old James Madison, felt like it fit him like a glove, given the legitimate and regal way in which Washington carried himself.

Madison—who would eventually become the fourth President of the United States of America—had been studying political theory and history for many years, looking closely at ancient Greece and Switzerland. After taking a closer look at the original 13 states and how they operated, Madison came to the conclusion that the Articles of the Confederation that the independent states lived by, had to be replaced. The Articles, which had been established in 1781 as

> "a league of friendship" and a constitution for the 13 sovereign and independent states after the Revolution . . . seemed to Madison woefully inadequate. With the states retaining considerable power, the central government, he believed, had insufficient power to regulate commerce. It could not tax and was generally impotent in setting commercial policy it could not effectively support a war effort. It had little power to settle quarrels between states. Saddled with this weak government, the states were on the brink of economic disaster.
>
> *(National Archives, n.d.)*

Madison felt that he had the perfect solution to this impending crisis: the creation of a central government that would provide the states with order and stability. He wrote, " 'Let it be tried then . . . whether any middle ground can be taken which will at once support a due supremacy of the national authority,' while maintaining state power only when 'subordinately useful.' " That's when Madison—with the help of a young Alexander Hamilton, at the time a lawyer in

New York—issued a report in the hopes of gathering the delegates from every state into one location in order to discuss the Articles of the Confederation (National Archives, n.d.).

Edmund Randolph, a delegate from Virginia, opened the Convention by supporting Madison's idea of creating a strong national government and stating that it should have a legislative, executive, and judiciary branch. While many approved of the three branches, some raised doubts over referencing to it as the national government. Given problems with the verbiage controversy, the delegates decided to refer to it as the United States of America, a term that appeased all. However, the compromising atmosphere that had nicely settled in the Convention after choosing the official name did not last long, as many delegates began expressing their opinions on just how much power and independence each state should have under this new plan. In fact, one of the main challenges they faced was over commerce regulation—the southern states, which exported several products, including rice and tobacco, were afraid that Congress might impose export taxes, thus severely damaging the South's economy.

Aside from trade, another major issue for the Framers was slavery and what it meant for the morality of the new government. South Carolina delegate John Rutledge argued that slavery should not affect the morality of the new government as it had nothing to do with it. Roger Sherman, delegate of Connecticut, invited fellow delegates to simply drop the issue before it became too much for them to bear and reminded them what was at stake during the Convention. Eventually, after much debate, the South Carolina and Georgia delegates agreed to require only a majority vote on navigation laws if the New Englanders supported the slave trade to continue for another 20 years. This resulted in minister Samuel Hopkins, an abolitionist, to declare that in his opinion the Convention had sold out,

> How does it appear . . . that these States, who have been fighting for liberty and consider themselves as the highest and most noble example of zeal for it, cannot agree in any political Constitution, unless it indulge and authorize them to enslave their fellow men. . . . Ah! these unclean spirits, like frogs, they, like the Furies of the poets are spreading discord, and exciting men to contention and war.
>
> *(National Archives, n.d.)*

The issue of slavery did cause many more problems to the delegates, including

> the method by which slaves were to be counted for purposes of taxation and representation. On July 12 Oliver Ellsworth proposed that representation for the lower house be based on the number of free persons and three-fifths of "all other persons," a euphemism for enslaved people. In the following week the members finally compromised, agreeing that direct taxation be according to representation and that the representation of the lower house be based on the white inhabitants and three-fifths of the "other people."
>
> *This is remembered as the Great Compromise, also known as the three-fifths compromise (National Archives, n.d.)*

Once these and many other issues that arose had been dealt with, on September 17, 1787, 39 of the 55 delegates signed the final draft of the Constitution of the United States of America. The Constitution presented a preamble and seven articles that describe how the government is shaped and how it operates. The first three articles explain the three different branches of the US Government—legislative, executive, and judicial—what each branch is for, and what their power is, making sure to add a system of checks and balances so that no branch could ever outpower another. The remaining four articles describe what the relationship is between each state and the federal government, establish the Constitution as the supreme law of the land, and explain the ratification and amendment process.

Although the Constitution had just been signed, it didn't take long for amendments to be proposed following the bitter debates that had characterized the Constitutional Convention, which left the majority of the tired delegates—who more than likely were simply longing to return home as soon as possible after spending months debating—feeling that the Constitution did not actually mirror the ideal form of government they wished for. The anti-Federalists, in particular, took issues with the verbiage, as they believed it did not specify well and clearly enough what the rights of the people were and how limited the power of the government was—thus claiming that the non-specific wording left too much room for interpretation. It was young Madison who stepped in and began supporting the need for amendments. By doing so, he was able to pilot 17 amendments, which were eventually reduced to 12.

> On October 2, 1789, President Washington sent to each of the states a copy of the 12 amendments adopted by the Congress in September. By December 15, 1791, three-fourths of the states had ratified the 10 amendments now so familiar to Americans as the "**Bill of Rights**."
>
> *(National Archives, n.d.)*

Just like the Constitution, the Bill of Rights starts with a preamble and presents ten amendments, some of which are more well-known than others, such as the First Amendment, which support freedom of religion, speech, and the press:

> Congress shall make no law respecting an establishment of religion, or prohibiting the free exercise thereof; or abridging the freedom of speech, or of the press; or the right of the people peaceably to assemble, and to petition the Government for a redress of grievances.
>
> *(National Center for Constitutional Studies, n.d.)*

After the Bill of Rights, 17 more amendments have been added to the US Constitution, bringing the total to 27 amendments.

How the Supreme Court Interprets the Constitution

The Supreme Court, being the final arbiter of the law, is tasked with the extremely important duty of interpreting the Constitution—something that is somewhat unique to the United States of America, since even though a few other countries in the world have courts with the same task, none of them have done it for as long as the Supreme Court has. The Constitution was

> designed to provide for a national government sufficiently strong and flexible to meet the needs of the republic, yet sufficiently limited and just to protect the guaranteed rights of citizens; it permits a balance between society's need for order and the individual's right to freedom. To assure these ends, the Framers of the Constitution created three independent and coequal branches of government. That this Constitution has provided continuous democratic government through the periodic stresses of more than two centuries illustrates the genius of the American system of government.
>
> *(SCOTUSblog, n.d.)*

The Framers of the Constitution had written the document using broad terms—which, as previously stated, had caused major disputes among the delegates themselves, eventually leading to the creation of the first ten amendments—in order to leave room for interpretation to future generations facing different problems, which is why the Justices on the Supreme Court rely on a few different factors when it is time to interpret the document.

For starters, some Justices may prefer to focus on textualism, which

> emphasizes how the terms in the Constitution would be understood by people at the time they were ratified, as well as the context in which those terms appear. Textualists usually believe there is an objective meaning of the text, and they do not typically inquire into questions regarding the intent of the drafters, adopters, or ratifiers of the Constitution and its amendments when deriving meaning from the text.

Others might instead prefer to focus on the original meaning that the Framers wanted the text to convey, and they agree "that the Constitution's text had an 'objectively identifiable' or public meaning at the time of the Founding that has not changed over time, and the task of judges and Justices (and other responsible interpreters) is to construct this original meaning" (Murrill, 2015, p. 2). Then, there are also pragmatists, whose approach usually focuses on the Supreme Court's ability to weigh and balance how one interpretation of the US Constitution measures up to another interpretation—as well as what the consequences of one interpretation against another might be.

Regardless of which method each Justice uses to interpret the Constitution, it is clear that the decision made in 1803 during the *Marbury v. Madison* case established the principle the Supreme Court is best known for: the authority that every Justice has to judicial review.

Conclusion

It took many months, many debates, and probably just as many compromises for the 39 delegates to finally sign the official version of the Constitution of the United States of America, which eventually led to the creation of the Supreme Court, the highest court in the federal system. In the 230 years since its establishment, there have been 17 courts—each Justice nominated by the President and approved by the Senate. While all of their decisions had constitutional importance, some "landmark decisions" were to significantly impact US institutions. In the chapters to come, we will explore ten of these landmark decisions. Although rather underutilized at the beginning, with only a few cases presented every year (the very first case ended in a settlement) the Supreme Court has increasingly established itself as the truly powerful institution that it is today, the beacon of the national conscience, the majestic presence whose mission is to preserve and protect the civil rights, freedom, and independence of the citizens of the United States of America, the country whose fundamental values the Supreme Court Justices are tasked to protect in an everchanging society.

Review Questions

1. Why did the Framers of the Constitution establish a third branch of the US government? What did the Judiciary Act of 1789 accomplish?
2. How has the shape of the Supreme Court changed since it was first established? How many Justices are there now?

3. How many Courts have there been since the establishment of the Supreme Court? Which Court is the most recent one?
4. How are Supreme Court Judges chosen and selected? Does their political affiliation matter? What criteria are *not* taken into account when choosing a new Justice?
5. What is a Supreme Court opinion? What is the best and most efficient way to read a Supreme Court opinion?
6. What was the Constitutional Convention? Where did it take place? What was discussed during the Convention?

References

American Bar Association. (n.d.). *How to read a US supreme court opinion*. Retrieved February 20, 2020, from www.americanbar.org/groups/public_education/publications/teaching-legal-docs/how-to-read-a-u-s-supreme-court-opinion/

Landmark Cases of the US Supreme Court. (n.d.). *Marbury v. Madison (1803)*. Retrieved from www.landmarkcases.org/cases/marbury-v-madison

Laws. (n.d.). *John Jay*. Retrieved from https://supreme-court.laws.com/john-jay

Library of Congress. (n.d.a). *Judiciary act of 1789: Primary documents of American history*. Retrieved from www.loc.gov/rr/program/bib/ourdocs/judiciary.html

Library of Congress. (n. d.b). *US constitution*. Retrieved from www.loc.g ov/item/48034353/

Longley, R. (2019, August 29). How do cases reach the supreme court? *ThoughtCo*. Retrieved February 18, 2020, from www.thoughtco.com/how-do-cases-reach-supreme-court-4113827

Murrill, B. J. (2015). *Modes of constitutional interpretation*. Congressional Research Service. Retrieved February 18, 2020, from https://fas.org/sgp/crs/misc/R45129.pdf

National Archives. (n.d.). *Constitution of the United States—a history*. Retrieved from www.archives.gov/founding-docs/more-perfect-union

National Center for Constitutional Studies. (n.d.). *The bill of rights (amendments 1–10)*. Retrieved from https://nccs.net/blogs/americas-founding-documents/bill-of-rights-amendments-1-10

O'Connor, S. D. (2014). *Out of order: Stories from the history of the supreme court*. New York: Random House Trade Paperbacks.

SCOTUSblog. (n.d.). *Whole woman's health v. Hellerstedt*. Retrieved from www.scotusblog.com/case-files/cases/whole-womans-health-v-cole/

The Supreme Court Historical Society. (n.d.). *The Jay court 1789–1795*. Retrieved from https://supremecourthistory.org/timeline_court_jay.html

Supreme Court of the United States (SCOTUS). (n.d.). *Syllabus: Whole woman's health et al. v. Hellerstedt, commissioner, Texas department of state health services, et al., October term 2015*. Retrieved from www.supremecourt.gov/opinions/15pdf/15-274_new_e18f.pdf

Supreme Court of the United States of America (SCOTUS). (n.d.). *The court and constitutional interpretation*. Retrieved from www.supremecourt.gov/about/constitutional.aspx

Texas Department of State Health Services. (2015, October). *Supreme court of the United States, syllabus: Whole woman's health et al v. Hellerstedt*. Retrieved from www.supremecourt.gov/opinions/15pdf/15-274_new_e18f.pdf

Yale Law School Lillian Goldman Law Library. (n.d.). *The judiciary act, September 24, 1789*. Retrieved from https://avalon.law.yale.edu/18th_century/judiciary_act.asp

2

US INSTITUTIONS

A Brief Introduction

Learning Objectives

- Understand the sociological definition of a social institution
- Identify and explain the five primary US institutions
- Describe current trends in the US in family, education, religion, politics/government, and economy
- Familiarize oneself with key sociological vocabulary and theorists as they relate to the five social institutions

Key Terms

Authority
Capitalism
Credentialism
Democracy
Economy
Education
Family
Government
Habits
Institution
Labor
Law
Marriage
Mixed economy
Norms
Pluralism
Politics
Power
Religion
Rights
Secularism
Socialism
State

Introduction to the Sociology of Institutions

Before investigating how the Supreme Court and landmark decisions have affected institutions in the United States, we need to explore first what institutions *are* from a sociological perspective. Sociologists have, indeed, played a large role in their study. One of the most prominent US-based sociologists of the 20th century, Harvard professor Talcott Parsons emphasized the importance of analyzing institutions: "I conceive of institutions to be one of the principal branches of general sociological theory, hence the theory of all social life" (Parsons, 1990).

DOI: 10.4324/9781003021438-3

This chapter will give us foundational knowledge about institutions: what characterizes them? What functions do they serve? How are they changed and who gets to decide? What are the primary types of institutions and their features?

There are several usages of the word "institution." Journalist H.L. Mencken's humorous quip, "Marriage is a wonderful institution, but who wants to live in an institution?" exemplifies the difference between two such usages—and the importance of keeping them separate for the purpose of this text. When Mencken jokes, "but who wants to live in an institution," he is referring to the most common usage of the term, meaning a large, formal organization, establishment, or facility. Sociologist Erving Goffman, in his classic book *Asylums*, talked about total institutions, or "of residence and work where a large number of like-situated individuals, cut off from the wider society for an appreciable period of time, together lead an enclosed, formally administered round of life" (Goffman, 1961, p. xiii). Examples of total institutions included mental asylums and prisons, but we can also extend the concept to cover other organizations like armies or monasteries or slave plantations (McEwen, 1980). Certainly, per Mencken, one wouldn't want a marital situation reminiscent of this type of institution.

However, another definition of institution is used in sociology to refer to the first type of institution implied by Mencken when he writes, "Marriage is a wonderful institution." In this usage, which will be the primary usage of the term throughout the text, an **institution** is a set of **norms** and/or rules that regulate human behavior and govern the structure of relationships of individuals to one another (Parsons, 1990; Coleman, 1990). Some categories of norms and rules within institutions include informal 'rules' like customs, habits, and routines, but also laws, all of which are enforced by sanctions, either positive or negative (Keizer, 2007; Garcelon, 2010). **Laws** are rules that are formally recognized by a government or controlling authority, and which therefore can carry official penalties and punishments. **Customs** are 'usual' ways of behaving or doing things over a period of time that is shared among a group of people. We expect people to follow the customs of the group, and if they do not, it may be offensive or appear unusual. For example, going from house to house asking for sweets at Halloween time dressed in a costume is a custom in the United States. **Habits** are socially acquired, repetitive behaviors performed by an individual with minimal conscious effort in a particular environment (Engman & Cranford, 2016). We can see how habits are socially contingent and acquired if we think about our hygiene and grooming habits, and how they vary by gender and cultural expectations. Routines are patterned, repetitive practices, but the term applies not to individuals, as habit does, but to groups and organizations (McKeown, 2008). Institutions, therefore, are a large part of the external social reality in which individuals find themselves. They shape all manner of assumptions we have about the way in which things 'work' and how others in our society behave. Parsons argues

> in so far as they regulate the relations of individuals to each other, [institutions] become a fundamental element of social structure which consists precisely in . . . a set of determinate relations of individuals. One element of social structure then is a system of norms defining what the relations of individuals *ought* to be.
>
> *(Parsons, 1990, p. 327)*

So, institutions don't only guide us to think about the way things are, but affect our views on what the ideal is, what our relationships, interactions, and the very trajectory of what our life should be. They constrain and guide our actions like rules of a game, in ways that have become so normalized, we may not realize their influence. Moreover, institutions are not normative contexts which are transitory, but have enduring power, although they do change and shift across time and vary across cultures.

Among the institutions that can be considered the building blocks of society, we will focus in this book on five of the primary institutions most frequently discussed in introductions to sociology texts: education, family, politics and government, the economy, and religion. The following chapters will explore how landmark Supreme Court cases have affected each of the institutions, both over time and immediately following the decision. The brief overviews of each of the five institutions provide basic vocabulary and understanding of the objects of study, as well as a snapshot of current trends in the United States.

Education

The education for which we receive degrees and diplomas predominantly takes place within the walls of a formal learning setting such as a high school, vocational school or university. But **education** as a social institution is more encompassing and abstract: it is that which confers academic and social knowledge, values, beliefs, and tools which are considered necessary in a particular time, place, and culture for social reproduction and indeed, for survival (Kendall, 2011). We learn informally from birth, through peers, mentors, family, friends, and the media. They convey to us an abundance of information, from normative behavior to technical skills, to language, to complex religious traditions. As sociologists from Edwin Sutherland to Elijah Anderson have pointed out, informal learning does not always induce prosocial behavior. People may learn to be deviant or engage in criminal behavior when they are surrounded by peers who provide law-breaking with an ideological underpinning and the technical skills for which to engage in crime.

Today in the US, the general contours of a uniform, foundational formal education is assumed for all children, though historically and currently marked by significant inequality on the basis of class, race, gender, and geography. We will discuss these inequalities in Chapter 3, when we cover the impact of the *Brown v. Board of Education* Supreme Court decision and its impact. Indeed, until the 19th century, formal education was largely restricted to wealthy white males. Legislation like the Virginia Revised Code of 1819 prohibited, under threat of arrest and physical punishment with the lash, the teaching of reading or writing to enslaved people or freemen. Women were also barred from obtaining higher education alongside male counterparts prior to the Civil War, with only two private colleges, Oberlin and Antioch, permitting coeducation (Parker, 2015).

Whereas in Colonial times and in the early 19th century, educational responsibilities were located largely in the family, over time private and public schools became legitimized as substitutes. The presence of mass education for all children regardless of sex, race, or wealth began after widespread calls in the mid-1800s for free, compulsory education. Educational reformer Horace Mann, Secretary of Massachusetts Board of Education, was at the center of this "Common School Movement," arguing for its political and civic necessity: "A republican form of government, without intelligence in the people, must be, on a vast scale, what a mad-house, without superintendent or keepers, would be on a small one." Mann furthermore was instrumental in fostering the professionalization and education of teachers ("Horace Mann", 2021). Such formal, universal, and bureaucratized education as Mann encouraged was widespread by the turn of the 20th century. The reason for this development of public schooling is debated, with some scholars arguing that they were established in order to inculcate compliant workers for manufacturers during rapid industrialization. Others (Vinovskis, 1992) argue that the expansion of mass education should be viewed as a natural extension of the religious fervor in the US, and a corresponding desire to have a population that could read the Bible and learn its moral tenets. It can furthermore be read as a recognition of the role of formal education in escaping poverty and social mobility, economic growth, the fostering of a sense of national unity and shared values, particularly during a time of mass migration of European immigrants to the United States (Open Textbook Library, "Sociology: Understanding and Changing the Social World", 2010). Even with the initial growth of mass education, however, the 19th century was marked by relatively low rates of enrollment. Only half of 5–19-year-olds enrolled in school, with rates of Black enrollment much lower than that of Whites. The proportion of young people enrolled in school remained relatively low in the last half of the 19th century. Literacy rates were generally also low compared to their late 20th century levels—between 80–90 percent prior to the 20th century—and disproportionately low for Black Americans (NCES, 2019a).

The US Educational System in Brief

The US has a highly decentralized system of public education, one of the most decentralized in a highly developed economy, owing partially to the Tenth Amendment to the Constitution, which leaves the authority to create public schools to the states. Compulsory school attendance laws therefore vary from state to state, with all requiring attendance starting from ages 5–8, and ending at ages 16–18. There are also maximum ages set by states for which they must provide free schooling, ranging from age 17 to 26 (NCES, 2017). States set the broad outlines for school curricula. In spite of this decentralization, beginning in the 1920s, the 'core' curricula that we recognize today had been introduced, including subjects like English, math, social studies, and science. This has since been expanded to include a plethora of subjects from health to computers, as needs and the functions of schooling have evolved, with much debate about what is being taught and how. Schools, in addition to providing education, now serve as de facto day care providers—nursery, pre-K, and full day kindergartens often offer necessary programs for working parents who cannot afford private daycare (Kendall, 2011). Consequently, education as an institution has become

> massive . . . involving millions of people and billions of dollars. About 75 million people, almost one-fourth of the US population, attend school at all levels. This number includes 40 million in grades pre-K through 8, 16 million in high school, and 19 million in college (including graduate and professional school) . . . they are taught by about 4.8 million teachers and professors.
>
> *(Barkan, 2020)*

The majority of schools in the US are public, with approximately 98,000 elementary, secondary, and combined elementary and secondary schools (NCES, 2021). However, a sizable number of elementary and secondary schools are private—approximately 34,500. These private schools receive funding primarily from non-public sources: tuition payments from students and their families, funding from religious organizations, alumni, and private donors. There are several demographic characteristics that differentiate private from public schools—students are more likely to be White, to come from two-parent backgrounds, and were less likely to have parents who had not completed high school, or to come from poor households (NCES, 2019b). Given the costs of private school education, the higher percentages of those in public schools from impoverished households may not be surprising. The average cost of private high school in New England, for example, is $39,200, and even in the most "affordable" region of the US, the Southeast, is over $15,000 (Wong, 2014). Studies have shown that private grammar and high schools, particularly Catholic schools, result in better outcomes for students like improved standardized test scores, keeping other variables constant. These differences may have more to do with the closeness of communities than the actual education in itself (Conley, 2013).

In addition to private schools, a growing number (1.6 million) of US students ages 5–17 receive their education through homeschooling, which is legal in all 50 states, thus eschewing both public and private elementary and secondary schools. The motives parents have for homeschooling include concerns about the potential for negative school environments, the need for moral or religious instruction, and dissatisfaction with academic instruction in schools (NCES, 2016). Although far from a normative practice, homeschooling has been shown to provide academic advantages vis-à-vis their public-school counterparts, earning higher scores on standardized tests like the ACT and SAT (Ray, 2016).

Higher Education, Educational Attainment, and Credentialism

The United States currently boasts approximately 4,500 institutions of higher learning—two- and four-year, private and public colleges (NCES, 2019b). Educational attainment in the US is at its highest point since 1940. The Census Bureau reported that more than one-third of all Americans have a bachelor's degree or higher. Approximately 89.1 percent had obtained a high school diploma or the equivalent (US Census Bureau, 2017). Recent statistics have shown that because of the abundance of college graduates, employers are looking to hire those with more education—nine out of ten jobs created in 2018 went to those with a bachelor's degree or higher (Goldstein, 2018). Higher education also generally results in higher rates of compensation. Those with professional degrees have median weekly earnings of around $1800, whereas those with a high school diploma earn around $700 (BLS, 2018b). This demonstrates the rise of **credentialism**, which as Kendall explains, is the "process of social selection in which class advantage and social status are linked to the possession of academic qualifications" (2011, p. 525). For all of the professional and monetary advantages conferred by higher education in the United States because of credentialism, student loan debt has become a major issue, with debt nationally rising to 1.4 trillion in 2019, with an average debt of $35,359 (Tatham, 2019).

Family

Keeping in mind our definition of an institution as a set of norms and/or rules that regulate human behavior and govern the structure of relationships of individuals to one another—how is family an institution? In what ways are our ideas of who our family members are, what types of relationships can exist among them, and what our responsibilities are to each other, shaped by societal norms and rules—including laws? How do we see the idea of family change historically and among different cultures? How are the possibilities for intimate relationships defined and confined by normative expectations and regulations? It is important for us to emphasize in this text, which focuses on the impact of landmark Supreme Court cases on US institutions, that family/intimate relationships are not just normative in an informal sense, where individuals may face a social sanction like disapproval or even extralegal violence, but are otherwise free to pick and choose family or lovers/sexual partners without the involvement of legal structures and the state. Intimate relationships—both in terms of who is defined as family, but also in terms of who we can love and/or engage with sexually—is and has always been regulated by the US government at the federal and state level, whether it is in terms of race, gender, sexual orientation, the presence or absence of 'blood' ties, age, the number of intimates, and so forth.

Defining Family

The **family** is one of the most foundational, universal units in human societies, crucial to ensuring successful reproduction and continuance of society, forging our identities, and providing for systems of economic support and emotional connection. And yet there is lack of consensus on a singular, measurable definition that can encompass its meaning due to varying normative ideas and values about the structure, roles, responsibilities, and function of the family. To give a few examples of the tricky questions raised: are cohabitating couples who are not married a family? What if they have children? Does the sexual orientation of those who cohabitate matter? Are adult siblings who live together in an apartment and share most expenses a family? The United States' Census Bureau provides a standard, limited definition of family which it uses for the purpose of its survey: a group of two people or more (one of whom is the householder) related by birth, marriage, or adoption and residing together; all such people (including related subfamily members) are considered as members of one family (USCB, 2019). Sociologists provide a more expansive definition that captures the way in which popularly understood conceptions of the family have changed, e.g. relationships in which people live together with commitment, form an economic unit and care for any young, and consider their identity to be significantly attached to the group (Kendall, 2011, p. 478).

Marriage, Domestic Partnership, and Cohabitation: Current Trends

The conception we have in the United States of the family has somewhat moved away from the "traditional" idealized nuclear family model that dominated the popular imagination during the mid-20th century, which consisted of a monogamous, heterosexual married couple (with a male breadwinner and female homemaker) and their underage children living in a single household. Yet, marriage itself remains a dominant and normative social institution. Though marriage rates have declined, half of adults over the age of 18 are married (Pew Research Center, 2017). And while the vast majority of the public believes that the most important reason for getting married is love, **marriage** is nevertheless the *legal* union of a couple as spouses. Marriage can only occur when two individuals are legally able to marry each other, mutually consent to doing so, and obtain a marriage contract (Legal Information Institute, 2017). Because marriage is a legal process, it can in turn only be dissolved through the legal processes of divorce or annulment, wherein a marriage is completely and retroactively erased. In the United States, social scientists have evidence that divorce rates are declining since the 1990s, that this decline may continue into the future, and this may be attributable to 'rarer' but more stable marriages (Cohen, 2019).

In Chapter 4, we will show how the Supreme Court expanded those legally able to marry on the basis of race and gender/sexual orientation. There are other prohibitions that remain in place, and which have also seen legal challenges. Polygamy—or marriage between more than two people—remains illegal in all 50 US states as well as at the federal level. Incest, or sexual relations and/or marriage among people within the same family who are spouses, is also illegal, though variably defined and punished according to the state (NDAA, 2013). Last, prohibitions remain in place on the basis of age of consent, also contingent upon state. Most states allow those who are above the age of 18 to marry without parental consent. Parental consent and/or permission of a judge may permit the marriage of consenting parties younger than 18. In New Hampshire, males can be 14 years of age, and females, 13 (Legal Information Institute, 2019).

Although most US adults will be married during their lifetime, with 77 percent of men and 83 percent of women (Pew Research Center, 2014) attitudes and norms have shifted over the past 40 years, allowing for other family arrangements to become prevalent, including

cohabitation, domestic partnerships, and **civil unions**. Cohabitation, where two people live together as a couple without being legally married, has increased in both prevalence and public approval, with 7 percent of US adults over 18 cohabitating (Pew Research Center, 2017). Civil unions and domestic partnerships are legally sanctioned relationships for couples which carry some of the same rights and benefits as those of marriage, and were for a time the only alternative for same-sex couples who wanted the legal protections afforded through marriage (although it is available for heterosexual couples as well). Yet, these legal relationships lack some federal benefits (NCLR, 2018).

The institution of the family has many points of overlap with the sociology of law beyond issues of marriage—parenting, childbearing, adoption, inheritance, violence within the family, extended families and kinship networks, and the varieties of intimacy.

Religion

Definitions and Sociological Approaches

There are obviously great differences in the theologies of Hinduism, Buddhism, Christianity, Islam, and Judaism. What, then, generally is the institution of **religion**; what is the common thread that underlies these traditions? Ethicist Arthur Dobrin provides the following definition:

> a set of beliefs and institutions, behaviors and emotions which binds human beings to something beyond their individual selves . . . it sets the tone of one's world-view and requires certain behavioral dispositions relative to that which transcends personal interests . . . it provides a story about one's place in the larger scheme of things, creates a sense of connection and it makes one feel grateful.
>
> *(2004, p. 5)*

Dobrin's definition allows for us to think of religious traditions which may not have any god or gods (such as Buddhism) or even the presence of the supernatural itself (such as Ethical Humanism). The influential sociologist Emile Durkheim, whose book *The Elementary Forms of Religious Life* (1995) pioneered the sociological study of religion, provides a slightly different definition. For him, religion is a "unified system of beliefs and practices relative to sacred things, that is to say set apart and forbidden, beliefs and practices which unite into one single moral community, called a church, all those who adhere to them" (p. 44). Durkheim was not concerned primarily with the study of different belief systems, but rather in understanding the role that religions generally perform in a given society. According to him, religions serve as a kind of social cement, unifying members of a community, and enhancing feelings of collectivity. The often-profound religious experience of believers of varied faiths can be explained fundamentally by the way it links the individual to society, "it awakens that feeling of support, safety, and protective guidance which binds a man of faith to his cult. It is this reality that makes him rise above himself" (p. 420).

Sociologists have also looked at the impact religions can have on other institutions, such as the economy and political systems. Max Weber's seminal *The Protestant Ethic and the Spirit of Capitalism* (1930/2007), posits that capitalism was able to develop and flourish in the United States and Western Europe because it possessed what he described as an 'elective affinity'—a kind of coherence or resonance—with Christian Protestantism, namely Calvinism. Calvinism as a religion emphasized certain behaviors and beliefs that were uniquely suited to foster a capitalist economic system. Weber states: "the religious valuation of restless, continuous, systematic work in a worldly calling, must have been the most powerful conceivable lever for the expansion of that attitude toward life which we have . . . called the spirit of Capitalism" (p. 241). Calvinism encouraged, indeed made it a duty, to pursue the accumulation of wealth in one's vocation or calling. Wealth gained through this pursuit was then a sign one was blessed by God for Calvinists, who further promoted worldly asceticism (self-discipline and avoidance of excess in consumption) in this pursuit. Weber cites quotations by Founding Father Benjamin Franklin which evidence how a Protestant belief-system nourished a capitalist mindset in the United States: "Remember that *time* is money . . . remember that *credit* is money . . . remember, that money is of a prolific, generating nature" (p. 231).

Current Trends in the United States

Alexis de Tocqueville, the French diplomat who wrote the influential *Democracy in America*, after his visit to the US in 1831, noted

> Upon my arrival in the United States, the religious aspect of this country was the first thing that struck my attention . . . there is no country in the whole world in which Christian religion retains a greater influence over the souls of men than in America.
>
> *(pp. 242, 245)*

Almost 200 years after de Tocqueville's arrival in the US, **secularism** is on the rise, in the US and around the world. A growing number of younger Americans in the Millennial generation report not having a religion, with 22.8 percent of the US population identifying as non-religious (Pew Research Center, 2019b). This was a large increase over a decade, as in 2007, 16 percent of Americans reported being unaffiliated with a religion (Shermer, 2018). Service attendance of those who identify with a religion has also declined over the past 30 years (Conley, 2013). Approximately 45 percent of Americans say that they attend services at least monthly, with a majority (54 percent) saying they attend religious services only a few times a year (Sherwood, 2019).

In spite of recent declines in religious affiliation and attendance at formal services, however, religion as an institution—and primarily Christianity—remains a dominant force in the United States among its residents, with approximately 70.6 percent of adults identifying as Christian (Protestants, Catholics, and other Christian sects), 1.9 percent as Jewish, 0.9 percent Muslim, 0.7 percent Buddhist, and 0.7 percent Hindu (Pew Research Center, 2019b). Though it is a **pluralistic** society, with a large amount of diversity in terms of cultures and religions, the US continues to be the most religious out of all other industrialized nations in terms of personal beliefs and affiliations (Conley, 2013). This is ironic, as unlike any of the 120 countries which have an 'official' or 'preferred' religion, (Pew Research Center, 2017), the US Constitution prevents such a relationship between religion and the state. There are several places in the US Constitution where religion is mentioned, specifically. Article IV states: "No religious test shall ever be required as a qualification to any office or public trust under the United States," and in the First Amendment: "Congress shall make no law respecting an establishment of religion, or prohibiting the free exercise thereof."

In Chapter 5, we will explore how the Supreme Court has interpreted the Constitution's limitations on government involvement in religion and the impact of landmark cases on religion in the United States. Here, though, we want to point out how religion is still embedded in Americans' lives and all the other social institutions we discuss in this book, from education (e.g. should natural selection, which is antithetical so some religious traditions, be taught?) to healthcare (should the US government mandate the employers provide birth control to their employees as part of their healthcare benefits? Should prayer be permitted in school?). As Kendall argues, "Religion . . . is a powerful, deeply felt, and influential force in human society" (2011). About 75 percent of Americans indicate that religion is, in fact, important in their lives (Gallup, 2019). We can see the power of this institution by looking at sheer numbers: There are 350,000 congregations in the US, 338,000 of which are Christian (Protestant, Catholic, and other Christian denominations). Larger evangelical Protestant churches known as megachurches have also been on the rise, as 37 percent of the American population identifies as 'born again' or evangelical. These churches, now numbering around 1,650 in the US, have an average of 2,000 weekend attendants, some drawing as many as 30,000. Attempting to be contemporary and embracing technology, megachurches have drawn diverse congregants (Thumma & Bird, 2015). While not in the majority, a full third of Americans indicated that they felt being Christian was very important to being a 'true American' (Briggs, 2016).

Politics and Government

Definitions and Approaches

The sociological institution of **politics** must be separated from its more colloquial connotations. When we say we 'talk politics,' this can mean anything from discussing a candidate for president, to arguing our opinion on a controversial topic like immigration policy, to discussing work-related power dynamics. For our purposes, the *institution* of politics is that which structures how power is gained and exercised by individuals, governments, and other social groups/actors. By this definition, we see, politics does not only refer to formal governments or nation-states, which we are accustomed to think about when we hear the term. Indeed, nation states, independent states with formal borders, written constitutions, and the notion of citizens with equal participation and rights, only became the ideal after the French and American Revolutions at the end of the 19th century. Prior to that time, kingdoms, city-states, empires, and other social configurations were dominant (Wimmer & Feinstein, 2010). **Government,** on the other hand, is the formal organization that has the legal and political authority to regulate the relationships among members of a society and between the society and those outside its borders (Kendall, 2011, p. 446). It is closely related to what sociologist Max Weber described as a **state:** a "human community that (successfully) claims the monopoly on the legitimate use of physical force within a given territory." His meaning becomes clear when we think about the criminal justice system in the US. We give over to the police and other law enforcement agencies the ability to use force—even deadly force—to enact the law. Citizens cannot 'take the law into their own hands,' which is known as vigilantism. Likewise, the majority of US states still retain the use of the death penalty, which gives the state the right to end the life of a citizen who has committed a capital offense. Insurrection, or rebellion, against the authority of the United States is also a crime. The state, then, has **power**, the ability to enforce its will even against opposition.

Sociologists have focused on the concepts of **authority** in their analyses of politics as a social institution. Notably, Max Weber distinguished among different types of authority or domination which are integral to the institution of politics. Authority for him is the legitimate right to and ability to exercise power (Conley, 2013, p. 575). Different types of authority he describes include charismatic authority, which relies on obedience through the personal magnetism of an individual leader, traditional authority, rooted in the claims of tradition and the past, and legal-rational authority, which is the type of authority dominant in the 21st century, and which we expect to find in the United States. This authority is rooted in the application of the law and rules without appeal to charisma or tradition. "Obey me because I am your lawfully appointed superior," is the grounds for claiming obedience under legal-rational authority (Parkin, cited in Swedburg, 2005, p. 64).

But what about the individuals who reside within the United States? What kind of power do they have, and how do they exercise this power?

Democracies, Rights, and the Political Process

The United States is a **democracy,** the form of government now in the majority around the globe (57 percent of countries with populations of at least 500,000 were democracies and 13 percent autocracies) (Desilver, 2019). While the term means "rule by the people," the US does not have a direct participatory democracy, relying instead on representatives (therefore we use the term representative democracy). In the bicameral legislature of the federal government, the US Congress, there are 100 elected Senators—two from each state—and 435 voting members of the House of Representatives and six non-voting members. There is also, of course, the opportunity for citizens to elect representatives at other levels of government, including at the state and local level. The citizens of the US have power as we have defined it earlier, to change their representatives through elections, and therefore lead to change in laws and policies. Still, not all Americans who are eligible to vote do so. The voting participation rate since 1980 has shown that more than a third of Americans do not cast a ballot in presidential elections (File, 2017). These rates vary by demographic categories, with White, college-educated, high-income, and older Americans more likely to be registered to vote. Local elections have even lower rates of participation, only about 25 percent (Hajnal, 2018).

More than 40 percent of Americans say democracy in their country is not working well, and a majority likewise express that they feel the US needs to do better at respecting the rights and freedom of all people (Geiger, 2018). In terms of Americans' rights if they are citizens, we focus here on two interrelated types of rights: civil rights and political rights (we will elaborate on these in Chapter 6) and the way the Supreme Court has affected both. **Civil rights** are the legal provisions that stem from notions of equality among the citizenry, and are meant to prevent discrimination from the government and individuals. **Political rights** are those which guarantee a citizen's ability to participate in the electoral process, including the right to vote or run for political office (with limitations—for example, naturalized citizens cannot run for President, and depending on the jurisdiction, people with felony records may be **disenfranchised**). The Civil Rights Act of 1964 and the Voting Rights Act of 1965 are two key pieces of legislation intended to safeguard these civil and political rights. The Civil Rights Act of 1965 was passed in response to the social pressure from the civil rights and women's rights movements, and "summarily outlawed the systematic, far-reaching, and in some cases, legally sanctioned discrimination that had prevailed for decades across a number of areas of American society" (Aiken , Salmon, & Hanges , 2013). The Voting Rights Act of 1965 prohibits the use of voting qualifications on the basis of race or color, and requires that districting plans for representatives do not dilute the votes of minority voters (Schuit & Rogowski, 2017).

Amplifying Power: Interest Groups and Lobbying

Beyond the individual citizen's power to use her or his vote, there are other legal routes to pursue for organized groups with specific issues of concern (running the gamut from oil corporations to teachers' unions to advocates for LGBTQ rights) to exercise power through a collective form of politics. Seven thousand of these types of organizations today can be labelled **interest groups**. These groups are organizations that seek to gain power and influence policy without direct election or appointment to office (Conley, 2013, p. 601). They may do so in any number of ways, from encouraging their membership to pressure elected officials to sponsor a piece of legislation, engage in marches, or write op-eds. They may also engage in **lobbying**: an attempt to influence public policy via communication methods by a person or group in a way that is personal, often in a social relationship with policymakers (Scott, 2018). The number of registered lobbyists in our nation's capital alone stands at approximately 19,000 (Holyoke, 2015). Tens of millions of dollars are spent each year by such interest groups to try to influence lawmakers. Facebook, for instance, spent almost $13 million in lobbying in 2018, Amazon spent $14 million, and Blue Cross Blue Shield, the health insurance company, spent $23 million (Perticone, 2019). Conflict and critical social theorists, building on the work of Karl Marx, would point to these enormous expenditures to demonstrate the way in which the wealthy elites are able to wield disproportionate power over political institutions, and thus bend the law and policies to favor themselves. In Chapter 6, we further explore this question of the power to influence the electoral process through wealth, through the *Citizens United vs. FEC* Supreme Court decision (2010).

Economy and Work

From the time we are children, one of the most frequent questions we receive is, "what do you want to be when you grow up?" Once we are adults, we are asked, "what do you do?" by strangers at parties. These questions demonstrate the normative power of the social institution of the economy, as we assume children will not only have free range to determine what their occupation will be, but also that they will need an occupation, and that this occupation will have a strong connection to their sense of identity and importance. Even our very acceptance of the use of a piece of paper or metal in the form of coins—**money**—in exchange for our labor or for food, demonstrates the way in which the economy is a social phenomenon. Economy, then as a social institution, is responsible for the production, distribution, and consumption of goods and services. The way in which societies have organized around different types of production—from humans' earliest hunter-gatherer economies, to those created after the agricultural revolution, to the industrial revolution, to the post-industrial revolution with its focus on information and services, all have a significant impact on all other social institutions.

We discuss the dominant mode of production in the US: capitalism, and contrast it with socialism. However, both of these systems are abstractions, ideal-types. In practice, we do not find 'perfect,' truly capitalist or socialist economies, and we will point out how elements of capitalism can be found in "socialist" countries, and elements of socialism, in "capitalist" countries.

Capitalism and Socialism

Capitalism began to take off after 1500, accompanied by colonialism and slavery, although some scholars argue that it predates this period and can be seen in the form of merchant capitalism in China, the Islamic and Western Middle Ages (Kocka, 2016). In its "ideal" form, **capitalism** is an economic system where property and the means of production (that is, the resources used to produce goods and services, from technology to raw materials to the facilities where goods are made to the machines) are privately owned. In this system, prices (including the price of **labor**, the physical or mental work we perform for wages) are freely set by supply and demand among consumers in a transparent, competitive marketplace which operates without government interference, under a *laissez faire* policy. In this context, goods are products offered for sale that are tangible (smartphones, food, cars) and services are intangible products (sports activities, education, tours). At the heart of the capitalist economy is the individual profit motive, each human being seeking to maximize his or her monetary gains. According to proponents of capitalism, this motive spurs innovation, economic growth, and an alignment between needs, wants, and products.

As mentioned, capitalism as an ideal type does not exist in practice. Most economies are **mixed economies,** allowing free market practices to exist side-by-side with government interventions. Although the United States is often thought of as the prototypical capitalistic nation, it does not rank in the top ten on the Index of Economic Freedom (2019), which measures variables like business freedom, trade freedom, fiscal freedom, investment freedom, and property rights. Hong Kong, Singapore, New Zealand, Switzerland, and Australia comprise the top five on this index. The United States does not conform to the abstract ideal of capitalism for various reasons. First, it does not operate without restrictions and interventions in the marketplace. The government regulates the market through a number of agencies which seek to protect consumers and businesses from harm and deceptive practices, such as the Securities and Exchange Commission (SEC). The SEC was created in the 1930s after the Great Depression to shield investors from fraud and market manipulation. The US government also injects itself into the economy through subsidies, bailouts, tax credits, and loan guarantees. For example, approximately 20 billion is spent on farm subsidies every year, including for the farming of corn, soybeans, rice, wheat, and cotton (Edwards, 2018). Last, the government also provides services, from public schooling to policing.

The most important social theorist to analyze and critique capitalism was Karl Marx, a German-born philosopher and economist. Although it is difficult to summarize Marx's vast writings on the subject in volumes one through three of *Capital*, his *Economic and Philosophical Manuscripts*, *Grundrisse*, *Communist Manifesto*, and many others, some key points about his arguments should be made. He argued that humans are, under capitalism, alienated from the labor process, the product of their labor, and indeed from others and the very nature of being human by the necessity to make products that do not 'belong' to them. Capitalism transforms all social relations into market relations to be bought and sold. The workers (for Marx, 'proletarians') are furthermore always exploited as they produce more value for the capitalist class through their labor than they are compensated for—their labor was the reason for the profit of the ruling class. There is always class conflict as a result. He also believed that capitalism as a system contained in it, inherently, contradictions (for example, the overproduction of goods to make a profit, but that the increasingly poorer workers of the world could not afford to buy) that would inevitably lead to growing number of ever-larger crises, and hence to its eventual end.

Marx's writings argue that the working class would eventually lead a revolution to overthrow the capitalist class and bring about a shift in the mode of production to socialism. He never laid a blueprint *per se*, though, for what he thought a communist or socialist society should look like. However, we can make some generalizations about this mode of production. Unlike capitalism, **socialism** as a mode of production does not assume the profit motive or private ownership of the means of production. In an ideal-type socialist economy, the government or collective owns the means of production and goods, with work and the resultant wealth from production divided equally among all members of society. Collectively made goods and services provide for the needs of the citizenry (such as for housing, food, healthcare, childcare, and education), rather than be determined on the basis of ability to pay. Decision-making is centralized because of the collective orientation of socialism as an economic system, with the government setting the prices for wages and goods (Kendall, 2011, p. 422). The prototypical example given of a socialist state is the Soviet Union, which came into existence after the Russian Revolution of 1917, and which collapsed in 1991. Socialist countries still in existence include Cuba, China, North Korea, Vietnam, and Laos.

In the United States today, a variant of socialism is endorsed among some left-leaning politicians. Democratic socialism is an economic and political philosophy also found in European nations like Norway and Denmark, which does not advocate for the overthrow of capitalism, but promotes more governmental regulation and intervention to distribute wealth more equally.

Working Conditions and Challenges

The deplorable conditions for many workers in factories, mines and mills during the Industrial Revolution ushered in the US Labor Movement in the mid-19th century, including the rise of unions. Labor unions allow workers to use **collective bargaining**, which is a way for workers to make negotiations on behalf of all members (thus increasing their leverage) with the union leadership. Some tactics that unions use to put pressure on employers include protests and strikes, which are work stoppages. Union membership in the US has been steadily declining after a peak in the 1950s of around 35 percent. Public sector workers, particularly those in protective services like the police, are more likely to be unionized, and because of this, African Americans (the population more likely to be in public sector jobs) are also more likely to have union jobs, and men are more likely to be unionized than women. Union membership in the US now stands at 10.5 percent, and union workers have higher median earnings than non-unionized workers (BLS, 2018a). Still, public opinion in the US about unions is mixed, with 55 percent of Americans holding a favorable view of unions, and 33 percent, an unfavorable view (Drew, 2018).

Although certainly working conditions have improved since the 19th century, with the implementation of the five-day, 40-hour workweek, sick leave, and other benefits and protections afforded to full-time workers, many challenges still confront workers today. The US still does not have a federal mandate for paid parental leave after the birth of a child, a rare exception among advanced democracies. There is the rise of contingent labor in a so-called "gig" economy, which means that individuals must work multiple part-time jobs ("gigs") or work as "temps" with a short-term contract in order to earn a livable salary. The unemployment rate at the start of the 2020s was at its lowest in 50 years, at 3.7 percent. People over 16 are classified as unemployed if they do not have a job, have actively looked for work in the prior four weeks, and are currently available for work. Yet, labor force participation, which is also a measure of labor market health, is around 62.9 percent, its lowest since 1977. Those who are underemployed (e.g. those who want to work full-time, but can only find part-time work), those who are employed but are looking for other work, and the long-term unemployed (those who have given up looking) are not counted in unemployment statistics, but are counted when measuring labor force participation. Ideally, unemployment rates are low, and participation rates are high. Those living in institutions such as jails and prisons are also not tallied in unemployment figures.

Conclusion

This chapter provided foundational knowledge about the primary sociological institutions which we encounter in any human society, in various manifestations historically and among different cultures. While we have given only brief glimpses of the current configurations of these institutions in the United States, it is important to consider that these are not unchangeable. If an institution, sociologically, is a set of norms and/or rules that regulate human behavior and govern the structure of relationships of individuals to one another, then they can evolve over time in response to major structural changes in other institutions, or, indeed, through daily changes in ways of relating to one another. "Every day we construct and change social institutions through ordinary interactions and the meanings we ascribe to them," Conley (2013, p. 15) observes. The landmark Supreme Court cases to be discussed in the following chapters demonstrate how legal changes influence society and institutions, but are also affected by social changes that evolve over time. The relationship is dialectical and ever-evolving.

Review Questions

- What is a social institution? Which sociologists are associated with the analysis of institutions?
- What are the five primary social institutions?
- Summarize the major characteristics of the five institutions.
- Choose two of the major social institutions. Give one example of how each might affect the other. For example, how does religion affect government? How does education affect economy?
- Do you think the laws are created out of social norms, or that social norms are created out of laws? Explain your answer.

References

Aiken, J., Salmon, E., & Hanges, P. (2013). The origins and legacy of the civil rights act of 1964. *Journal of Business and Psychology, 28*(4), 383–399.

Barkan, S. (2020). *Sociology*. Retrieved from https://socialsci.libretexts.org/@go/page/2003

Briggs, D. (2016). The rise and fall (and rise?) of Christian nationalism. *Christian Century, 133*(26), 16.

Bureau of Labor Statistics (BLS). (2018a). *Labor unions*. Retrieved from www.bls.gov/news.release/union2.nr0.htm

Bureau of Labor Statistics (BLS). (2018b). *Measuring the value of education*. Retrieved from www.bls.gov/careeroutlook/2018/data-on-display/education-pays.htm

Cohen, P. N. (2019). The coming divorce decline. *Socius, 5*. Retrieved from https://journals.sagepub.com/doi/full/10.1177/2378023119873497

Coleman, J. S. (1990). Commentary. *American Sociological Review, 55*(3), 333–339.

Conley, D. (2013). *You may ask yourself*. New York: W.W. Norton.

Desilver, D. (2019). *Despite global concerns about democracy, more than half of countries are democratic*. Pew Research Center. Retrieved from www.pewresearch.org/fact-tank/2019/05/14/more-than-half-of-countries-are-democratic/

Dobrin, A. (2004). *Religious ethics: A sourcebook*. Mumbai: Hindi Grantha Karyalay.

Drew, D. (2018). *Most Americans view unions favorably, though few workers belong to one*. Pew Research Center. Retrieved from www.pewresearch.org/fact-tank/2018/08/30/union-membership-2/

Durkheim, E. (1995). *The elementary forms of religious life*. New York: The Free Press.

Edwards, C. (2018). *Reforming federal farm policies*. Cato Institute. Retrieved from www.cato.org/people/policy-scholars

Engman, A., & Cranford, C. (2016). Habit and the body: Lessons for social theories of habit from the experience of people with physical disabilities. *Sociological Theory, 34*(1), 27–44.

File, Thom. (2017). Voting in America: A look at the 2016 US election. *US Census Bureau*. Retrieved from https://www.census.gov/newsroom/blogs/random-samplings/2017/05/voting_in_america.html

Gallup. (2019). *Religion*. Retrieved from https://news.gallup.com/poll/1690/religion.aspx

Garcelon, M. (2010). The missing key: Institutions, networks, and the project of neoclassical sociology. *Sociological Theory, 28*(3), 326–353.

Geiger, A. W. (2018). *How Americans see their country and their democracy*. Pew Research Center. Retrieved from www.pewresearch.org/fact-tank/2018/07/04/how-americans-see-their-country-and-their-democracy

Goffman, E. (1961). *Asylums*. New York: Doubleday/Anchor.

Goldstein, S. (2018, June 5). Nine out of 10 new jobs are going to those with a college degree. *Market-Watch*. Retrieved from https://www.marketwatch.com/story/nine-out-of-10-new-jobs-are-going-to-those-with-a-college-degree-2018-06-04

Hajnal, Z. (2018, October 22). Why does no one vote in local elections? *The New York Times*.

Holyoke, T. T. (2015). *The ethical lobbyist: Reforming Washington's influence industry*. Georgetown University Press.

"Horace Mann." (2021). *PBS*. Retrieved from https://www.pbs.org/onlyateacher/horace.html

Keizer, P. (2007). *The concept of institution in economics and sociology, a methodological exposition*. Utrecht School of Economics Tjalling C. Koopmans Research Institute, Discussion Paper Series 07–25. Retrieved from https://www.researchgate.net/publication/23696141_The_Concept_of_Institution_in_Economics_and_Sociology_a_Methodological_Exposition

Kendall, D. (2011). *Sociology in our times*. Belmont, CA: Wadsworth.

Kocka, J. (2016). Capitalism: A short history. Princeton University Press.

Legal Information Institute. (2017). *Marriage*. Cornell University Law School. Retrieved from www.law.cornell.edu/wex/marriage

Legal Information Institute. (2019). *Marriage laws*. Cornell University Law School. Retrieved from www.law.cornell.edu/wex/table_marriage

McEwen, C. A. (1980). Continuities in the study of total and nontotal institutions. *Annual Review of Sociology*, *6*(1), 143–185.

McKeown, T. (2008). Organizational routines in political science. In M. C. Becker (Ed.), *Handbook of organizational routines* (pp. 31–51). Cambridge, MA: Edward Elgar.

National Center for Education Statistics. (2016). *Homeschooling in the United States*. Retrieved from https://files.eric.ed.gov/fulltext/ED569947.pdf

National Center for Education Statistics. (2017). *Compulsory school attendance laws*. Retrieved https://nces.ed.gov/programs/statereform/tab5_1.asp

National Center for Education Statistics. (2019a). *National assessment of adult literacy*. Retrieved from https://nces.ed.gov/naal/lit_history.asp

National Center for Education Statistics. (2019b). *School choice in the United States*. Retrieved from https://nces.ed.gov/fastfacts/display.asp?id=55

National Center for Education Statistics. (2021). *Digest of Education Statistics, 2019*. Retrieved from https://nces.ed.gov/fastfacts/display.asp?id=84

National Center for Lesbian Rights (NCLR). (2018). *Marriage, domestic partnerships, and civil unions: An overview of relationship recognition for same-sex couples within the United States*. Retrieved from www.nclrights.org/legal-help-resources/resource/marriage-domestic-partnerships-and-civil-unions-an-overview-of-relationship-recognition-for-same-sex-couples-within-the-united-states/

National District Attorneys Association (NDAA). (2013). *Statutory compilation regarding incest statutes*. Retrieved from https://ndaa.org/wp-content/uploads/Incest-Statutes-2013.pdf

Open Textbook Library. (2010). *Sociology: Understanding and changing the social world*. Minneapolis: University of Minnesota.

Parker, P. (2015). The historical role of women in higher education. *Administrative Issues Journal: Connecting Education, Practice, and Research*, *5*(1), 3–14.

Parsons, T. (1990). Prolegomena to a theory of social institutions. *American Sociological Review*, *55*(3), 319–333.

Perticone, J. (2019, March 11). The 20 companies and groups that spent the most money to influence lawmakers. *Business Insider*. Retrieved from www.businessinsider.com/lobbying-groups-spent-most-money-washington-dc-2018-2019-3

Pew Research Center. (2014). *Record share of Americans have never been married*. Retrieved from https://www.pewresearch.org/social-trends/2014/09/24/record-share-of-americans-have-never-married/

Pew Research Center. (2017). *Many countries favor specific religions, officially or unofficially*. Retrieved from www.pewforum.org/2017/10/03/many-countries-favor-specific-religions-officially-or-unofficially/

Pew Research Center. (2019a). *Eight facts about love and marriage*. Retrieved from www.pewresearch.org/fact-tank/2019/02/13/8-facts-about-love-and-marriage/

Pew Research Center. (2019b). *Religious landscape study*. Retrieved from www.pewforum.org/religious-landscape-study/

Ray, B. D. (2016). *Homeschool SAT scores higher than national average*. National Home Education Research Institute. Retrieved from www.nheri.org/homeschool-sat-scores-for-2014-higher-than-national-average/

Sherwood, H. (2019, October 17). Americans becoming less Christian. *The Guardian*.

Schuit, S., & Rogowski, J. (2017). Race, representation, and the voting rights act. *American Journal of Political Science*, *61*(3), 513–526.

Scott, J. (2018). *Lobbying and society: A political sociology of interest groups*. Cambridge: Polity.

Shermer, M. (2018). The number of Americans with no religious affiliation is rising. In *Scientific American*

Tatham, M. (2019). Student loan debt climbs to $1.4 trillion in 2019. *Experian*. Retrieved from www.experian.com/blogs/ask-experian/state-of-student-loan-debt/

Thumma, S., & Bird, W. (2015). *Recent shifts in America's largest protestant Churches: Megachurches 2015 report* Hartford Institute for Religious Research. Retrieved from www.hartfordinstitute.org/megachurch/megachurches.html

United States Census Bureau. (2017). *Highest educational attainment levels since 1940*. Retrieved from www.census.gov/newsroom/press-releases/2017/cb17-51.html

United States Census Bureau (USCB). (2019). *Subject definitions*. Retrieved from www.census.gov/programs-surveys/cps/technical-documentation/subject-definitions.html#family

Vinovskis, M. A. (1992). Schooling and poor children in 19th-century America. *American Behavioral Scientist*, *35*(3), 313–331.

Weber, M. (1930/2007). The protestant ethic and the spirit of capitalism. In C. Calhoun, J. Gerteis, J. Moody, S. Pfaff & I. Virk (Eds.), *Classical sociological theory*. Maiden, MA: Blackwell Publishing.

Wimmer, A., & Feinstein, Y. (2010). The rise of the nation state across the world, 1816–2001. *American Sociological Review*, *75*(5), 764–790.

Wong, A. (2014). When private school tuition costs more than college. *The Atlantic*.

3

EDUCATION

Learning Objectives

After reading this chapter, students should be able to:

- Explain the roles Linda and Oliver Brown played in *Brown v. Board of Education*
- Describe the impact of the Brown decision on the institution of education
- Summarize the persistence of segregation within schools
- Detail how Brown influenced higher education
- Analyze the *San Antonio Independent School District v. Rodriguez case*
- Understand how public education is funded
- Generalize how income and wealth gaps impact learning and education
- Outline how informal learning links to the learning and achievement gaps between students

Key Terms

Ability Grouping and Tracking Systems
Affirmative Action
Brown v. Board of Education
Cultural Capital
Desegregation
Forced Busing
Hypersegregation
Income
San Antonio Independent School District v. Magnet Schools
Social Economic Status (SES)
Wealth

Brown v. Board of Education Introduction

The *Brown v. Board of Education* case argued by the Supreme Court, which in 1954 ruled racially segregated public schools to be unconstitutional, is one of the most well-known and pivotal cases in the history of the United States of America. Lesser known is perhaps the person behind the famous case: Linda Carol Brown.

Born in 1943 in Topeka, Kansas, Linda Brown was only eight years old when the *Brown v. Board of Education* case began in 1951. Daughter of Leola and Oliver Brown, Linda had two younger sisters and the Brown family lived in a culturally diverse neighborhood. "I played with

DOI: 10.4324/9781003021438-4

FIGURE 3.1 "Brown v Board of Education National Historic Site"

children that were Spanish-American," Linda Brown said in an interview in 1985. "I played with children that were white, children that were Indian, and black children in my neighborhood." However, after the *Plessy v. Ferguson* case of 1896 that dictated the segregation of all public facilities under the "separate but equal" doctrine, Linda Brown had to attend an all-black school, Monroe Elementary School, which was far away from her house and in an economically depressed neighborhood. Hers was one in four schools in Topeka for all-black students, a staggering difference when compared to the eighteen all-white schools. In order to reach Monroe Elementary School—which in December 1992 was declared a National Historic Site and has since been managed by the National Park Service—Linda Brown's daily routine consisted of a long walk through busy avenues and railroad tracks, along with a two-miles bus ride. "When I first started the walk it was very frightening to me," she stated, "and then when wintertime came, it was a very cold walk. I remember that. I remember walking, tears freezing up on my face, because I began to cry" (Genzlinger, 2018).

Given her young age, Linda Brown couldn't understand why she was not allowed to go to the school that was right in their neighborhood, which all the White children she played with attended. Leola and Oliver Brown tried to explain—using words that an eight-year-old could comprehend—the meaning of racial segregation to their daughter. In an interview, Leola Brown revealed that she explained that "It was because her face was black . . . and she just couldn't go to school with the white races at that time." As time went by, her father became more and more concerned about his daughter's upbringing. He wasn't so much worried about the quality of education that she was receiving at Monroe Elementary School, as he was about the distance she had to travel every day in order to reach the school. Something had to change, and it was time for him to take matters into his own hands. According to Leola Brown, her husband reassured their daughter that "he was going to try his best to do something about it and see that that was done away" (Romo, 2018).

Oliver Brown was born in 1918. A former Golden Gloves champion boxer who still maintained his dominant and heavyset appearance, he was now a welder for the Atchison Topeka and Santa Fe Railroad. He had also studied theology and became a pastor at the African Methodist Episcopal Church. Brown was a member of the Topeka National Association for the Advancement of Colored People (NAACP), an organization founded in 1919 by American writer and sociologist W.E.B. DuBois—among other people—with the mission of securing "the political, educational, social, and economic equality of rights in order to eliminate race-based discrimination and ensure the health and well-being of all persons" (NAACP, 2021).

In the fall of 1950, Oliver Brown joined a group of other 12 parents that had been assembled by the Topeka NAACP to press a test case in federal court. According to Cheryl Brown Henderson, Linda Brown's younger sister, the 13 parents were instructed by the NAACP to "Find the nearest white school to your home and take your child or children and a witness, and attempt to enroll in the fall, and then come back and tell us what happened" (History Now, 2017). For the Brown family, the closest school was Sumner Elementary School—only four blocks away from their residence.

On a sunny morning of September 1950, Linda Brown held her father's hand and walked with him to the all-White school—although it was hard for her to keep up with the fast pace her determined father kept, as she herself recalled in an interview: "Being very small, the steps seemed very large and tall, and we walked into this building." Once they reached the school, Oliver Brown instructed her to wait outside the principal's office, as he went in to talk about the possibility of his daughter attending the school. According to Linda Brown's recollections, the meeting did not go well. Voices were getting louder and soon after her father stormed out of the office, visibly aggravated. Although he did not share the details of the meeting with her on their way back home, young Linda Brown "could feel the tension in his hand, the tension from his body being generated to my hand, because he was very upset about something" (Brown Smith, 1985).

Five months later, in February 1951, attorney Charles S. Scott led the Topeka National Association for the Advancement of Colored People (NAACP) to file a lawsuit against the Topeka Board of Education. After three judges ruled in favor of the school district—thus allowing the district to keep its segregated schools—the case was appealed directly to the Supreme Court by NAACP chief counsel, Thurgood Marshall, who would one day become the first African American Supreme Court Justice. Although Oliver Brown was only one of 13 plaintiffs who had joined the case to fight the law on behalf of their 20 children, his last name was the first to appear in alphabetical order, hence the case was recorded as *Oliver L. Brown et al. v. Board of Education of Topeka* and why it is now commonly referred to as *Brown v. Board of Education*.

While the Court argued the case, deciding the question of whether the Equal Protection Clause of the Fourteenth Amendment of the Constitution (see Box 3.1)—which was not the only one that had been brought to their attention, as similar cases had been filed in Delaware, South Carolina, Virginia, and Washington, D.C.—life went on as usual at the Brown household. Three years went by and Linda Brown was in junior high school. On May 17, 1954, she had just returned home from school when she saw her father had tears in his eyes, and her mother told her that the Supreme Court had ruled in their favor and against the Board of Education of Topeka: schools in the entire country were to be desegregated. Linda Brown and her two sisters would never attend Sumner School—although one of her sisters eventually became a teacher for the Topeka School District—because during the lengthy case the family had moved to Springfield, Missouri, where her father had been offered a position at the African Methodist

Episcopal Church. A few years later after their move, Oliver Brown had a heart attack and died at the age of 42.

Linda Brown, who went on to become an educator, was proud of the role that she and her family played in the advancement for African American civil rights and equal opportunities. She died on March 25, 2018, at the age of 75, and was remembered by many people, including Kansas Governor Jess Colyer and President of the NAACP Legal Defense and Educational Fund, Sherrilyn Ifill, as an unlikely hero who, as a young woman and with the support of her family, fought for the greater good of African Americans in the United States.

BOX 3.1 FOURTEENTH AMENDMENT AND THE EQUAL PROTECTION CLAUSE

What is the Equal Protection Clause described in the Fourteenth Amendment? It is the idea that the federal and state government must treat people who are in similar circumstances the same way regardless of their race, gender, religion, or sex. The categorizing of people within similar circumstances is called Classification. For example, while the state can require all people who wish to receive a driver's license to be a minimum of 16 years old, the state cannot prevent—and therefore, discriminate against—16-year-olds who identify themselves as part of a racial minority from earning their driver's license because of their race. Another example of classification of people within similar circumstances can be found in the case of single parents who are financially challenged and are eligible to receive government aid regardless of whether it is a single mother or father—therefore, regardless of their gender. However, if said single parents are financially stable and can afford to provide for their own child(ren), they will not be eligible for government aid, regardless of their gender.

So, what happens if individuals feel that the state or federal government have not treated them impartially? After proving to the court that they have indeed been discriminated against and that said discrimination resulted in damage to the people, the court will have to choose which judicial level of scrutiny they have to apply: strict scrutiny, intermediate scrutiny, or rational basis review.

Strict scrutiny, which is the highest level of scrutiny that a court can apply—and that requires the burden of proof to fall on the government—is the judicial review that is generally applied when there is a case of discrimination or prejudice. This level of scrutiny was brought on by Chief Justice Earl Warren (1953–1968), who recognized the need for a clearer examination and evaluation of laws under the Equal Protection Clause. If the plaintiff is suing because of a perceived violation of fundamental rights—which include those highlighted in the Bill of Rights as well as others, such as privacy, marriage, voting, and more—the court will have to determine whether the government applied a law that is to be deemed unconstitutional. Some of the most notorious cases in which the Supreme Court applied a strict scrutiny are: *Brown v. Board of Education of Topeka*, *Roe v. Wade*, and *Loving v. Virginia*.

Intermediate scrutiny is a test that the court relies on to decide whether a statute is unconstitutional—in this case, government must present proof. It was first applied in 1976 when the Supreme Court—under the Warren E. Burger Court—argued the *Craig v. Boren, Governor of Oklahoma* case, which determined that discrimination on the basis of gender is unconstitutional as it affects a protected class of people. In the *Craig v. Boren* case, the

Burger Court decided that the Oklahoma statue that allowed the sale of non-intoxicating 3.2 percent beer to females over the age of 18 but prohibited it to males of under 21 years of age went against the Equal Protection Clause as it was based on gender and not age.

The rational basis review is the lowest level and determines whether a statute or ordinance has a legitimate state interest and is therefore constitutional. It was formally used for the first time in the *Nebbia v. People of State of New York* case (1934) under the Charles E. Hughes Court, which decided that New York had the right to regulate the price of milk. Unlike the previous levels of scrutiny, the rational test must be proven by the challenger.

Brown v. Board of Education Decision

BROWN V. BOARD OF EDUCATION OF TOPEKA, 347 U.S. 483 (1954)

MR. CHIEF JUSTICE WARREN delivered the opinion of the Court.

These cases come to us from the States of Kansas, South Carolina, Virginia, and Delaware. They are premised on different facts and different local conditions, but a common legal question justifies their consideration together in this consolidated opinion.

In each of the cases, minors of the Negro race, through their legal representatives, seek the aid of the courts in obtaining admission to the public schools of their community on a non-segregated basis. In each instance, they had been denied admission to schools attended by White children under laws requiring or permitting segregation according to race. This segregation was alleged to deprive the plaintiffs of the equal protection of the laws under the Fourteenth Amendment. In each of the cases other than the Delaware case, a three-judge federal district court denied relief to the plaintiffs on the so-called "separate but equal" doctrine announced by this Court in *Plessy v. Ferguson*, 163 U. S. 537. Under that doctrine, equality of treatment is accorded when the races are provided substantially equal facilities, even though these facilities be separate. In the Delaware case, the Supreme Court of Delaware adhered to that doctrine, but ordered that the plaintiffs be admitted to the White schools because of their superiority to the Negro schools.

The plaintiffs contend that segregated public schools are not "equal" and cannot be made "equal," and that hence they are deprived of the equal protection of the laws. Because of the obvious importance of the question presented, the Court took jurisdiction. Argument was heard in the 1952 Term, and reargument was heard this Term on certain questions propounded by the Court.

Reargument was largely devoted to the circumstances surrounding the adoption of the Fourteenth Amendment in 1868. It covered exhaustively consideration of the Amendment in Congress, ratification by the states, then-existing practices in racial segregation, and the views of proponents and opponents of the Amendment. This discussion and our own investigation convince us that, although these sources cast some light, it is not enough to resolve the problem with which we are faced. At best, they are inconclusive. The most avid proponents of the post-War Amendments undoubtedly intended them to remove all legal distinctions among "all persons born or naturalized in the United States." Their opponents, just as certainly, were antagonistic to both the letter and the spirit of the Amendments and wished them to have the most limited effect. What others in Congress and the state legislatures had in mind cannot be determined with any degree of certainty.

An additional reason for the inconclusive nature of the Amendment's history with respect to segregated schools is the status of public education at that time. In the South, the movement toward free common schools, supported by general taxation, had not yet taken hold. Education of White children was largely in the hands of private groups. Education of Negroes was almost non-existent, and practically all of the race were illiterate. In fact, any education of Negroes was forbidden by law in some states. Today, in contrast, many Negroes have achieved outstanding success in the arts and sciences, as well as in the business and professional world. It is true that public school education at the time of the Amendment had advanced further in the North, but the effect of the Amendment on Northern States was generally ignored in the congressional debates. Even in the North, the conditions of public education did not approximate those existing today. The curriculum was usually rudimentary; ungraded schools were common in rural areas; the school term was but three months a year in many states, and compulsory school attendance was virtually unknown. As a consequence, it is not surprising that there should be so little in the history of the Fourteenth Amendment relating to its intended effect on public education.

In the first cases in this Court construing the Fourteenth Amendment, decided shortly after its adoption, the Court interpreted it as proscribing all state-imposed discriminations against the Negro race. The doctrine of "separate but equal" did not make its appearance in this Court until 1896 in the case of *Plessy v. Ferguson, supra*, involving not education but transportation. American courts have since labored with the doctrine for over half a century. In this Court, there have been six cases involving the "separate but equal" doctrine in the field of public education. In *Cumming v. County Board of Education*, 175 U. S. 528, and *Gong Lum v. Rice*, 275 U. S. 78, the validity of the doctrine itself was not challenged. In more recent cases, all on the graduate school level, inequality was found in that specific benefits enjoyed by White students were denied to Negro students of the same educational qualifications. *Missouri ex rel. Gaines v. Canada*, 305 U. S. 337; *Sipuel v. Oklahoma*, 332 U. S. 631; *Sweatt v. Painter*, 339 U. S. 629; *McLaurin v. Oklahoma State Regents*, 339 U. S. 637. In none of these cases was it necessary to reexamine the doctrine to grant relief to the Negro plaintiff. And in *Sweatt v. Painter, supra*, the Court expressly reserved decision on the question whether *Plessy v. Ferguson* should be held inapplicable to public education.

In the instant cases, that question is directly presented. Here, unlike *Sweatt v. Painter*, there are findings below that the Negro and White schools involved have been equalized, or are being equalized, with respect to buildings, curricula, qualifications and salaries of teachers, and other "tangible" factors. Our decision, therefore, cannot turn on merely a comparison of these tangible factors in the Negro and White schools involved in each of the cases. We must look instead to the effect of segregation itself on public education.

In approaching this problem, we cannot turn the clock back to 1868, when the Amendment was adopted, or even to 1896, when *Plessy v. Ferguson* was written. We must consider public education in the light of its full development and its present place in American life throughout the nation. Only in this way can it be determined if segregation in public schools deprives these plaintiffs of the equal protection of the laws.

Today, education is perhaps the most important function of state and local governments. Compulsory school attendance laws and the great expenditures for education both demonstrate our recognition of the importance of education to our democratic society. It is required in the performance of our most basic public responsibilities, even service in the armed forces. It is the very foundation of good citizenship. Today it is a principal instrument in awakening the child to cultural values, in preparing him for later professional training, and in helping him to adjust normally to his environment. In these days, it is doubtful that any child may reasonably be expected to succeed in life if he is denied the opportunity of an education. Such an opportunity, where the state has undertaken to provide it, is a right which must be made available to all on equal terms.

We come then to the question presented: does segregation of children in public schools solely on the basis of race, even though the physical facilities and other "tangible" factors may be equal, deprive the children of the minority group of equal educational opportunities? We believe that it does.

In *Sweatt v. Painter, supra*, in finding that a segregated law school for Negroes could not provide them equal educational opportunities, this Court relied in large part on "those qualities which are incapable of objective measurement but which make for greatness in a law school." In *McLaurin v. Oklahoma State Regents, supra*, the Court, in requiring that a Negro admitted to a White graduate school be treated like all other students, again resorted to intangible considerations: ". . . his ability to study, to engage in discussions and exchange views with other students, and, in general, to learn his profession."

Such considerations apply with added force to children in grade and high schools. To separate them from others of similar age and qualifications solely because of their race generates a feeling of inferiority as to their status in the community that may affect their hearts and minds in a way unlikely ever to be undone. The effect of this separation on their educational opportunities was well stated by a finding in the Kansas case by a court which nevertheless felt compelled to rule against the Negro plaintiffs:

> Segregation of white and colored children in public schools has a detrimental effect upon the colored children. The impact is greater when it has the sanction of the law, for the policy of separating the races is usually interpreted as denoting the inferiority of the negro group. A sense of inferiority affects the motivation of a child to learn. Segregation with the sanction of law, therefore, has a tendency to [retard] the educational and mental development of negro children and to deprive them of some of the benefits they would receive in a racial[ly] integrated school system.

Whatever may have been the extent of psychological knowledge at the time of *Plessy v. Ferguson*, this finding is amply supported by modern authority. Any language in *Plessy v. Ferguson* contrary to this finding is rejected.

We conclude that, in the field of public education, the doctrine of "separate but equal" has no place. Separate educational facilities are inherently unequal. Therefore, we hold that the plaintiffs and others similarly situated for whom the actions have been brought are, by reason of the segregation complained of, deprived of the equal protection of the laws guaranteed by the Fourteenth Amendment. This disposition makes unnecessary any discussion whether such segregation also violates the Due Process Clause of the Fourteenth Amendment.

Because these are class actions, because of the wide applicability of this decision, and because of the great variety of local conditions, the formulation of decrees in these cases presents problems of considerable complexity. On reargument, the consideration of appropriate relief was necessarily subordinated to the primary question—the constitutionality of segregation in public education. We have now announced that such segregation is a denial of the equal protection of the laws. In order that we may have the full assistance of the parties in formulating decrees, the cases will be restored to the docket, and the parties are requested to present further argument on Questions 4 and 5 previously propounded by the Court for the reargument this Term. The Attorney General of the United States is again invited to participate. The Attorneys General of the states requiring or permitting segregation in public education will also be permitted to appear as *amici curiae* [e.g, a "friend of the court"--a person who isn't party to the case but who has strong interest in or views on the subject matter of an action] upon request to do so by September 15, 1954, and submission of briefs by October 1, 1954.

It is so ordered.

The Impact of *Brown v. Board of Education* on Education

Almost 70 years after the *Brown v. Board of Education* decision, what can we say has been the impact on the institution of education of its major injunction: that separate but equal is inherently unequal, and that therefore segregation in schools is unconstitutional? Here, we will focus on the question of if and to what extent schools have been desegregated in grammar and high schools, the policies implemented to try to achieve integration, as well as *Brown v. Board of Education*'s effect on post-secondary educational attainment for racial minorities.

Integration in K-12 Education: Benefits and Controversies

Chief Justice Warren's statement in the unanimous opinion of *Brown v. Board of Education*,

> To separate [black students] from others of similar age and qualifications solely because of their race generates a feeling of inferiority as to their status in the community that may affect their hearts and minds in a way unlikely ever to be undone

hinted at the belief that not only was segregation unconstitutional, but lack of integration would lead to negative outcomes for Black students. Since this time there has been extensive research on how integration affects student outcomes—both racial minority as well as White students. Black adults have been found to have higher educational attainment in integrated schools, including being less likely to drop out of high school and obtaining higher standardized test scores. More positive outcomes in non-educational arenas such as in occupational attainment, health, and lower incarceration rates were also correlated with the move away from segregation. At the same time, adverse effects on White students' educational attainment has not been demonstrated, but in fact shown to be unaffected by integration. Racial diversity in the learning environment has been shown to have positive impacts on learning across racial groups (Ayscue, Frankenberg, & Siegel-Hawley, 2017).

As discussed in Chapter 2, education as a social institution is not only about "book learning," and transmission of specific facts, but also learning about cultural values and norms. Integrated schooling provides young people with exposure and positive contact with peers of different racial and ethnic backgrounds, and therefore has been shown to reduce racial animosity, anxieties, stereotyping, and prejudice into adulthood (Kahlenberg, Potter, & Quick, 2019). Contact with those who are different, learning to negotiate differences in common pursuits, then, becomes an educational goal in itself, a form of positive socialization and cognitive challenge that can spark innovation and even encourage people to work harder (Phillips, 2014). Especially in the United States with its multicultural society, where by 2045 the US Census projects that White Americans will be in the minority, the ability to learn and work across racial divides and foster social cohesion is of great importance. Parents, regardless of race, income, gender, or political party now support racial integration in schools, although whiter and more affluent parents lean more often to choosing whiter and more socio-economically advantaged schools for their own children, even if they believe in the principle of integration (Torres & Weissbourd, 2020).

Yet, some have challenged the idea that integration brought only positive outcomes in education or is sufficient, if nominally achieved, to remedy inequalities not only between Black and White students but other racial groups. Students even in integrated schools may experience a form of segregation through academic **ability grouping** and **tracking systems**. This system was devised in the early 20th century—well before the *Brown v. Board of Education* decision—following an influx of immigrant children into the public school system, and was found in a majority of schools by the mid-20th century (Futtrell & Gomez, 2008). The practice has continued, and led to Blacks and Latinos being underrepresented in more academically challenging 'tracks' vis-à-vis Whites and Asians. Compared to their peers, Blacks and Latinos are less likely to be in programs for the gifted or talented and accelerated/advanced placement courses (collectively known as GATE—gifted and talented education programs), which can result in persistent educational achievement gaps (Kohli & Quarts, 2014).

Integration's benefits were challenged by the Black community as well. Critical race scholar Derrick Bell argued that Black-only schools should be preserved and created (1980). Among some of the concerns are integration's not taking the needs of Black children and communities fully into account (Boddie & Parker, 2018). W.E.B. DuBois, founder of the NAACP, asserted that Black-only schools helped build a sense of Black pride, enhanced community cohesion, and allowed students to be taught by Black teachers. Lutz (2017) shows that after *Brown*, 38,000 black teachers in the southern and border states lost their jobs as schools were integrated. This has affected the educational landscape in the current day, where currently, fewer than 7 percent of public school teachers are black, and 20 percent overall belong to a minority group, whereas over 50 percent of the student body is non-White (Geiger, 20 1 8). This may lead to negative results for students, as recent research has shown that **role model effects** exist, and Black students who encounter Black teachers in their K-12 years are more likely than their peers who have not, to enter college (Gersehenson, Hart, Hyman, Lindsay, & Papgeorge, 2018). Encountering someone of one's own race who has gone on for a college degree demonstrates for children that effort given in one's education can lead to professional success.

Desegregation/forced busing, transporting students to schools outside of their own neighborhoods so as to racially integrate, began a few years after *Brown v. Board of Education*, as courts ordered schools to desegregate, and another Supreme Court decision *Swann v. Charlotte-Mecklenburg Board of Education*, ruled it constitutional. Large protests against busing by Whites ensued, not only in the South but also the North, such as in New York City in 1964, when 10,000 White parents gathered to rally for maintaining their children in "neighborhood schools" (Hannah-Jones, 2019). These protests were sometimes violent. While forced busing has declined since the 1980s, and hundreds of school districts are still under court order to desegregate, some do maintain busing (Prasad, 2019).

Persistent Segregation

It should be emphasized that desegregation after *Brown v. Board of Education* was not immediate nor easily achieved. To the contrary, the reason why, as we read earlier, forced busing was mandated, was the existence of opposition to integration. "The Massive Resistance" in the South, which included the Southern Manifesto, signed by 20 percent of all members of Congress, all from the former Confederate States, called *Brown* an abuse of judicial power and urged legislative resistance to the ruling. Unlawful acts of resistance, such as the 1958 bombing of the integrated Clinton High School in Tennessee—brought fear (Hannah-Jones, 2019). By the end of the 1950s, the deep South had not made even a slight headway into integrating its school children, and stronger measures were necessitated. President Dwight Eisenhower famously signed an executive order to bring in troops from the Army's 101st Airborne Division to keep the peace as nine Black students attempted to integrate in Little Rock, Arkansas (Berlin & Rumore, 2017). Deliberate attempts at desegregating school reached their apex from 1964 through the 1980s (Boddie & Parker, 2018) with mandated busing, court-supervised desegregation, and race-based admissions to the magnet schools. Desegregation was especially effective in the southern states, with a high of 40 percent of Black students attending a formerly all-White school (Tatum, 2017). Since that time in the South, the gains made have been eroding, and the North remains even more segregated in its schools. New York, especially New York City, provides a glaring example of segregation—one of the most diverse cities in the country, its public schools are also the most segregated in the United States. Astonishingly, 73 percent of New York's City's charter schools are "apartheid schools," with less than 1 percent White enrollment (Kucsera & Orfield, 2014).

"Severe" segregation persists for African Americans, with stalled progress from Latinos (Orfield & Frankenberg, 2014). This reality exists in spite of the fact that nationwide in the US, some extensive measures have been taken in the US to integrate K-12 schools, including court-ordered desegregation busing, redrawing neighborhood school boundaries, and the creation of magnet schools. **Magnet schools,** otherwise known as "alternative" schools, are typically located in urban school districts. They began to be established in the 1970s after their approval by federal courts to serve as a means of desegregating schools. They are offered as a public school choice that would allow parents to choose schools with an explicitly integrative focus, but also other advantages, including innovative curricular focuses, such as in the performing arts, talented programs, business, or math (Davis, 2014). Although voluntary, magnet schools are popular choices—there are 4,340 magnet schools educating 3.5 million children in the US (MSA, 2020). They often cannot accommodate demand, relying on lottery systems, and receive a sizable amount of funding from their districts and the federal government's Magnet School Assistance Program. While some districts yielded positive results in improving the quality of education and promoting diverse student bodies, yet, research on the wholesale effectiveness of magnet schools on diversity or on learning outcomes is mixed (Goldring & Smrekar, 2002; Arcia, 2006).

The student body as a whole has become more diverse, with White children now under 50 percent of that population. Currently, 40 percent of Black and Latino children go to schools where the student body is 90–100 percent minority, leading to what is known as **hypersegregation**. This number has tripled since the 1980s. Approximately 80 percent of Latinos and 75 percent of Black students attend majority-minority schools, and 40 percent of Latinos and 38 percent of Black students attend schools with a White population of 10 percent or less (Tatum, 2017). And White students are the most segregated group of all: about 70 percent of their classmates are White, far in excess of what their representation in the population would predict (Orfield & Frankenberg, 2014). Whites, therefore, have little exposure to Black, Latino, and Asian students. The reason for this segregation is complex, but segregated housing is a primary driver of segregated schools, the consequence of discrimination in housing, unequal knowledge, and access to financing options, and redlining (Torres & Weissbourd, 2020). So-called "White flight" as public schools were integrating is another reason for hypersegregation (Zirkel & Cantor, 2004).

Among the consequences of segregation, Chen notes (2019): "Schools with large numbers of minority and low-income students face many obstacles: less qualified teachers, tighter budgets, facilities in poor condition, lack of adequate school supplies and texts, violence, health issues, and highly mobile populations." In the next section of this chapter, we will explore wealth and poverty-segregated schooling and the impacts this has upon student populations.

Impact of Brown v. Board of Education *on Higher Education*

The *Brown v. Board of Education* decision did not only impact K-12, but also post-secondary education. Before *Brown,* **Historically Black Colleges and Universities (HBCUs)** served as the primary sites for Black Americans wishing to pursue their degree. These institutions were established largely with the support of Black churches, the American Missionary Association and the Freedman's Bureau. The second Morrill Act of 1890 led to land-grants for institutions for Black students if they were denied admission elsewhere, as they were especially in the Confederate states (NMAAHC, 2020). Very prominent leaders and figures in Black history attended HBCUs, including W.E.B DuBois and Martin Luther King, Jr. Into the 1960s, 70 percent of Black students continued to attend these colleges. However, by 2018, that number hovered around 10 percent (NCES, 2020), with 101 HBCUs across the United States, and 292,000 students. About 24 percent of HBCU students are now non-Black students.

Strayhorn and Johnson point out that a shift (2014), with more Black students attending what are known as PWIs—Predominantly White Institutions—required much more than the *Brown* decision, including the legal changes that ushered in affirmative action. **Affirmative action** includes active efforts to increase educational or employment opportunities for groups who have been historically excluded. Affirmative action has brought controversy from those who claim it unfairly uses race as a basis for evaluating candidates; however recent analyses have shown that even after its use over decades, Black and Latino students are no closer to having more representation in the most selective colleges than they were 35 years ago. For example, Blacks consist of 15 percent of college -age Americans, but make up only 6 percent of college freshmen (Ashkenas, Park, & Pearce, 2017). More Blacks and Latino students are seeing enrollment increase at less-selective colleges, however.

Across all racial minority groups, and even Whites, college enrollment rates have increased in the 21st century. Asian Americans lead college enrollment, with 58 percent of Asian young adults enrolled (DeBrey, Musu, & McFarland, 2019). Blacks have increased enrollment since 2000, from 30 to 36 percent and Latinos from 22 to 39 percent, as have Whites, from 39 to 42 percent.

In thinking about the impact of *Brown v. Board of Education* on the institution of education broadly—including post-secondary education, we see that there is a complex picture, where some advances have been made, but also some retrenchment. However, as the report, "Brown at 60" concluded: "The consensus of nearly 60 years of social science research on the harms of school segregation is clear: separate remains extremely unequal" (2014).

Introduction to *San Antonio Independent School District v. Rodriguez*

Demetrio Rodriguez was only six years old when he moved to San Antonio. His parents, hard-working farmers, wanted to provide him with a better quality of education than the one he could receive in Rio Grande Valley. Rodriguez, however, dropped out of school when World War II broke and joined the Navy. Once a veteran, his parents' dream turned into his own, when he became a father. Unsatisfied with the level of quality education three of his four sons were receiving at Edgewood Elementary School, Rodriguez—at the time 42 years old and working at Kelly Air Force Base just outside of San Antonio—joined forces with many other parents by forming the Edgewood District Concerned Parents Association and suing Texas for the unequal way it financed its public schools.

It all began in May 1968—14 years after the Supreme Court ruled over the landmark *Brown v. Board of Education* decision, declaring that segregated schools were unconstitutional—when hundreds of students decided to protest the quality of education they were receiving by walking out of Edgewood High School in San Antonio, Texas. The high school was located in a rather poor neighborhood, inhabited by mostly Latino families—including the Rodriguez family—a demographic mirrored by the student body that was made up of 90 percent Hispanic and 6 percent African American. The 400 high schoolers had been facing underprivileged conditions in school: forced into overcrowded classrooms, they lacked textbooks and many of their teachers were not only underqualified, but almost half of them were working on emergency teaching permits and did not hold a college degree, which affected the quality of education they were able to impart.

These were not the same issues faced by the nearby Alamo Heights high schoolers, who came from wealthier neighborhoods—as their more expensive homes and businesses attested to. The Alamo Heights students were mostly White—only 18 percent of the entire student body were Latino and 1 percent African American. Their classrooms were not overcrowded, their teachers were not underqualified, their textbooks were not lacking. They also could take advantage of high-quality school amenities, like their Olympic-size swimming pool and a clubhouse that had a fully functioning air conditioning system and even a disco ball that the students would use to make their school gatherings memorable.

Less than 20 miles apart, Edgewood and Alamo Heights offered very different high school experiences to their students, which could eventually result in highly different outcomes for the students' future as well. The sharp divide was due to the tax base: Edgewood had roughly $5,000 in taxable property per student, while Alamo Heights had over $45,000—the state of Texas had imposed a limit on the local tax rates as well, making the situation even more complicated. This clearly caused a large gap in funding to the school in the poorer neighborhood and the school in the wealthier neighborhood. This discrepancy was not limited to the city of San Antonio either. It was actually found to be the case in the entire state of Texas, where rich neighborhoods could afford their students to benefit from better quality of education, while poor neighborhoods could not afford the same luxuries and, as a result, their school districts could barely guarantee the minimum educational and safety requirements. Staff who worked at the Edgewood Elementary School, for example, commented on the level of safety of the building they worked at, admitting that they would not even feel safe getting down the fire escape because they were crumbling, "That would be as much a hazard as the fire," stated a member of the school staff at the same elementary school that Rodriguez's children attended.

The situation was clear for all to see. Children who came from lower-income families and poor neighborhoods could not expect to receive the same level of education of their wealthier peers, as the quality of education was not equal for all. The Edgewood District Concerned Parents Association secured the expert guidance of civil rights lawyer Arthur Gochman, who believed they had a good cause rooted in solid ground, given how the inequality in school funding had been gaining momentum not only in Texas, but also in the rest of the country. In fact, around the same time as the Edgewood students' protest, a graduate student from the University of Chicago, Arthur Wise, published a book titled *Rich School, Poor Schools: The Promise of Equal Educational Opportunities*, in which he indicated how the differences in school funding were a direct violation of the Equal Protection Clause, a clause of the Fourteenth Amendment of the United States Constitution.

The Equal Protection Clause stated that states should not "deny to any person within its jurisdiction the equal protection of the laws." The Equal Protection Clause took effect in 1868 and played a major role in the *Brown v. Board of Education* case. In fact, it was the basis on which the Supreme Court placed its decision to declare that racial segregation was unconstitutional.

The Edgewood students and parents wanted to base their case on the same clause that had been so decisive in the *Brown* case.

In previous years, the Supreme Court had developed a tiered system of **scrutiny** separated into strict scrutiny, mostly used for discrimination cases; intermediate scrutiny, mostly used for gender classification cases; and rationale basis scrutiny, also known as judicial review test, used to determine the constitutionality of an ordinance or a statute. Arthur Gochman had the uphill challenge of not only having to prove that the students had been discriminated against by the governing body, but also that the discrimination resulted in a harmful outcome for the students. The court in San Antonio decided that the *Rodriguez v. San Antonio School District* case—named after the lead plaintiff, Demetrio Rodriguez, just as it had happened for the *Brown v. Board of Education* case when Oliver Brown, father of Linda Brown, became the lead plaintiff—would be subjected to strict scrutiny, based on two arguments: *Rodriguez* was a case of wealth discrimination and education was a fundamental right—one of the most important roles of the Supreme Court is to protect the fundamental rights identified in the US Constitution, such as the right to freedom of religion, the right to property, and the right to equality.

The case, although it was first filed in the District Court for the Western District of Texas, moved through the courts and eventually reached the United States Supreme Court in 1972—four years after the suit was filed. The main question facing the Supreme Court was: Did Texas discriminate against the Edgewood students by violating the Fourteenth Amendment's Equal Protection Clause and, as a result, denying students their fundamental right to an education because it did not distribute funding equally among its school districts?

In 1973, the Supreme Court declined to examine Texas' public education finance system through strict scrutiny and declared that Texas had not discriminated against the Edgewood students. According to Justice Lewis Powell, who was the swing vote in the case, "Education is not among the rights afforded explicit protection under our Federal Constitution. Nor do we find any basis for saying it is implicitly so protected." Therefore, the Supreme Court ruled that Texas did not deny Edgewood students their fundamental right to an education, mainly because education was not recognized as a fundamental right.

San Antonio Independent School District v. Rodriguez Decision

SAN ANTONIO INDEP. SCH. DIST. V. RODRIGUEZ, 411 U.S. 1 (1973)

MR. JUSTICE POWELL delivered the opinion of the Court.

This suit attacking the Texas system of financing public education was initiated by Mexican-American parents whose children attend the elementary and secondary schools in the Edgewood Independent School District, an urban school district in San Antonio, Texas. They brought a class action on behalf of school children throughout the State who are members of minority groups or who are poor and reside in school districts having a low property tax base. Named as defendants were the State Board of Education, the Commissioner of Education, the State Attorney General, and the Bexar County (San Antonio) Board of Trustees. The complaint was filed in the summer of 1968, and a three-judge court was impaneled in January, 1969. In December, 1971, the panel rendered its judgment in a *per curiam* opinion holding the Texas school finance system unconstitutional under the Equal Protection Clause of the Fourteenth Amendment. The State appealed, and we noted probable jurisdiction to consider the far-reaching constitutional questions presented. For the reasons stated in this opinion, we reverse the decision of the District Court.

I

The school district in which appellees reside, the Edgewood Independent School District, has been compared throughout this litigation with the Alamo Heights Independent School District. This comparison between the least and most affluent districts in the San Antonio area serves to illustrate the manner in which the dual system of finance operates, and to indicate the extent to which substantial disparities exist despite the State's impressive progress in recent years. Edgewood is one of seven public school districts in the metropolitan area. Approximately 22,000 students are enrolled in its 25 elementary and secondary schools. The district is situated in the core-city sector of San Antonio in a residential neighborhood that has little commercial or industrial property. The residents are predominantly of Mexican-American descent: approximately 90% of the student population is Mexican-American and over 6% is Negro. The average assessed property value per pupil is $5,960—the lowest in the metropolitan area—and the median family income ($4,686) is also the lowest. At an equalized tax rate of $1.05 per $100 of assessed property—the highest in the metropolitan area—the district contributed $26 to the education of each child for the 1967–1968 school year above its Local Fund Assignment for the Minimum Foundation Program. The Foundation Program contributed $222 per pupil for a state-local total of $248. Federal funds added another $108, for a total of $356 per pupil.

Alamo Heights is the most affluent school district in San Antonio. Its six schools, housing approximately 5,000 students, are situated in a residential community quite unlike the Edgewood District. The school population is predominantly "Anglo," having only 18% Mexican-Americans and less than 1% Negroes. The assessed property value per pupil exceeds $49,000, and the median family income is $8,001. In 1967–1968 the local tax rate of $.85 per $100 of valuation yielded $333 per pupil over and above its contribution to the Foundation Program. Coupled with the $225 provided from that Program, the district was able to supply $558 per student. Supplemented by a $36 per-pupil grant from federal sources, Alamo Heights spent $594 per pupil.

Although the 1967–1968 school year figures provide the only complete statistical breakdown for each category of aid, more recent partial statistics indicate that the previously noted trend of increasing state aid has been significant. For the 1970–1971 school year, the Foundation School Program allotment for Edgewood was $356 per pupil, a 62% increase over the 1967–1968 school year. Indeed, state aid alone in 1970–1971 equaled Edgewood's entire 1967–1968 school budget from local, state, and federal sources. Alamo Heights enjoyed a similar increase under the Foundation Program, netting $491 per pupil in 1970–1971. These recent figures also reveal the extent to which these two districts' allotments were funded from their own required contributions to the Local Fund Assignment. Alamo Heights, because of its relative wealth, was required to contribute out of its local property tax collections approximately $100 per pupil, or about 20% of its Foundation grant. Edgewood, on the other hand, paid only $8.46 per pupil, which is about 2.4% of its grant. It appears then that, at least as to these two districts, the Local Fund Assignment does reflect a rough approximation of the relative taxpaying potential of each.

Despite these recent increases, substantial inter-district disparities in school expenditures found by the District Court to prevail in San Antonio and in varying degrees throughout the State still exist. And it was these disparities, largely attributable to differences in the amounts of money collected through local property taxation, that led the District Court to conclude that Texas' dual system of public school financing violated the Equal Protection Clause. The District Court held that the Texas system discriminates on the basis of wealth in the manner in which education is provided for its people. Finding that wealth is a "suspect" classification, and that education is a "fundamental" interest, the District Court held that the Texas system could be sustained only if the State could show that it was premised upon some compelling state interest. On this issue the court concluded that

> [n]ot only are defendants unable to demonstrate compelling state interests . . . they fail even to establish a reasonable basis for these classifications.

This, then, establishes the framework for our analysis. We must decide, first, whether the Texas system of financing public education operates to the disadvantage of some suspect class or impinges upon a fundamental right explicitly or implicitly protected by the Constitution, thereby requiring strict judicial scrutiny. If so, the judgment of the District Court should be affirmed. If not, the Texas scheme must still be examined to determine whether it rationally furthers some legitimate, articulated state purpose, and therefore does not constitute an invidious discrimination in violation of the Equal Protection Clause of the Fourteenth Amendment.

II

The District Court's opinion does not reflect the novelty and complexity of the constitutional questions posed by appellees' challenge to Texas' system of school financing. In concluding that strict judicial scrutiny was required, that court relied on decisions dealing with the rights of indigents to equal treatment in the criminal trial and appellate processes, and on cases disapproving wealth restrictions on the right to vote. Those cases, the District Court concluded, established wealth as a suspect classification. Finding that the local property tax system discriminated on the basis of wealth, it regarded those precedents as controlling. It then reasoned, based on decisions of this Court affirming the undeniable importance of education, that there is a fundamental right to education, and that, absent some compelling state justification, the Texas system could not stand.

We are unable to agree that this case, which in significant aspects is *sui generis*, may be so neatly fitted into the conventional mosaic of constitutional analysis under the Equal Protection Clause. Indeed we find neither the suspect classification nor the fundamental interest analysis persuasive.

We thus conclude that the Texas system does not operate to the peculiar disadvantage of any suspect class.

But in recognition of the fact that this Court has never heretofore held that wealth discrimination alone provides an adequate basis for invoking strict scrutiny, appellees have not relied solely on this contention. They also assert that the State's system impermissibly interferes with the exercise of a "fundamental" right, and that, accordingly, the prior decisions of this Court require the application of the strict standard of judicial review. It is this question—whether education is a fundamental right, in the sense that it is among the rights and liberties protected by the Constitution—which has so consumed the attention of courts and commentators in recent years.

B

In *Brown v. Board of Education*, a unanimous Court recognized that "education is perhaps the most important function of state and local governments." What was said there in the context of racial discrimination has lost none of its vitality with the passage of time:

> Compulsory school attendance laws and the great expenditures for education both demonstrate our recognition of the importance of education to our democratic society. It is

> required in the performance of our most basic public responsibilities, even service in the armed forces. It is the very foundation of good citizenship. Today it is a principal instrument in awakening the child to cultural values, in preparing him for later professional training, and in helping him to adjust normally to his environment. In these days, it is doubtful that any child may reasonably be expected to succeed in life if he is denied the opportunity of an education. Such an opportunity, where the state has undertaken to provide it, is a right which must be made available to all on equal terms.

This theme, expressing an abiding respect for the vital role of education in a free society, may be found in numerous opinions of Justices of this Court writing both before and after *Brown* was decided.

Nothing this Court holds today in any way detracts from our historic dedication to public education. We are in complete agreement with the conclusion of the three-judge panel below that "the grave significance of education both to the individual and to our society" cannot be doubted. But the importance of a service performed by the State does not determine whether it must be regarded as fundamental for purposes of examination under the Equal Protection Clause. Mr. Justice Harlan, dissenting from the Court's application of strict scrutiny to a law impinging upon the right of interstate travel, admonished that "[v]irtually every state statute affects important rights" *Shapiro v. Thompson*. In his view, if the degree of judicial scrutiny of state legislation fluctuated, depending on a majority's view of the importance of the interest affected, we would have gone "far toward making this Court a *super-legislature.'" Ibid. We would, indeed, then be assuming a legislative role, and one for which the Court lacks both authority and competence. But MR. JUSTICE STEWART's response in Shapiro to Mr. Justice Harlan's concern correctly articulates the limits of the fundamental rights rationale employed in the Court's equal protection decisions:*

The Court today does *not* "pick out particular human activities, characterize them as *'fundamental,' and give them added protection . . ."* To the contrary, the Court simply recognizes, as it must, an established constitutional right, and gives to that right no less protection than the Constitution itself demands.

The Court explained:

> We do not denigrate the importance of decent, safe, and sanitary housing. But the Constitution does not provide judicial remedies for every social and economic ill. We are unable to perceive in that document any constitutional guarantee of access.

The lesson of these cases in addressing the question now before the Court is plain. It is not the province of this Court to create substantive constitutional rights in the name of guaranteeing equal protection of the laws. Thus, the key to discovering whether education is "fundamental" is not to be found in comparisons of the relative societal significance of education, as opposed to subsistence or housing. Nor is it to be found by weighing whether education is as important as the right to travel. Rather, the answer lies in assessing whether there is a right to education explicitly or implicitly guaranteed by the Constitution.

Education, of course, is not among the rights afforded explicit protection under our Federal Constitution. Nor do we find any basis for saying it is implicitly so protected. As we have said, the undisputed importance of education will not, alone, cause this Court to depart from the usual standard for reviewing a State's social and economic legislation. It is appellees' contention, however, that education is distinguishable from other services and benefits provided by the State, because it bears a peculiarly close relationship to other rights and liberties accorded protection under the Constitution. Specifically, they insist that education is itself a fundamental personal right, because it is essential to the effective exercise of First Amendment freedoms and to intelligent utilization of the right to vote. In asserting a nexus between speech and education, appellees urge that the right to speak is meaningless unless the speaker is capable of articulating his thoughts intelligently and persuasively. The "marketplace of ideas" is an empty forum for those lacking basic communicative tools. Likewise, they argue that the corollary right to receive information becomes little more than a hollow privilege when the recipient has not been taught to read, assimilate, and utilize available knowledge.

Even if it were conceded that some identifiable quantum of education is a constitutionally protected prerequisite to the meaningful exercise of either right, we have no indication that the present levels of educational expenditures in Texas provide an education that falls short. Whatever merit appellees' argument might have if a State's financing system occasioned an absolute denial of educational opportunities to any of its children, that argument provides no basis for finding an interference with fundamental rights where only relative differences in spending levels are involved and where—as is true in the present case—no charge fairly could be made that the system fails to provide each child with an opportunity to acquire the basic minimal skills necessary for the enjoyment of the rights of speech and of full participation in the political process.

Furthermore, the logical limitations on appellees' nexus theory are difficult to perceive. How, for instance, is education to be distinguished from the significant personal interests in the basics of decent food and shelter? Empirical examination might well buttress an assumption that the ill-fed, ill-clothed, and ill-housed are among the most ineffective participants in the political process, and that they derive the least enjoyment from the benefits of the First Amendment. If so, appellees' thesis would cast serious doubt on the authority of *Dandridge v. Williams, supra*, and *Lindsey v. Normet, supra*.

We have carefully considered each of the arguments supportive of the District Court's finding that education is a fundamental right or liberty, and have found those arguments unpersuasive. In one further respect, we find this a particularly inappropriate case in which to subject state action to strict judicial scrutiny. The present case, in another basic sense, is significantly different from any of the cases in which the Court has applied strict scrutiny to state or federal legislation touching upon constitutionally protected rights. Each of our prior cases involved legislation which "deprived," "infringed," or "interfered" with the free exercise of some such fundamental personal right or liberty. A critical distinction between those cases and the one now before us lies in what Texas is endeavoring to do with respect to education. MR. JUSTICE BRENNAN, writing for the Court in *Katzenbach v. Morgan*, expresses well the salient point:

> This is not a complaint that Congress . . . has unconstitutionally denied or diluted anyone's right to vote, but rather that Congress violated the Constitution by not extending the relief effected [to others similarly situated] . . . .

The Texas system of school financing is not unlike the federal legislation involved in *Katzenbach* in this regard. Every step leading to the establishment of the system Texas utilizes today—including the decisions permitting localities to tax and expend locally, and creating and continuously expanding state aid—was implemented in an effort to extend public education and to improve its quality. Of course, every reform that benefits some more than others may be criticized for what it fails to accomplish. But we think it plain that, in substance, the thrust of the Texas system is affirmative and reformatory, and, therefore, should be scrutinized under judicial principles sensitive to the nature of the State's efforts and to the rights reserved to the States under the Constitution.

C

It should be clear, for the reasons stated above and in accord with the prior decisions of this Court, that this is not a case in which the challenged state action must be subjected to the searching judicial scrutiny reserved for laws that create suspect classifications or impinge upon constitutionally protected rights.

We need not rest our decision, however, solely on the inappropriateness of the strict scrutiny test. A century of Supreme Court adjudication under the Equal Protection Clause affirmatively supports the application of the traditional standard of review, which requires only that the State's system be shown to bear some rational relationship to legitimate state purposes. This case represents far more than a challenge to the manner in which Texas provides for the education of its children. We have here nothing less than a direct attack on the way in which Texas has chosen to raise and disburse state and local tax revenues. We are asked to condemn the State's judgment in conferring on political subdivisions the power to tax local property to supply revenues for local interests. In so doing, appellees would have the Court intrude in an area in which it has traditionally deferred to state legislatures. This Court has often admonished against such interferences with the State's fiscal policies under the Equal Protection Clause:

> The broad discretion as to classification possessed by a legislature in the field of taxation has long been recognized. . . . [T]he passage of time has only served to underscore the wisdom of that recognition of the large area of discretion which is needed by a legislature in formulating sound tax policies. . . .
>
> It has . . . been pointed out that in taxation, even more than in other fields, legislatures possess the greatest freedom in classification. Since the members of a legislature necessarily enjoy a familiarity with local conditions which this Court cannot have, the presumption of constitutionality can be overcome only by the most explicit demonstration that a classification is a hostile and oppressive discrimination against particular persons and classes. . .

Thus, we stand on familiar ground when we continue to acknowledge that the Justices of this Court lack both the expertise and the familiarity with local problems so necessary to the making of wise decisions with respect to the raising and disposition of public revenues. Yet we are urged to direct the States either to alter drastically the present system or to throw out the property tax altogether in favor of some other form of taxation. No scheme of taxation, whether the tax is imposed on property, income, or purchases of goods and services, has yet been devised which is free of all discriminatory impact. In such a complex arena in which no perfect alternatives exist, the Court does well not to impose too rigorous a standard of scrutiny lest all local fiscal schemes become subjects of criticism under the Equal Protection Clause.

In addition to matters of fiscal policy, this case also involves the most persistent and difficult questions of educational policy, another area in which this Court's lack of specialized knowledge and experience counsels against premature interference with the informed judgments made at the state and local levels. Education, perhaps even more than welfare assistance, presents a myriad of "intractable economic, social, and even philosophical problems." *Dandridge v. Williams.* The very complexity of the problems of financing and managing a state-wide public school system suggests that "there will be more than one constitutionally permissible method of solving them," and that, within the limits of rationality, "the legislature's efforts to tackle the problems" should be entitled to respect, *Jefferson v. Hackney.* On even the most basic questions in this area, the scholars and educational experts are divided. Indeed, one of the major sources of controversy concerns the extent to which there is a demonstrable correlation between educational expenditures and the quality of education—an assumed correlation underlying virtually every legal conclusion drawn by the District Court in this case. Related to the questioned relationship between cost and quality is the equally unsettled controversy as to the proper goals of a system of public education. And the question regarding the most effective relationship between state boards of education and local school boards, in terms of their respective responsibilities and degrees of control, is now undergoing searching reexamination. The ultimate wisdom as to these and related problems of education is not likely to be divined for all time even by the scholars who now so earnestly debate the issues. In such circumstances, the judiciary is well advised to refrain from imposing on the States inflexible constitutional restraints that could circumscribe or handicap the continued research and experimentation so vital to finding even partial solutions to educational problems and to keeping abreast of ever-changing conditions.

It must be remembered, also, that every claim arising under the Equal Protection Clause has implications for the relationship between national and state power under our federal system. Questions of federalism are always inherent in the process of determining whether a State's laws are to be accorded the traditional presumption of constitutionality, or are to be subjected instead to rigorous judicial scrutiny. While

> [t]he maintenance of the principles of federalism is a foremost consideration in interpreting any of the pertinent constitutional provisions under which this Court examines state action," it would be difficult to imagine a case having a greater potential impact on our federal system than the one now before us, in which we are urged to abrogate systems of financing public education presently in existence in virtually every State.

The foregoing considerations buttress our conclusion that Texas' system of public school finance is an inappropriate candidate for strict judicial scrutiny. These same considerations are relevant to the determination whether that system, with its conceded imperfections, nevertheless bears some rational relationship to a legitimate state purpose. It is to this question that we next turn our attention.

III

The basic contours of the Texas school finance system have been traced at the outset of this opinion. We will now describe in more detail that system and how it operates, as these facts bear directly upon the demands of the Equal Protection Clause.

Apart from federal assistance, each Texas school receives its funds from the State and from its local school district. On a state-wide average, a roughly comparable amount of funds is derived from each source. The State's contribution, under the Minimum Foundation Program, was designed to provide an adequate minimum educational offering in every school in the State. Funds are distributed to assure that there will be one teacher—compensated at the state supported minimum salary—for every 25 students. Each school district's other supportive personnel are provided for: one principal for every 30 teachers; one "special service" teacher—librarian, nurse, doctor, etc.—for every 20 teachers; superintendents, vocational instructors, counselors, and educators for exceptional children are also provided. Additional funds are earmarked for current operating expenses, for student transportation, and for free textbooks.

The program is administered by the State Board of Education and by the Central Education Agency, which also have responsibility for school accreditation and for monitoring the statutory teacher-qualification standards. As reflected by the 62 increase in funds allotted to the Edgewood School District over the last three years, the State's financial contribution to education is steadily increasing. None of Texas' school districts, however, has been content to rely alone on funds from the Foundation Program.

By virtue of the obligation to fulfill its Local Fund Assignment, every district must impose an *ad valorem* tax on property located within its borders. The Fund Assignment was designed to remain sufficiently low to assure that each district would have some ability to provide a more enriched educational program. Every district supplements its Foundation grant in this manner. In some districts, the local property tax contribution is insubstantial, as in Edgewood, where the supplement was only $26 per pupil in 1967. In other districts, the local share may far exceed even the total Foundation grant. In part, local differences are attributable to differences in the rates of taxation or in the degree to which the market value for any category of property varies from its assessed value. The greatest inter-district disparities, however, are attributable to differences in the amount of assessable property available within any district. Those districts that have more property, or more valuable property, have a greater capability for supplementing state funds. In large measure, these additional local revenues are devoted to paying higher salaries to more teachers. Therefore, the primary distinguishing attributes of schools in property-affluent districts are lower pupil-teacher ratios and higher salary schedules.

This, then, is the basic outline of the Texas school financing structure. Because of differences in expenditure levels occasioned by disparities in property tax income, appellees claim that children in less affluent districts have been made the subject of invidious discrimination. The District Court found that the State had failed even "to establish a reasonable basis" for a system that results in different levels of per-pupil expenditure. We disagree.

In its reliance on state, as well as local, resources, the Texas system is comparable to the systems employed in virtually every other State. The power to tax local property for educational purposes has been recognized in Texas at least since 1883. When the growth of commercial and industrial centers and accompanying shifts in population began to create disparities in local resources, Texas undertook a program calling for a considerable investment of state funds.

The "foundation grant" theory upon which Texas legislators and educators based the Gilmer-Aikin bills was a product of the pioneering work of two New York educational reformers in the 1920's, George D. Strayer and Robert M. Haig. Their efforts were devoted to establishing a means of guaranteeing a minimum state-wide educational program without sacrificing the vital element of local participation. The Strayer-Haig thesis represented an accommodation between these two competing forces. As articulated by Professor Coleman:

> The history of education since the industrial revolution shows a continual struggle between two forces: the desire by members of society to have educational opportunity for all children and the desire of each family to provide the best education it can afford for its own children.

The Texas system of school finance is responsive to these two forces. While assuring a basic education for every child in the State, it permits and encourages a large measure of participation in and control of each district's schools at the local level. In an era that has witnessed a consistent trend toward centralization of the functions of government, local sharing of responsibility for public education has survived. The merit of local control was recognized last Term in both the majority and dissenting opinions in *Wright v. Council of the City of Emporia*, 407 U. S. 451 (1972). MR. JUSTICE STEWART stated there that "[d]irect control over decisions vitally affecting the education of one's children is a need that is strongly felt in our society." *Id.* at 407 U. S. 469. THE CHIEF JUSTICE, in his dissent, agreed that

> [l]ocal control is not only vital to continued public support of the schools, but it is of overriding importance from an educational standpoint as well.

The persistence of attachment to government at the lowest level where education is concerned reflects the depth of commitment of its supporters. In part, local control means, as Professor Coleman suggests, the freedom to devote more money to the education of one's children. Equally important, however, is the opportunity it offers for participation in the decision making process that determines how those local tax dollars will be spent. Each locality is free to tailor local programs to local needs. Pluralism also affords some opportunity for experimentation, innovation, and a healthy competition for educational excellence. An analogy to the Nation-State relationship in our federal system seems uniquely appropriate. Mr. Justice Brandeis identified as one of the peculiar strengths of our form of government each State's freedom to "serve as a laboratory; and try novel social and economic experiments." No area of social concern stands to profit more from a multiplicity of viewpoints and from a diversity of approaches than does public education.

Appellees do not question the propriety of Texas' dedication to local control of education. To the contrary, they attack the school financing system precisely because, in their view, it does not provide the same level of local control and fiscal flexibility in all districts. Appellees suggest that local control could be preserved and promoted under other financing systems that resulted in more equality in educational expenditures. While it is no doubt true that reliance on local property taxation for school revenues provides less freedom of choice with respect to expenditures for some districts than for others, the existence of "some inequality" in the manner in which the State's rationale is achieved is not alone a sufficient basis for striking down the entire system. *McGowan v. Maryland*, 366 U. S. 420, 366 U. S. 425–426 (1961). It may not be condemned simply because it imperfectly effectuates the State's goals. *Dandridge v. Williams*, 397 U.S. at 397 U. S. 485. Nor must the financing system fail because, as appellees suggest, other methods of satisfying the State's interest, which occasion "less drastic" disparities in expenditures, might be conceived. Only where state action impinges on the exercise of fundamental constitutional rights or liberties must it be found to have chosen the least restrictive alternative. *Cf. Dunn v. Blumstein*, 405 U.S. at 405 U. S. 343; *Shelton v. Tucker*, 364 U. S. 479, 364 U. S. 488 (1960). It is also well to remember that even those districts that have reduced ability to make free decisions with respect to how much they spend on education still retain, under the present system, a large measure of authority as to how available funds will be allocated. They further enjoy the power to make numerous other decisions with respect to the operation of the schools. The people of Texas may be justified in believing that other systems of school financing, which place more of the financial responsibility in the hands of the State, will result in a comparable lessening of desired local autonomy. That is, they may believe that along with increased control of the purse strings at the state level will go increased control over local policies.

Appellees further urge that the Texas system is unconstitutionally arbitrary because it allows the availability of local taxable resources to turn on "happenstance." They see no justification for a system that allows, as they contend, the quality of education to fluctuate on the basis of the fortuitous positioning of the boundary lines of political subdivisions and the location of valuable commercial and industrial property. But any scheme of local taxation—indeed the very existence of identifiable local governmental units—requires the establishment of jurisdictional boundaries that are inevitably arbitrary. It is equally inevitable that some localities are going to be blessed with more taxable assets than others. Nor is local wealth a static quantity. Changes in the level of taxable wealth within any district may result from any number of events, some of which local residents can and do influence. For instance, commercial and industrial enterprises may be encouraged to locate within a district by various actions—public and private.

Moreover, if local taxation for local expenditures were an unconstitutional method of providing for education, then it might be an equally impermissible means of providing other necessary services customarily financed largely from local property taxes, including local police and fire protection, public health and hospitals, and public utility facilities of various kinds. We perceive no justification for such a severe denigration of local property taxation and control as would follow from appellees' contentions. It has simply never been within the constitutional prerogative of this Court to nullify state-wide measures for financing public services merely because the burdens or benefits thereof fall unevenly depending upon the relative wealth of the political subdivisions in which citizens live.

In sum, to the extent that the Texas system of school financing results in unequal expenditures between children who happen to reside in different districts, we cannot say that such disparities are the product of a system that is so irrational as to be invidiously discriminatory. Texas has acknowledged its shortcomings, and has persistently endeavored—not without some success—to ameliorate the differences in levels of expenditures without sacrificing the benefits of local participation. The Texas plan is not the result of hurried, ill-conceived legislation. It certainly is not the product of purposeful discrimination against any group or class. On the contrary, it is rooted in decades of experience in Texas and elsewhere, and, in major part, is the product of responsible studies by qualified people. In giving substance to the presumption of validity to which the Texas system is entitled, *Lindsley v. Natural Carbonic Gas Co.*, 220 U. S. 61, 220 U. S. 78 (1911), it is important to remember that, at every stage of its development, it has constituted a "rough accommodation" of interests in an effort to arrive at practical and workable solutions. *Metropolis Theatre Co. v. City of Chicago*, 228 U. S. 61, 228 U. S. 69–70 (1913). One also must remember that the system here challenged is not peculiar to Texas or to any other State. In its essential characteristics, the Texas plan for financing public education reflects what many educators for a half century have thought was an enlightened approach to a problem for which there is no perfect solution. We are unwilling to assume for ourselves a level of wisdom superior to that of legislators, scholars, and educational authorities in 50 States, especially where the alternatives proposed are only recently conceived and nowhere yet tested. The constitutional standard under the Equal Protection Clause is whether the challenged state action rationally furthers a legitimate state purpose or interest. We hold that the Texas plan abundantly satisfies this standard.

IV

The complexity of these problems is demonstrated by the lack of consensus with respect to whether it may be said with any assurance that the poor, the racial minorities, or the children in overburdened core-city school districts would be benefited by abrogation of traditional modes of financing education. Unless there is to be a substantial increase in state expenditures on education across the board—an event the likelihood of which is open to considerable question—these groups stand to realize gains in terms of increased per-pupil expenditures only if they reside in districts that presently spend at relatively low levels, *i.e.*, in those districts that would benefit from the redistribution of existing resources. Yet recent studies have indicated that the poorest families are not invariably clustered in the most impecunious school districts. Nor does it now appear that there is any more than a random chance that racial minorities are concentrated in property-poor districts. Additionally, several research projects have concluded that any financing alternative designed to achieve a greater equality of expenditures is likely to lead to higher taxation and lower educational expenditures in the major urban centers, a result that would exacerbate, rather than ameliorate, existing conditions in those areas.

These practical considerations, of course, play no role in the adjudication of the constitutional issues presented here. But they serve to highlight the wisdom of the traditional limitations on this Court's function. The consideration and initiation of fundamental reforms with respect to state taxation and education are matters reserved for the legislative processes of the various States, and we do no violence to the values of federalism and separation of powers by staying our hand. We hardly need add that this Court's action today is not to be viewed as placing its judicial imprimatur on the *status quo*. The need is apparent for reform in tax systems which may well have relied too long and too heavily on the local property tax. And certainly innovative thinking as to public education, its methods, and its funding is necessary to assure both a higher level of quality and greater uniformity of opportunity. These matters merit the continued attention of the scholars who already have contributed much by their challenges. But the ultimate solutions must come from the lawmakers and from the democratic pressures of those who elect them.

Reversed.

The impact of *San Antonio Independent School District v. Rodriguez* on Education

The impact of *San Antonio Independent School District v. Rodriguez* on the institution of education in the United States went far beyond the confines of Texas. By ruling that the US Constitution does not specifically provide for education as a fundamental right (no matter how important it might be for full civic, social, political, and economic participation) and that therefore Fourteenth Amendment equal protection challenges to school funding systems through property taxes did not apply, this meant that addressing inequitable financing of schools would be left to the discretion of individual states and voters (Imazeki & Reschovsky, 2006). The court also distanced itself in their decision from issuing any type of statement on whether money had an impact on the quality of education a child received. At the heart of the *Rodriguez* case, then, is how class, socioeconomic status, **wealth inequality** and **income inequality** (see Box 3.2 on wealth and income inequality and how these have changed in the United States), variables that often intersect with race, affect education and its outcomes. Here, we look at the influence of such inequality on both formal and informal educational settings since the *Rodriguez* decision 50 years ago.

Informal Education and Income Inequality

As described in Chapter 2, learning does not only occur within the walls of a formal institution, but also informally from birth—through peers, mentors, family, friends, and the media. Income and wealth inequality (see Box 3.2: Wealth and Income Inequality in the United States after *Rodriguez*) affects educational outcomes that do not have to do exclusively with formal education. The **socio-economic status (SES)** of parents is one of the strongest predictors of educational achievement and attainment (Reardon, 2011), as it may influence not only the schools a child goes to, the support they have in the schools, but also what happens outside of the classroom. Researchers have demonstrated that SES begins to predict differences in learning attainment very early in life. For example, by 18 months of age, children from those in lower SES families—a term that implies income but also educational attainment—begin to fall behind their wealthier counterparts in language proficiency. Children from lower SES families between 18–24 months were learning 30 percent fewer words (Fernald, Marchman, & Weisleder, 2013). This leads to lower levels of language acquisition and skills which can persist, and gaps become even wider as the child ages. Several mechanisms behind this deficiency have been explored, including children being spoken to less in lower SES homes, or not being exposed to the kind of speech that supports language growth (Ribot & Hoff, 2015).

BOX 3.2: WEALTH AND INCOME INEQUALITY IN THE UNITED STATES

While income and wealth are often used interchangeably, they describe two different measures. **Income** includes money flows which come from sources such as employment in the form of salaries, wages, tips, state benefits, dividends from stock or rent, interest on savings accounts, and sales of items, products, and services. **Wealth** includes the value of assets owned by an individual, such as property, bonds and stocks, excluding debts. Inequality—or the degree to which something is distributed unevenly among a population, is high among those in the US for income and wealth, however wealth inequality is even higher.

In 1973, the year of the *Rodriguez* decision, the income of those in US's top 0.1 percent of income was 37x greater than the bottom 90 percent. By 2018, income inequality increased dramatically, and the multiple was 198x greater (Saez, 2020). Differences among racial groups in income can exacerbate educational inequalities: Whites and Asians have significantly higher median household incomes, with Asian American families garnering approximately 81,331, dollars Whites, 68,145, Hispanics, 50,486, and Blacks, 40, 258 (US Census, 2018). One way to measure income inequality is through the **Gini coefficient,** also known as a **Gini index**. This statistic shows how incomes are dispersed across the entirety of the income distribution. The larger the Gini coefficient, the greater the inequality, with the number ranging from 0 (total income equality) to 1 (all income goes to a single person or group) (Census Bureau, 2021). The US Gini Coefficient is 0.434, the highest among the G-7 countries. Other measures, such as the 90/10 ratio, which looks at the ratio between the income of the top 10 percent of earners to the bottom 10 percent of earners, also shows increasing inequality, from 9.1 in 1980 to 12.6 in 2018 (Pew, 2020). Furthermore, those at the highest rung of the income bracket—the top 1 percent, have seen the greatest gains in income since the 1970s—226 percent, versus the next 19 percent of income earners—79 percent, or the middle 60 percent of income earners—47 percent (CBPP, 2020). The coronavirus pandemic of 2020–2021 had the effect of hitting those with low incomes the hardest, further exacerbating inequalities.

Wealth inequality also increased in the past five decades, with the share of wealth owned by the top 1 percent of families growing since the late 1970s, the period of the *Rodriguez* decision, with most of the change brought by increases in the wealth of the top 0.1 percent (Saez & Zucman, 2016). The wealth owned in the United States by the top 1 percent is around 40 percent, whereas that owned by the bottom 90 percent of the wealth distribution is around 20 percent (Ingraham, 2017). Even more dramatically, three of the wealthiest men in the United States (Warren Buffet, Bill Gates, and Jeff Bezos) currently have as much wealth as the bottom half of Americans (Kirsch, 2017). During the coronavirus pandemic of 2020–2021, similar to its impact on income, the wealth of the wealthiest soared, with American billionaires adding more than a trillion dollars to their net worth (Guardian, 2020).

Educational enrichment experiences outside of the classroom to which families can expose their children are another form of informal education. The National Center for Education Statistics (NCES) investigated how kindergartners spent their summer. They gave evidence that poor children were less likely to have educationally enriching experiences outside of the classroom which could develop their knowledge and **cultural capital**. Sociologists have emphasized the importance of such cultural capital, which are the social assets of a person, including their education, tastes, and experiences, which promote social mobility. For example, 33 percent of non-poor children were taken to see a play or concert during the summer, whereas 15 percent of poor children did. About 63 percent of children from non-poor households visited an art gallery, museum, or historical site, versus 32 percent of children from poor households. Additionally, access to computer use for educational purposes was higher among non-poor households. Only 16 percent of children from non-poor houses reported not using a computer for educational purposes, versus 32 percent of children in poor households (NCES, 2018). Lower SES children, conversely, watched more TV and spent less time in verbal communication with their parents in lower income households. Exposure to plays, libraries, museums, and the like are experiences that give children professional, educational, and personal advantages, but are often confined to those whose parents have been educated to understand the value of these experiences, and who have the resources and time to provide them to their children.

Last, informal educational inequalities arise as a direct result of socioeconomic segregation in housing that, as mentioned in the discussion about *Brown v. Board of Education*, is a problem intimately connected to "nonschool social contexts that may affect educational success, including the prevalence of adult role models and monitoring or safety, as the neighborhood effects literature describes" (Owens, 2018).

Low SES can influence informal learning; also it predicts less non-compulsory formal learning in the form of early childhood education programs, which wealthier children are more likely to be enrolled in. Because poverty rates in the United States are higher than in peer countries in the Organization for Economic Cooperation and Development (OECD), with 23.1 percent of American children living in households with income below half of the household-size adjusted median income (Gould & Wething, 2012), this has an effect on a substantial number of children. While the Supreme Court decision in *Rodriguez*'s direct effect was on formal schooling, an understanding of the way in which income and wealth inequality creates an uneven playing field even before a child enters kindergarten shows just how important a role compulsory schooling plays to try to provide children with equal opportunities to education and its benefits.

Formal Education: School Districts, Spending per Pupil, and Outcomes

If there were no relationship between the amount of money spent per student and indicators of positive educational outcomes—scores on standardized tests, reading at or above grade level, enrollment in advanced classes, graduating high school, or going on to a college degree—then there would be no cause for the concerns about educational equity on the basis of resources allocated raised by *Rodriguez*. However, this is not the case. The National Bureau of Economic (NBER) research found that

> For children from low income families, increasing per-pupil spending yields large improvements in educational attainment, wages, family income, and reductions in the annual incidence of adult poverty . . . improved access to school resources can profoundly shape the life outcomes of economically disadvantaged children, and thereby significantly reduce the intergenerational transmission of poverty.
>
> *(2015)*

Even for children from higher-income families, per-child spending increased educational attainment and adulthood family income, but the magnitude of the effect is less. While there may not be a perfect relationship between dollars spent and educational outcomes, there is a strong correlation, and one that is especially strong for children in lower grades, when they are undergoing their most foundational learning experiences (Stone, 2017). A 10 percent increase in per pupil expenditures has been shown, in fact, to increase graduation rates up to 4.4 percent, and the standard deviation of test scores by up to 0.09 (Miller, 2018).

About 75 percent of children in the United States end up attending their neighborhood public school (Owens, 2018), and so it is an important question whether, post-*Rodriguez*, schools are being funded equitably given the linkage of spending to educational outcomes. After the *Rodriguez* ruling, indeed, there was movement in the states' judicial and legislative systems to remedy some of the disparities caused by school districts' borders, which can cause economic segregation and poverty concentration. Now, although schools moved away from being primarily funded through local taxes, they still derive about half of funding from local property taxes. States are obligated to reduce the discrepancy in spending, and also contribute about half of funding, with the federal government providing a much smaller source (Mervosh, 2019; Chingos & Blagg, 2017). Yet, funding inequities in public schools continue across school district lines, often on the overlapping bases of class and race. "Income segregation between school districts may contribute to the income achievement gap by exacerbating inequalities in spending in high-and low-income students' school districts" (Owens, 2013, p. 3). Consequently, for every student, non-White school districts across the United States receive $2,226 less than a White school district (EdBuild, 2021).

The US Department of Education's Equity and Excellence Commission found in its 2013 report that "students, families and communities are burdened by the broken system of education funding in America." State funding systems are not closely linked to desired educational outcomes: despite the fact that all states have adopted educational standards, the commission found that only a few states have developed funding systems that enable schools to teach all students the content of state standards (Ogletree & Robinson, 2017).

New York State provides an example of these continued educational problems that went unresolved after *Rodriguez*. Despite its reputation for being a cosmopolitan and diverse state, New York has some of the most persistent economic and racial segregation in its school districts. In 2006, the state's highest court ruled in *Campaign for Fiscal Equity, Inc. v. State of New York* that the state had not met its constitutional responsibility to ensure all schools had adequate funding, especially in New York City. Following this, New York adopted a new "Fair student" formula for funding schools that took into account the needs of student populations who are poor, disabled, non-English speakers, and learning disabled. Presumably, these students require extra support to even the educational opportunity playing field. However, the formula was never funded adequately ("The Central Crisis in New York Education," 2015).

With rising income inequality that led to increased residential segregation, the income achievement gap has also increased steadily since the *Rodriguez* ruling in the 1970s (defined as the income difference between a child from a family at the 90th percentile of the income distribution and a child from a family at the 10th percentile) (Reardon, 2011). High-income students are more likely in the decades after *Rodriguez* to enter college and finish higher education degrees in more selective schools than lower income students, which has ramifications for future earning potential, intergenerational mobility, marrying someone also with a college degree, and life chances in general. For example, 37 percent of children from high-income families enrolled at selective colleges, whereas only 7 percent of lower income students did. Only one-third of the students in the lowest quintile of family incomes enroll in college within a year of graduating, whereas 79 percent of students from the top quintile do. Wealthier students furthermore were more likely to enroll in a four-year college than their poorer counterparts (Fain, 2020). If we look at lifetime earnings by educational attainment, we can see the consequences of these inequalities. The median lifetime earnings of someone with a high school diploma is approximately $1.3 million. With an associate's degree, this rises to $1.7 million, and with a bachelor's degree, $2.3 million. With a doctoral or professional degree, the number surpasses 3 million (Carnevale, Rose, & Cheah, n.d.). Chances of unemployment are lower as one achieves more education, too, with only 1.5 percent of those with a doctoral or professional degree unemployed, but 4.1 percent of those with a high school diploma (BLS, 2018).

If wealthier children begin with informal educational advantages, then proceed to formal education which has the advantages of better funding and resources—which the Supreme Court in *Rodriguez* said was not a matter that the Constitution directly addresses—and then go on to higher education which results in higher earnings over the life course, the United States risks reproducing and exacerbating inequalities.

Review Questions

1. What functions does education play in American society as written in the *Brown v. Board of Education* decision?
2. How does segregation persist within education?
3. What rationale did the court provide in their decision of *San Antonio Independent School District v. Rodriguez*?
4. Is education still the greatest equalizer in America? Please provide points to affirm and negate this adage.
5. How does socioeconomic status influence education?

References

Arcia, E. (2006). Comparison of the enrollment percentages of magnet and non-magnet schools in a large urban school district. *Educational Policy Analysis Archives*, *14*(33), 1–14.

Ashkenas, J., Park, H., & Pearce, A. (2017, August 24). Even with affirmative action, Blacks and Hispanics are more underrepresented at top colleges than 35 years ago. *New York Times*.

Ayscue, J., Frankenberg, E., & Siegel-Hawley, G. (2017). *The Complementary Benefits of Racial and Socioeconomic Diversity in Schools*. Research Brief No. 10. National Coalition on School Diversity. Retrieved from: https://school-diversity.org/research-briefs/

Bell, D. A. (1980). *Brown v. Board of Education* and the interest-convergence dilemma. *Harvard Law Review*, *93*(3), 518.

Berlin, J., & Rumore, K. (2017, January 27). 12 times the president called the military domestically. *The Chicago Tribune*.

Boddie, E. C., & Parker, D. D. (2018, March 30). Linda Brown and the unfinished work of school integration. *The New York Times*.

Brown Smith, L. (1985, October 26). *Eyes on the prize: America's civil rights years (1954–1965)*. Interview with Linda Brown Smith, Conducted by Blackside, Inc. Washington University Libraries, Film and Media Archive, Henry Hampton Collection. Retrieved from http://digital.wustl.edu/e/eop/eopweb/smi0015.0647.098lindabrownsmith.html

Bureau of Labor Statistics (BLS). (2018). *Unemployment rates and earnings by educational attainment*. Retrieved from www.bls.gov/emp/chart-unemployment-earnings-education.htm

Carnevale, A. P., Rose, S. J., & Cheah, B. (n.d.). *The college payoff: Education, occupations, and lifetime earnings*. Washington, DC: Georgetown Center on Education and the Workforce.

Center for Budget and Policy Priorities (CBPP). (2020). *A guide to statistics on historical income inequality*. Retrieved from www.cbpp.org/research/poverty-and-inequality/a-guide-to-statistics-on-historical-trends-in-income-inequality

"The Central Crisis in New York Education." (2015, January 4). *The New York Times*.
Chen, G. (2019, November 14). New York's schools are the most segregated in the nation. *Public School Review*. Retrieved from https://www.publicschoolreview.com/blog/new-yorks-schools-are-the-most-segregated-in-the-nation
Chingos, M., & Blagg, K. (2017). *Making sense of state school funding policy*. Washington, DC: Urban Institute.
Davis, T. (2014). School choice and segregation: "Tracking" racial equity in magnet schools. *Education and Urban Society, 46*(4).
DeBrey, C., Musu, L., & McFarland, J. (2019). *Status and trends in the education of racial and ethnic groups 2018*. Washington, DC: US Department of Education, National Center for Education Statistics.
EdBuild. 2021. *23 billion*. Retrieved from https://edbuild.org/content/23-billion
Fain, P. (2020). Wealth's Influence on College Enrollment and Completion. The Scandal of Standardized Tests: Why We Need to Drop the SAT and ACT, 44.
Fernald, A., Marchman, V. A., & Weisleder, A. (2013). SES differences in language processing skill and vocabulary are evident at 18 months. *Developmental Science, 16*(2), 234–248.
Futtrell, M. H., & Gomez, J. (2008). How tracking creates a poverty of learning. *Educational Leadership, 65*(8), 74–78.
Genzlinger, N. (2018, March 26). Linda Brown, symbol of landmark desegregation case, dies at 75. *New York Times*.
Gersehenson, S., Hart, C., Hyman, J., Lindsay, C., & Papgeorge, N. W. (2018, November). *The long-run impacts of same-race teachers*. NBER Working Paper No. 25254. Retrieved from https://www.nber.org/system/files/working_papers/w25254/w25254.pdf
Goldring, E., & Smrekar, C. (2002). Magnet schools: Reform and race in urban education. *The Clearing House, 76*(1), 13–15.
Gould, E., & Wething, H. (2012). *US poverty rates higher, safety net weaker than in peer countries*. Economic Policy Institute, Issue Brief, 339. Retrieved from: https://www.epi.org/publication/ib339-us-poverty-higher-safety-net-weaker/
The Guardian. (2020, December 19). Ten billionaires reap $400bn to boost wealth during the pandemic. *The Guardian*. Retrieved from www.theguardian.com/technology/2020/dec/19/ten-billionaires-reap-400bn-boost-to-wealth-during-pandemic
Hannah-Jones, N. (2019, July 12). It was never about busing. *The New York Times*.
History Now. (2017). *Cheryl Brown Henderson reflects on Brown v. Board of Education*. Retrieved from www.youtube.com/watch?v=zurRCk3vNFE
Hoff, E., & Ribot, K. (2015). Language development: Influence of socio-economic status. *International Encyclopedia of the Social & Behavioral Sciences*. doi:10.1016/B978-0-08-097086-8.23132-2
Imazeki, J., & Reschovsky, A. (2006, April 27–28). *Rethinking Rodriguez: Education as a fundamental right*. Paper prepared for the symposium, sponsored by the Earl Warren Institute on Race, Ethnicity, and Diversity, Boalt Hall School of Law, University of California, Berkeley, CA.
Ingraham, C. (2017, December 8). The nation's top 1% how have greater wealth than the bottom 90%. *The Seattle Times*.
Kahlenberg, R. D., Potter, H., & Quick, K. (2019). School integration: How it can promote social cohesion and combat racism. *American Educator*. Retrieved from www.aft.org/ae/fall2019/kahlenberg_potter_quick
Kendall, D. (2011). *Sociology in our times*. Belmont, CA: Wadsworth.
Kirsch, N. (2017, November 9). The Richest 3 Americans hold more wealth than the bottom 50% of the country. *Forbes*.
Kohli, S., & Quartz. (2014, November 18). Modern-day segregation in public schools. *The Atlantic*.
Kucsera, J., & Orfield, G. (2014). *New York State's extreme school segregation: Inequality, inaction and a damaged future*. Retrieved from Escholarship.org.
Lutz, M. (2017). The hidden cost of Brown v. Board: African American educators' resistance to desegregating schools. Online Journal of Rural Research & Policy, *12*(4).
Magnet Schools of America. (2020). Retrieved from https://magnet.edu/about/what-are-magnet-schools
Mervosh, S. (2019, February 27). How much wealthier are white school districts than non-White ones? 23 billion, report says. *The New York Times*.
Miller, C. L. (2018, January). The effect of education spending on student achievement. In *Proceedings. Annual Conference on Taxation and Minutes of the Annual Meeting of the National Tax Association* (Vol. 111, pp. 1–121). National Tax Association, Washington, DC.

NAACP. (2021). *What is the mission of the NAACP?* NAACP Website. Retrieved from www.naacp.org/about-us/

National Bureau of Economic Research. (2015). *The effects of school spending on educational and economic outcomes: Evidence from school finance reforms.* Working Paper 20847. Retrieved from www.nber.org/papers/w20847

National Center for Education Statistics (NCES). (2018). *The Summer after kindergarten: Children's experiences by socio-economic characteristics.* Retrieved from https://nces.ed.gov/pubsearch/pubsinfo.asp?pubid=2018160

National Center for Education Statistics (NCES). (2020). *Historically Black colleges and universities.* Retrieved from https://nces.ed.gov/fastfacts/display.asp?id=667

National Museum of African American History and Culture (NMAAHC). (2020). *5 things to know.* HBCU Edition. Retrieved from https://nmaahc.si.edu/blog-post/5-things-know-hbcu-edition

Ogletree, C., & Robinson, K. (2017). Inequitable schools demand a federal remedy. *EducationNext, 17*(2). Retrieved from www.educationnext.org/inequitable-schools-demand-federal-remedy-forum-san-antonio-rodriguez/

Orfield, G., & Frankenberg, E. (2014). Increasingly segregated and unequal schools as courts reverse policy. *Educational Administration Quarterly, 50*(5), 718–734.

Owens, A. (2018). Income segregation between school districts and inequality in students' achievement. *Sociology of Education, 91*(1), 1–27.

Pew. (2020). *Trends in income and wealth inequality.* Retrieved from www.pewresearch.org/social-trends/2020/01/09/trends-in-income-and-wealth-ineq uality/#:~:text=Ranging%20from%200%20to%201,Cooperation%20and%20Developme nt%20(OECD)

Phillips, K. W. (2014, October 1). How diversity makes us smarter. *Scientific American.* Retrieved from https://www.scientificamerican.com/article/how-diversity-makes-us-smarter/

Prasad, R. (2019, June 28). Kamala Harris–Joe Biden row: What is desegregation busing? *BBC News.*

Reardon, S. F. (2011). *The widening academic achievement gap between the rich and the poor: New evidence and possible explanations. Whither opportunity? Rising inequality, schools, and children's life chances.* New York: Russell Sage Foundation.

Romo, V. (2018, March 26). Linda Brown, who was at center of *Brown v. Board of Education*, dies. *NPR.*

Saez, E. (2020). Striking it richer: The evolution of top incomes in the United States (updated with 2018 estimates). *Pathways Magazine, Stanford Center for the Study of Poverty and Inequality, Winter 2008*, 6–7.

Saez, E., & Zucman, G. (2016). Wealth inequality in the United States since 1913: Evidence from capitalized income data. *The Quarterly Journal of Economics, 131*(2), 519–578.

Stone, G. (2017). How a 1973 supreme court decision has contributed to our inequality. *The Daily Beast.* Retrieved from www.thedailybeast.com/how-a-1973-supreme-court-decision-has-contributed-to-our-inequality

Strayhorn, T. L., & Johnson, R. M. (2014). Why are all the White students sitting together in college? Impact of *Brown v. Board of Education* on cross-racial interactions among Blacks and Whites. *The Journal of Negro Education, 83*(3), 385–399, 426.

Tatum, B. D. (2017, September 14). Segregation worse in schools 60 years after Brown v. Board of education. *Seattle Times.*

Torres, E., & Weissbourd, R. (2020). *Do parents really want school integration?* Retrieved from https://mcc.gse.harvard.edu/

United States Census Bureau. (2018). *Real median household income by race and Hispanic origin: 1967 to 2017.* Retrieved from www.census.gov/content/dam/Census/library/visualizations/2018/demo/p60-263/figure1.pdf

United States Census Bureau. (2021). *Gini index.* Retrieved from www.census.gov/topics/income-poverty/income-inequality/about/metrics/gini-index.html

US Department of Education (DOE). (2016). *The state of diversity in the educator workforce.* Washington, DC: DOE.

Zirkel, S., & Cantor, N. (2004). 50 years after Brown v. Board of education: The promise and challenge of multicultural education. *Journal of Social Issues, 60*(1). Retrieved from www.bbc.com/news/world-us-canada-48803864

4

FAMILY

Learning Objectives

After reading this chapter, students should be able to:

- Discuss the US Supreme Court case *Loving v. Virginia*
- Describe the impact of the *Loving* decision on the institution of Family
- Explain the history of interracial marriages in the US
- Summarize the evolution of societal attitudes toward interracial marriages
- Provide an overview of the *Obergefell v. Hodges* case
- Understand how marriage and family were changed by the *Obergefell* ruling
- Expound on same sex marriage and parenting
- Paraphrase the changing of attitudes toward same-sex marriage

Key Terms

Anti-miscegenation
Colorism
Domestic Partnerships
Family
Hegemonic
Heteronormative
Homogeny Perspective
Loving v. Virginia
Nuclear Family
Obergefell v. Hodges
Patriarchy
Repronormative

Introduction to *Loving v. Virginia*

On July 14, 1958, at two o'clock in the morning, the police knocked on the Loving's residence in Central Point, Virginia. Richard Loving and his wife Mildred, who had been married for six weeks, were sound asleep. Richard was startled by the second knocking, opened his eyes, and began moving out of bed to go open the door. But he didn't have time because the police had forced their way in their house by breaking down the door. The police stormed into their bedroom and pointed a flashlight at Mildred, who was momentarily blinded by the bright light. The police officers asked Richard who the woman in his bed was and Mildred replied on his behalf

DOI: 10.4324/9781003021438-5

by identifying herself as Richard's wife. The newly married couple was placed under arrest and taken into custody right away. They were charged with violating Virginia's Racial Integrity Act of 1924, which criminalized interracial marriage.

Richard Loving, a White American, was 17 years old when he met 11-year-old Mildred, who was biracial, African American and Native American. The two struck a friendship and eventually began dating, not realizing that, at the time, interracial relationships were against the law in Virginia—as well as in other 15 states. Central Point was a small town and it was not unusual for White people and people of color, including Native Americans, to mingle and get together. Many young men and women would gather at Mildred's house and listen to music or race cars, which was one of the most common pastimes for young people living in the area. The more time Richard spent at Mildred's house, the more he became part of her family. It wasn't long, for example, that he began working for her father, who had a lumber mill, which is where Richard honed his skills as a carpenter—he would eventually be the one to build a house for him and his brand-new wife.

On January 27, 1957, Richard and Mildred welcomed their first child—out of wedlock—and they named him Sidney. The baby was delivered by Richard's mother, Lola Jane Loving, who was a highly experienced midwife who delivered most of the babies in the area. Since the couple wasn't married, Mildred and the baby lived at her parents' house until the two decided to finally marry. Knowing that he would have a hard time finding any pastor in the area willing to marry them, Richard decided to drive up to Washington, D.C., where he was sure he would find somebody who would marry them. After getting a marriage license on May 24, they went back to D.C. on June 2, to get married. Now respectively 23 and 19 years old, Richard and Mildred were happily married and living in the house he built for them in Central Point. More good news kept coming as Mildred found out she was pregnant with their second son, who was due in October 1958.

The night they were arrested, Mildred and Richard were separated from each other and placed in two different jail cells. After their trial took place, the couple was convicted and sentenced to one year in prison or to 25 years away from Caroline County, Virginia. Mildred—who by then had already given birth to their second son, Donald—had a cousin living in the D.C. area, so they opted to move there and avoid jail time, even though the couple was heartbroken at the thought of having to leave their family and friends behind. Even though their marriage was accepted in Washington D.C., Mildred was not happy there, nor were her children. The Loving family moved to a mostly all-black neighborhood, where most of the families came from Trinidad. Mildred knew that her children were not safe playing in the street, but she also didn't want them to feel caged, so she allowed them to play outside. One day, Donald was hit by a car and, even though he recovered, Mildred—who had also welcomed a daughter by then, Peggy—had had enough. Venting to her cousin, she expressed her sadness about being so far away from her family members and longed to go back to her hometown. Her cousin, who had listened to many of Mildred's venting sessions and just wanted to do something to help her, suggested she write a letter to United States Attorney General Robert F. Kennedy to ask for his assistance. Much to her surprise, Mildred received a letter from Kennedy who advised her to reach out to the American Civil Liberties Union (ACLU), which agreed to represent their case.

In 1963, Bernard Cohen and Philip Hirschkop, two young lawyers working at ACLU, filed a motion asking the judge in Virginia to vacate the Loving's sentence, but the judge refused. Having had no success with the judge, the two young lawyers decided to take the case to the Virginia Supreme Court of Appeals, which also turned them down by upholding the original ruling that the Lovings were guilty of **miscegenation**—meaning, the interbreeding of different races. Hirschkop revealed that the Virginia Supreme Court said that, "*Plessy* [the 1896 case that upheld racial segregation in public facilities] is still good law and that *Pace* [the 1883 decision that upheld Alabama's anti-miscegenation law] is still good law. It was an outrageous decision" (Kelly, 2016). Meanwhile, as Cohen and Hirschkop were busy moving the case through the courts, the Loving family secretly made their way back to Virginia because they could no longer handle life in the Washington D.C. and longed to be close to family. Unfortunately, though, they were stopped and arrested yet again. This time, however, their lawyers talked the judge out of charging them with any crime and they were allowed to legally reside in Virginia—although not in Central Point.

In 1964, the **Civil Rights Act**—a landmark civil rights law—was passed. The Act "outlawed discrimination on the basis of race, color, religion, sex, or national origin, required equal access to public places and employment, and enforced desegregation of schools and the right to vote" (NPS, 2016b). A year later, in 1965, the Voting Rights Act was passed, and it "expanded the Fourteenth and Fifteenth Amendments by banning racial discrimination in voting practices. The act was a response to the barriers that prevented African Americans from voting for nearly a century" (NPS, 2016a).

Encouraged by the recent landmark rulings in civil rights legislature, the two lawyers decided to appeal the Loving case to the United States Supreme Court. Cohen and Hirschkop asked Richard and Mildred Loving if they wanted to go to D.C. with them and attend the Supreme Court hearing, but the couple declined the invitation because they didn't want the attention of the media. Instead, they preferred to stay home with their children and simply hoped for a positive outcome. The Warren Court heard the *Loving v. Virginia* case in 1967. According to Hirschkop, Virginia Assistant Attorney General McIlwaine explained that there were studies showing the perils of interbreeding on children, calling it a slippery slope, but was quickly interrupted by Chief Justice Warren who questioned the solidity of Virginia's positioning on the case: "Isn't that the exact same argument made in *Brown v. Board of Education*, that if black children were allowed in schools, all sorts of terrible things would happen, and it was that slippery slope, and that never happened, either?" (Kelly, 2016).

On June 12, 1967, the Warren Court announced the unanimous decision of the United States Supreme Court that the Virginia's Racial Integrity Act of 1924, which criminalized interracial marriage, violated the Fourteenth Amendment of the United States Constitution. Chief Justice Warren said that, "Under our Constitution, the freedom to marry, or not marry, a person of another race resides with the individual, and cannot be infringed by the state."

The *Loving v. Virginia* Decision

LOVING V. VIRGINIA, 388 U.S. 1 (1967)

MR. CHIEF JUSTICE WARREN delivered the opinion of the Court.

This case presents a constitutional question never addressed by this Court: whether a statutory scheme adopted by the State of Virginia to prevent marriages between persons solely on the basis of racial classifications violates the Equal Protection and Due Process Clauses of the Fourteenth Amendment. For reasons which seem to us to reflect the central meaning of those constitutional commands, we conclude that these statutes cannot stand consistently with the Fourteenth Amendment.

In June, 1958, two residents of Virginia, Mildred Jeter, a Negro woman, and Richard Loving, a White man, were married in the District of Columbia pursuant to its laws. Shortly after their marriage, the Lovings returned to Virginia and established their marital abode in Caroline County. At the October Term, 1958, of the Circuit Court of Caroline County, a grand jury issued an indictment charging the Lovings with violating Virginia's ban on interracial marriages. On January 6, 1959, the Lovings pleaded guilty to the charge, and were sentenced to one year in jail; however, the trial judge suspended the sentence for a period of 25 years on the condition that the Lovings leave the State and not return to Virginia together for 25 years. He stated in an opinion that:

> Almighty God created the races white, black, yellow, malay and red, and he placed them on separate continents. And, but for the interference with his arrangement, there would be no cause for such marriage. The fact that he separated the races shows that he did not intend for the races to mix.

After their convictions, the Lovings took up residence in the District of Columbia. On November 6, 1963, they filed a motion in the state trial court to vacate the judgment and set aside the sentence on the ground that the statutes which they had violated were repugnant to the Fourteenth Amendment. The motion not having been decided by October 28, 1964, the Lovings instituted a class action in the United States District Court for the Eastern District of Virginia requesting that a three-judge court be convened to declare the Virginia anti-miscegenation statutes unconstitutional and to enjoin state officials from enforcing their convictions. On January 22, 1965, the state trial judge denied the motion to vacate the sentences, and the Lovings perfected an appeal to the Supreme Court of Appeals of Virginia. On February 11, 1965, the three-judge District Court continued the case to allow the Lovings to present their constitutional claims to the highest state court.

The Supreme Court of Appeals upheld the constitutionality of the anti-miscegenation statutes and, after modifying the sentence, affirmed the convictions. The Lovings appealed this decision, and we noted probable jurisdiction on December 12, 1966.

The two statutes under which appellants were convicted and sentenced are part of a comprehensive statutory scheme aimed at prohibiting and punishing interracial marriages. The Lovings were convicted of violating § 258 of the Virginia Code:

> Leaving State to evade law.—If any white person and colored person shall go out of this State, for the purpose of being married, and with the intention of returning, and be married out of it, and afterwards return to and reside in it, cohabiting as man and wife, they shall be punished as provided in § 20–59, and the marriage shall be governed by the same law as if it had been solemnized in this State. The fact of their cohabitation here as man and wife shall be evidence of their marriage.

Section 259, which defines the penalty for miscegenation, provides:

> Punishment for marriage.—If any white person intermarry with a colored person, or any colored person intermarry with a white person, he shall be guilty of a felony and shall be punished by confinement in the penitentiary for not less than one nor more than five years.

Other central provisions in the Virginia statutory scheme are § 20–57, which automatically voids all marriages between "a White person and a colored person" without any judicial proceeding, and §§ 20–54 and 1–14 which, respectively, define "White persons" and "colored persons and Indians" for purposes of the statutory prohibitions. The Lovings have never disputed in the course of this litigation that Mrs. Loving is a "colored person" or that Mr. Loving is a "White person" within the meanings given those terms by the Virginia statutes.

Virginia is now one of 16 States which prohibit and punish marriages on the basis of racial classifications. Penalties for miscegenation arose as an incident to slavery, and have been common in Virginia since the colonial period. The present statutory scheme dates from the adoption of the Racial Integrity Act of 1924, passed during the period of extreme nativism which followed the end of the First World War. The central features of this Act, and current Virginia law, are the absolute prohibition of a "White person" marrying other than another "White person," a prohibition against issuing marriage licenses until the issuing official is satisfied that the applicants' statements as to their race are correct, certificates of "racial composition" to be kept by both local and state registrars, and the carrying forward of earlier prohibitions against racial intermarriage.

I

In upholding the constitutionality of these provisions in the decision below, the Supreme Court of Appeals of Virginia referred to its 1965 decision in *Naim v. Naim*, as stating the reasons supporting the validity of these laws. In Naim, the state court concluded that the State's legitimate purposes were "to preserve the racial integrity of its citizens," and to prevent "the corruption of blood," "a mongrel breed of citizens," and "the obliteration of racial pride," obviously an endorsement of the doctrine of White Supremacy. The court also reasoned that marriage has traditionally been subject to state regulation without federal intervention, and, consequently, the regulation of marriage should be left to exclusive state control by the Tenth Amendment.

While the state court is no doubt correct in asserting that marriage is a social relation subject to the State's police power, Maynard v. Hill, the State does not contend in its argument before this Court that its powers to regulate marriage are unlimited notwithstanding the commands of the Fourteenth Amendment. Nor could it do so in light of Meyer v. Nebraska, and Skinner v. Oklahoma. Instead, the State argues that the meaning of the Equal Protection Clause, as illuminated by the statements of the Framers, is only that state penal laws containing an interracial element as part of the definition of the offense must apply equally to Whites and Negroes in the sense that members of each race are punished to the same degree. Thus, the State contends that, because its miscegenation statutes punish equally both the White and the Negro participants in an interracial marriage, these statutes, despite their reliance on racial classifications, do not constitute an invidious discrimination based upon race. The second argument advanced by the State assumes the validity of its equal application theory. The argument is that, if the Equal Protection Clause does not outlaw miscegenation statutes because of their reliance on racial classifications, the question of constitutionality would thus become whether there was any rational basis for a State to treat interracial marriages differently from other marriages. On this question, the State argues, the scientific evidence is substantially in doubt and, consequently, this Court should defer to the wisdom of the state legislature in adopting its policy of discouraging interracial marriages.

Because we reject the notion that the mere "equal application" of a statute containing racial classifications is enough to remove the classifications from the Fourteenth Amendment's proscription of all invidious racial discriminations, we do not accept the State's contention that these statutes should be upheld if there is any possible basis for concluding that they serve a rational purpose. The mere fact of equal application does not mean that our analysis of these statutes should follow the approach we have taken in cases involving no racial discrimination where the Equal Protection Clause has been arrayed against a statute discriminating between the kinds of advertising which may be displayed on trucks in New York City, Railway Express Agency, Inc. v. New York, or an exemption in Ohio's ad valorem tax for merchandise owned by a non-resident in a storage warehouse, Allied Stores of Ohio, Inc. v. Bowers. In these cases, involving distinctions not drawn according to race, the Court has merely asked whether there is any rational foundation for the discriminations, and has deferred to the wisdom of the state legislatures. In the case at bar, however, we deal with statutes containing racial classifications, and the fact of equal application does not immunize the statute from the very heavy burden of justification which the Fourteenth Amendment has traditionally required of state statutes drawn according to race.

The State argues that statements in the Thirty-ninth Congress about the time of the passage of the Fourteenth Amendment indicate that the Framers did not intend the Amendment to make unconstitutional state miscegenation laws. Many of the statements alluded to by the State concern the debates over the Freedmen's Bureau Bill, which President Johnson vetoed, and the Civil Rights Act of 1866, enacted over his veto. While these statements have some relevance to the intention of Congress in submitting the Fourteenth Amendment, it must be understood that they pertained to the passage of specific statutes, and not to the broader, organic purpose of a constitutional amendment. As for the various statements directly concerning the Fourteenth Amendment, we have said in connection with a related problem that, although these historical sources "cast some light" they are not sufficient to resolve the problem;

> [a]t best, they are inconclusive. The most avid proponents of the post-War Amendments undoubtedly intended them to remove all legal distinctions among "all persons born or naturalized in the United States." Their opponents, just as certainly, were antagonistic to both the letter and the spirit of the Amendments, and wished them to have the most limited effect.
>
> *(Brown v. Board of Education)*

We have rejected the proposition that the debates in the Thirty-ninth Congress or in the state legislatures which ratified the Fourteenth Amendment supported the theory advanced by the State, that the requirement of equal protection of the laws is satisfied by penal laws defining offenses based on racial classifications so long as White and Negro participants in the offense were similarly punished. McLaughlin v. Florida.

The State finds support for its "equal application" theory in the decision of the Court in Pace v. Alabama. In that case, the Court upheld a conviction under an Alabama statute forbidding adultery or fornication between a White person and a Negro which imposed a greater penalty than that of a statute proscribing similar conduct by members of the same race. The Court reasoned that the statute could not be said to discriminate against Negroes because the punishment for each participant in the offense was the same. However, as recently as the 1964 Term, in rejecting the reasoning of that case, we stated "Pace represents a limited view of the Equal Protection Clause which has not withstood analysis in the subsequent decisions of this Court." McLaughlin v. Florida. As we there demonstrated, the Equal Protection Clause requires the consideration of whether the classifications drawn by any statute constitute an arbitrary and invidious discrimination. The clear and central purpose of the Fourteenth Amendment was to eliminate all official state sources of invidious racial discrimination in the States.

There can be no question but that Virginia's miscegenation statutes rest solely upon distinctions drawn according to race. The statutes proscribe generally accepted conduct if engaged in by members of different races. Over the years, this Court has consistently repudiated "[d]istinctions between citizens solely because of their ancestry" as being "odious to a free people whose institutions are founded upon the doctrine of equality." Hirabayashi v. United States. At the very least, the Equal Protection Clause demands that racial classifications, especially suspect in criminal statutes, be subjected to the "most rigid scrutiny," Korematsu v. United States, and, if they are ever to be upheld, they must be shown to be necessary to the accomplishment of some permissible state objective, independent of the racial discrimination which it was the object of the Fourteenth Amendment to eliminate. Indeed, two members of this Court have already stated that they "cannot conceive of a valid legislative purpose . . . which makes the color of a person's skin the test of whether his conduct is a criminal offense."

McLaughlin v. Florida.

There is patently no legitimate overriding purpose independent of invidious racial discrimination which justifies this classification. The fact that Virginia prohibits only interracial marriages involving White persons demonstrates that the racial classifications must stand on their own justification, as measures designed to maintain White Supremacy. We have consistently denied the constitutionality of measures which restrict the rights of citizens on account of race. There can be no doubt that restricting the freedom to marry solely because of racial classifications violates the central meaning of the Equal Protection Clause.

II

These statutes also deprive the Lovings of liberty without due process of law in violation of the Due Process Clause of the Fourteenth Amendment. The freedom to marry has long been recognized as one of the vital personal rights essential to the orderly pursuit of happiness by free men.

Marriage is one of the "basic civil rights of man," fundamental to our very existence and survival. Skinner v. Oklahoma. To deny this fundamental freedom on so unsupportable a basis as the racial classifications embodied in these statutes, classifications so directly subversive of the principle of equality at the heart of the Fourteenth Amendment, is surely to deprive all the State's citizens of liberty without due process of law. The Fourteenth Amendment requires that the freedom of choice to marry not be restricted by invidious racial discriminations. Under our Constitution, the freedom to marry, or not marry, a person of another race resides with the individual, and cannot be infringed by the State.

These convictions must be reversed.

It is so ordered.

The Impact of *Loving v. Virginia* on the Institution of the Family in the US

As we described in Chapter 2, the institution of the family is defined, for sociologists, as comprised of relationships in which people live together with commitment, form an economic unit and care for any young, and consider their identity to be significantly attached to the group (Kendall, 2011, p. 478). The institution of the **family** is one that is socio-historically situated and constructed, meaning that what society acknowledges as normative and legitimizes changes over time and place. While family by no means is limited to those who are married and their children, most US adults will be married during their lifetime, with 77 percent of men and 83 percent of women (Pew, 2014), and the **nuclear family** (legally married parents and their biological offspring) remains the dominant cultural conception. Given this reality, the importance of the *Loving v. Virginia* decision on the institution of the family in the United States—while it should not be overstated, should not also be overlooked. As sociologist Erica Chito Childs notes, "Regulating sexual relationships by preventing or discouraging marriage through legal means or societal pressure constructs interracial relationships as deviant" (2002). Once legal means were removed, how did social pressures in regard to interracial marriages change? How has interracial marriage changed since before *Loving?* Here, we look at interracial marriages and pre and post *Loving*, interracial marriage stability, children in such multiracial families, and attitudes in the United States.

Interracial Marriages pre Loving v. Virginia

Anti-**miscegenation** laws (laws which govern/ban the sexual relationships between races) which prohibited marriage and the formation of families on the basis of racist ideology were in effect in the United States for over 300 years. They began in the colonial period, from the 1660s onward, when Maryland became the first state to ban interracial marriage, declaring that any White woman who married a Black man and their children would become slaves, and when Virginia mandated exile for Whites who married people of color (Brown, Williams, & Durtschi, 2019). Forty-one American colonies or states—primarily those in the South but also the western states—at some point in US history had anti-miscegenation laws, which carried formal punishment ranging from enslavement to imprisonment. Depending on which state one lived in, these laws continued into the 20th century, bolstered by scientific racism. Eugenicists, some backed by large 'reputable' foundations like the Carnegie Institution, supported measures that would strengthen state control over limiting interracial marriages and maintaining the White supremacist notion of racial purity (Pascoe, 1996) and gave the veneer of science to the justifications for maintaining legal barriers. To give an example of the language used in these laws, consider the below text from Virginia in 1924:

> It shall hereafter be unlawful for any white person in this State to marry any save a white person, or a person with no other admixture of blood than white and American Indian. For the purpose of this act, the term "white person" shall apply only to the person who has no trace whatsoever of any blood other than Caucasian; but persons who have one-sixteenth or less of the blood of the American Indian and have no other non-Caucasic blood shall be deemed to be white persons.
>
> *(cited in Pascoe, 1996, p. 59)*

As sociologists and anthropologists have long argued, race itself is a social construction, and so as ideas about race changed, a patchwork of laws banned marriage between Whites and a spectrum of other shifting racial categories of people, from American Indians to Japanese, Mongolians to Hindus and other cross-group pairings (Pascoe, 1996; de Guzman & Nishina, 2017). For example, in the mid-19th century, California prohibited marriage between Whites and Black people or "mulattoes," those with mixed Black ancestry, and by the end of the 19th century, this had been extended to ban marriages between Chinese and White people (Volpp, 2005). Notably, most anti-miscegenation laws generally did not ban marriage between two different racial groups who were non-White (Pratt, 2012), as one of the key pillars of White supremacist ideology is maintaining the mythical purity of the White race. Because the focus of this chapter is on the influence of the Supreme Court of the family, we will not include discussions of sexual relationships broadly, but it should be noted that legal enforcement of sex was much less the target than marriage. Marriage brings with it legal, economic, and social privileges that are not found in other types of sexual partnerings (Pascoe, 1996).

While the anti-miscegenation laws that persisted until 1967 remained in the South, it should be noted that the North was not immune from the racist thinking that motivated these laws. In fact, "the early 20th century saw lively debates in the North about whether Black and white couples should have the right to formalize their unions and what the consequences of such marriages might be" (Syrett, 2018, p. 54).

Interracial Relationships Post Loving v. Virginia

Loving v. Virginia did not of course mark the beginning of an era where interracial sexuality, partnerships, child-rearing or cohabitation began to take place. But the legal rights and privileges conferred on sexual relationships through marriage only began in states that did not permit interracial marriage in 1967. As such, dramatic differences can be observed when looking at the rates of legal marriage since that time. When the *Loving* decision was rendered, interracial marriage rates in the United States stood at only 0.4 percent of all marriages (Garcia, Lewis, & Ford-Robertson, 2015), and a full 17 out of 50 states—more than a third—had anti-miscegenation laws on the books. Since then, not only because of the lifting of legal limitations on marriage, but changing racial attitudes more broadly, this number has climbed substantially. In 2015, 17 percent of all newly married people had a spouse of a different race or ethnicity, a fivefold increase since *Loving*. Even when looking at the rate of change since 1980, there has been an increase over the past 40 years in both the percentages of Black and White people who choose to marry a spouse of a different race or ethnicity, with Latinos also going up slightly and Asians declining slightly. In 2015 29 percent of Asians married outside of their racial group, 27 percent of Latinos, 18 percent of Blacks and 11 percent of Whites (Livingston & Brown, 2017). Other demographic characteristics predict intermarriage. Currently, it is more common in those with a college education, and in metropolitan areas versus more rural areas (18 percent versus 11 percent, respectively). Of intermarried couples, White/Latino pairings make up the largest percentage: 42 percent, White-Asian, 15 percent, White-Multiracial, 12 percent, White-Black, 11 percent, Hispanic/Black, 5 percent, White-American Indian, 3 percent, Hispanic/Asian, 3 percent, and Hispanic/Multiracial, 3 percent (Livingston & Brown, 2017). The reasons for the differences in rates of intermarriage are complex, but they are affected by racial attitudes, contact between groups, and the availability of potential partners (for example, members of racial groups that are a small percentage of the population may be more likely to intermarry).

Interestingly, interracial dating is more common than interracial marriage and having children (de Guzman & Nishina, 2017), which may speak to still extant unconscious or conscious unwillingness to commit to sharing of power and resources. "The examination of interracial relationships can be insightful for understanding race relations in general" (Garcia et al., 2015).

Interracial Marriage Stability

With the increased number of interracial marriages, social scientists have been interested in the outcomes of these unions in terms of martial quality, or assessments of relationships between spouses. **Homogeny perspective** predicts that couples with similar characteristics (such as race, ethnicity, religion, and/or culture) are less likely to have conflict, social support, and understanding from peers and family (de Guzman & Nishina, 2017). There is a lot of mixed evidence, with some showing no difference between relationship quality, while other have shown that interracial marriages may indeed be more vulnerable to dissolution/divorce, with Asian and White marriages being an exception (de Guzman & Nishina, 2017). National data from 23,000 participants revealed that interracial couples were 15–21 percent more likely to dissolve their marriage than their same-race counterparts, and to have shorter marriages (Brown et al., 2019). The reasons for this are complex, but we can see social pressures are exerted on interracial couples that are not present for same-race couples. Because of **colorism,** where lighter-skinned individuals are valued more highly in certain societies including in the US, acceptance of Black–White marriages versus Latino–White or Asian–White (Garcia et al., 2015) is lower, and they may face more negative society reactions, like staring in public, jokes or discrimination. Parental approval is of great importance for the survival of the marriage—even more so than the presence of negative societal reactions. But in Black–White couples, positive feelings about the Black spouse's racial identity were also shown to increase marriage quality, as did the White spouse's not possessing feelings of racial superiority, but rather of cultural and racial acceptance (Garcia et al., 2015).

In looking at how marital quality changes longitudinally (over the duration of a relationship) (e.g. do couples start out with different assessments of marriage quality than later on in their marriage?), some social scientists have yielded positive findings. In one of the largest and most robust studies on the question (Toosi, Babbitt, Ambady, & Sommers, 2012, cited in Brown et al., 2019) it was discovered "the nature of romantic relationships is converging and becoming more similar across time between same-race and interracial couples," in feeling positive about their relationship, and exhibiting more friendly non-verbal behavior in their interactions.

Interracial Children

The status of mixed-race children in the United States has a troubled past, with hundreds of thousands born out of the sexual assault of enslaved women, and consequently unrecognized, or born out of the relationships between indentured White women and freed Black men. "The effect of these laws was often to create entire generations of mixed-race indentured laborers" (Syrett, 2018, p. 3). The children of interracial couples were at the heart of early arguments in favor of legalization of interracial marriage. In 1913, in arguing against miscegenation laws in Illinois, the Illinois Protective League, composed of 100 Black men and women, posited that those made most vulnerable by these laws were biracial children. Afterall, without the ability for two people of different races to marry legally, this meant that the child would not have a legal father, and led to the stigma of being born—without recourse—"illegitimately" (Syrett, 2018). Children became a way to advocate for interracial marriage (even if the parents may not have desired this outcome). Still, little sympathy was afforded to these children, as bills to protect them in the 20th century met with fierce opposition. For example, in Missouri, the president of the Negro Republican League introduced a bill, "an act making legitimate the illegitimate children of Negro women, begotten by white fathers," which got no votes from either political party (55).

The number of biracial children also increased in the US dramatically since *Loving v. Virginia*. Among those children younger than one who are living with both parents (which leads to underestimating the population) 14 percent are multiracial or multiethnic, compared to only 5 percent in 1980. Of these children, the 42% have one parent who is Hispanic and one who is non-Hispanic White. About 22 percent have at least one multiracial parent, and 14 percent have one parent who is White and the other Asian, and 10 percent have one parent who is Black and the other White (Livingston, 2017).

This may be a positive sign for racial relations, as intermarriage and multiracial/multiethnic children may soften group identities and prejudice in subsequent generations. Recent surveys of multiracial adults also show that the majority express pride in their backgrounds, feel more open to new cultures because of those backgrounds, and 20 percent see their backgrounds as providing them with an advantage, despite a majority also indicating they had been subjected to racial slurs or jokes (Parker, Menasce Horowitz, Morin, & Hugo Lopez, 2015).

Attitudes Toward Interracial Marriages

Changes to laws do not always lead to shift changes in attitudes, and the *Loving* decision exemplified this disconnect. "It took until 1991 for most Americans to accept the idea of interracial marriages" (de Guzman & Nishina, 2017), and even in the 2010s, evidence exists that negative attitudes were still persisting. Historically and presently, White supremacist ideas of White biological and cultural superiority have meant opposition to racial mixing, relying on ideals of "racial purity," promoting racial social segregation (Perry & Whitehead, 2015). Yet, through social and media validation and affirmation of the validity of these unions (Edmonds, 2018), there has been a movement toward more widespread acceptance in the United States.

The number of those who say they disapprove of interracial marriage or would oppose a relative marrying someone of a different race has fallen. In 2017, only 9 percent of Americans said that interracial marriage is a "bad thing," whereas 39 percent said it was a "good thing" and 52 percent said it doesn't make a difference. In 2010, only 24 percent indicated it was a "good thing." Attitudes about whether intermarriage is a "good thing" vary by age, education, race, and gender. In general, older people (65+) are less likely to see it as a good thing (26 percent) than the younger cohorts (such as 18–29, 42 percent of which expressed that it is a good thing.) Those with a college education are more likely than those without to say it is a good thing, men are more likely than women. Black Americans express less support for interracial marriage (18 percent) than Whites (9 percent) or Hispanics (3 percent).

In terms of support for a relative marrying a member of the opposite race, a Pew Center Analysis of the General Social Survey showed that Whites are the least likely to report opposing this (4 percent), Asians and Hispanics at 9 percent, and Blacks the most opposed, at 14 percent. However, these numbers have all seen declines (Livingston & Brown, 2017). Sociologist Erica Chito Childs cautions though against easily inferring from survey responses. "Responses to interracial relationships are complex, and there is a discrepancy between people's words and their actions," she states. In her studies of interracial marriages and attitudes toward them, she found that while Whites may express acceptance, they may still live in overwhelmingly White spaces and express **colorblind** reasons for not wanting to get into interracial relationships personally. Black people may, conversely, state opposition to interracial marriages on the basis of their experiences of discrimination, yet accept interracial couples as family and friends (Chito Childs, 2008).

In the over 50 years since *Loving*, the idea of what the US family can be has shifted, although "society and law continue to work together to frame the normative ideal of intimate couples and families as . . . monoracial" (Onwuachi-Willing & Onwuachi-Willing, 2012) Cultural shifts in the United States in the conception of the family include coming to terms with the idea that members of the same family may not identify with the same racial groups (Bedley, 2018), and against the collective notion of the family as monoracial/ethnic.

Introduction to *Obergefell v. Hodges*

> "This morning, the Supreme Court recognized that the Constitution guarantees marriage equality. In doing so, they've reaffirmed that all Americans are entitled to the equal protection of the law. That all people should be treated equally, regardless of who they are or who they love," the 44th President of the United States Barack Obama announced in the Rose Garden of the White House on June 26, 2015
>
> ("Remarks from the President").

FIGURE 4.1 "Protest against a constitutional amendment banning same sex marriage."

License: Protest against a constitutional amendment banning same sex marriage_ by Fibonacci Blue is licensed under CC BY 2.0

The Supreme Court had ruled in favor of Jim Obergefell, the lead plaintiff in the *Obergefell v. Hodges* case, a landmark case that quickly placed Obergefell on the same list of history makers as *Brown* and *Roe*—a spotlight Obergefell had a hard time coming to terms with, especially because the only reason why he became the lead plaintiff, as it usually happens in Supreme Court cases, was because he had the lowest case number, 14–556. "It's just Jim," Obergefell stated in an interview, "I just stood up for our marriage" (Rosenwald, 2015).

Obergefell and his late husband, John Arthur, had been married only three months and eleven days when Arthur succumbed to amyotrophic lateral sclerosis (ALS), a degenerative and often fatal disease that attacks the nervous system and impacts body functions by weakening muscles. Arthur and Obergefell met in the early 1990s and quickly moved in together. The two both worked in information technology and shared a passion for art. Then, in 2011, Arthur began having trouble walking. Soon, he found himself falling often, and it wasn't long before he had a hard time getting into their car. The couple visited several doctors, who all diagnosed Arthur with ALS. By the time the two shared their "With this ring I thee wed," Arthur could barely speak. Hospice care had already started, and he was bedbound. Although they lived in Ohio, they had to fly to the state of Maryland in order to get married—Ohio did not recognize same-sex marriage. But getting to Maryland wasn't easy or cheap. Although they had been together for 20 years, Obergefell and Arthur decided to get married only after the Supreme Court had ruled in favor of same-sex married couples by striking down a portion of the Defense of Marriage Act, which had been signed into law by former President Bill Clinton in 1996 and that, for all federal intents and purposes, described marriage as the union between one man and one woman, and allowed states the freedom to refuse to recognize same-sex marriages.

Although their friends often pushed them to get married as it was clear that their union was going to be lifelong, both Obergefell and Arthur often declared that they didn't want just a symbolic marriage. They wanted a marriage that was going to be recognized by the law. So, when Obergefell heard the news of the Supreme Court decision, he told Obergefell that it was finally time for them to make their union official under the law. Obergefell agreed but the two quickly faced setbacks due to Arthur's physical disability. Obergefell knew that in order to get to Maryland—a state suggested by one of their friends—they needed to fly, and they needed medical assistance as well.

Thanks to the emotional, moral, and financial support from their friends and family members, Obergefell and Arthur were able to afford the $13,000 fee for a medically assisted flight to Maryland. On July 11, 2013, Obergefell and Arthur arrived at the airport with an ambulance and boarded the medically assisted flight with a nurse and Arthur's aunt, Paulette Roberts. As soon as they landed in Maryland, Roberts—who had become an ordained minister online—married the couple on the tarmac. "If marriage vows mean anything," Roberts said, "then those two were more married than anyone I have ever known" (Rosenwald, 2015).

Soon after getting married, Obergefell and Arthur—who had recently moved into a one-level condo in Cincinnati after the couple decided that their two-level condo was not going to fit their new normal after Arthur had been diagnosed with ALS—received an unexpected visit from Al Gerhardstein, a local civil rights attorney. He had learned about the couple's story through one of their neighbors and Gerhardstein felt compelled to help. "I knew right away they had a problem," Gerhardstein said. "And I knew they probably weren't thinking about it. Who thinks about a death certificate after getting married?" (Rosenwald, 2015). Gerhardstein pointed out to the couple that, should Arthur pass away, Obergefell would not be listed as the surviving spouse of his death certificate because their marriage was not going to be recognized by the state of Ohio. Together, they decided to file a lawsuit and a judge agreed that Obergefell's name would appear on Arthur's death certificate as his surviving spouse. The sweetness of their legal victory was short lived, however. Arthur died soon after of ALS.

At the same time Obergefell was mourning the loss of his husband, he had to face yet another terrible news: Ohio had filed an appeal to a higher court and won. Obergefell knew this was not the time to back down. He wanted to keep John's memory and legacy alive, and he wanted for people to understand the true meaning of spouse. "We need to protect their interest for posterity, for the end of time," Gerhardstein said. "For many people, marriage is some kind of theoretical thing. There are so many ways that this case is about marriage, about that enduring commitment." Obergefell brought the case to the Supreme Court. Although his name appeared as the lead plaintiff, there were other same-sex couples involved in the case. Between January 2012 and February 2014, they had sued their state agencies in Ohio, Michigan, Kentucky, and Tennessee. The plaintiffs argued that their respective states' statutes went against the Equal Protection Clause and Due Process Clause of the Fourteenth Amendment.

In April 2015, the Roberts Court agreed to hear the case—whose full name is *James Obergefell v. Richard Hodges, Director, Ohio Department of Health, et al.* After the Supreme Court ruled on June 26, 2015, in favor of Obergefell—a decision that was not unanimous, as five of the nine Supreme Court Justices ruled in favor—Justice Kennedy stated that,

> No union is more profound than marriage, for it embodies the highest ideals of love, fidelity, devotion, sacrifice, and family. In forming a marital union, two people become something greater than once they were. As some of the petitioners in these cases demonstrate, marriage embodies a love that may endure even past death.

After the Supreme Court's ruling, Obergefell, who had both wedding rings fused into one, went back to living in the couple's Cincinnati condo, surrounded by the artwork they had collected through the years and plenty of photos that depict the happy years they had lived together. Obergefell has since become a public figure and a speaker. Although both of these roles still feel foreign to him, he appreciates the opportunity of talking about the love he shared with Arthur and he knows that this is a great way to keep his late husband's legacy alive.

Obergefell v. Hodges Decision

JAMES OBERGEFELL, et al., PETITIONERS

Justice Kennedy delivered the opinion of the Court.

The Constitution promises liberty to all within its reach, a liberty that includes certain specific rights that allow persons, within a lawful realm, to define and express their identity. The petitioners in these cases seek to find that liberty by marrying someone of the same sex and having their marriages deemed lawful on the same terms and conditions as marriages between persons of the opposite sex.

I

These cases come from Michigan, Kentucky, Ohio, and Tennessee, States that define marriage as a union between one man and one woman. The petitioners are 14 same-sex couples and two men whose same-sex partners are deceased. The respondents are state officials responsible for enforcing the laws in question. The petitioners claim the respondents violate the Fourteenth Amendment by denying them the right to marry or to have their marriages, lawfully performed in another State, given full recognition.

Petitioners filed these suits in United States District Courts in their home States. Each District Court ruled in their favor. The respondents appealed the decisions against them to the United States Court of Appeals for the Sixth Circuit. It consolidated the cases and reversed the judgments of the District Courts. The Court of Appeals held that a State has no constitutional obligation to license same-sex marriages or to recognize same-sex marriages performed out of State.

The petitioners sought certiorari. This Court granted review, limited to two questions. The first, presented by the cases from Michigan and Kentucky, is whether the Fourteenth Amendment requires a State to license a marriage between two people of the same sex. The second, presented by the cases from Ohio, Tennessee, and, again, Kentucky, is whether the Fourteenth Amendment requires a State to recognize a same-sex marriage licensed and performed in a State which does grant that right.

III

Under the Due Process Clause of the Fourteenth Amendment, no State shall "deprive any person of life, liberty, or property, without due process of law." The fundamental liberties protected by this Clause include most of the rights enumerated in the Bill of Rights. See *Duncan v. Louisiana*. In addition these liberties extend to certain personal choices central to individual dignity and autonomy, including intimate choices that define personal identity and beliefs. See, *e.g.*, *Eisenstadt v. Baird*, *Griswold v. Connecticut*.

The identification and protection of fundamental rights is an enduring part of the judicial duty to interpret the Constitution. That responsibility, however, "has not been reduced to any formula." *Poe v. Ullman*. Rather, it requires courts to exercise reasoned judgment in identifying interests of the person so fundamental that the State must accord them its respect. That process is guided by many of the same considerations relevant to analysis of other constitutional provisions that set forth broad principles rather than specific requirements. History and tradition guide and discipline this inquiry but do not set its outer boundaries. See *Lawrence*. That method respects our history and learns from it without allowing the past alone to rule the present.

The nature of injustice is that we may not always see it in our own times. The generations that wrote and ratified the Bill of Rights and the Fourteenth Amendment did not presume to know the extent of freedom in all of its dimensions, and so they entrusted to future generations a charter protecting the right of all persons to enjoy liberty as we learn its meaning. When new insight reveals discord between the Constitution's central protections and a received legal stricture, a claim to liberty must be addressed.

Applying these established tenets, the Court has long held the right to marry is protected by the Constitution. In *Loving v. Virginia*, which invalidated bans on interracial unions, a unanimous Court held marriage is "one of the vital personal rights essential to the orderly pursuit of happiness by free men." The Court reaffirmed that holding in *Zablocki v. Redhail*, which held the right to marry was burdened by a law prohibiting fathers who were behind on child support from marrying. The Court again applied this principle in *Turner v. Safley*, which held the right to marry was abridged by regulations limiting the privilege of prison inmates to marry. Over time and in other contexts, the Court has reiterated that the right to marry is fundamental under the Due Process Clause.

It cannot be denied that this Court's cases describing the right to marry presumed a relationship involving opposite-sex partners. The Court, like many institutions, has made assumptions defined by the world and time of which it is a part. This was evident in *Baker v. Nelson*, a one-line summary decision issued in 1972, holding the exclusion of same-sex couples from marriage did not present a substantial federal question.

Still, there are other, more instructive precedents. This Court's cases have expressed constitutional principles of broader reach. In defining the right to marry these cases have identified essential attributes of that right based in history, tradition, and other constitutional liberties inherent in this intimate bond. And in assessing whether the force and rationale of its cases apply to same-sex couples, the Court must respect the basic reasons why the right to marry has been long protected.

This analysis compels the conclusion that same-sex couples may exercise the right to marry. The four principles and traditions to be discussed demonstrate that the reasons marriage is fundamental under the Constitution apply with equal force to same-sex couples.

A first premise of the Court's relevant precedents is that the right to personal choice regarding marriage is inherent in the concept of individual autonomy. This abiding connection between marriage and liberty is why *Loving* invalidated interracial marriage bans under the Due Process Clause. Like choices concerning contraception, family relationships, procreation, and childrearing, all of which are protected by the Constitution, decisions concerning marriage are among the most intimate that an individual can make. Indeed, the Court has noted it would be contradictory "to recognize a right of privacy with respect to other matters of family life and not with respect to the decision to enter the relationship that is the foundation of the family in our society." *Zablocki*

Choices about marriage shape an individual's destiny. As the Supreme Judicial Court of Massachusetts has explained, because "it fulfils yearnings for security, safe haven, and connection that express our common humanity, civil marriage is an esteemed institution, and the decision whether and whom to marry is among life's momentous acts of self-definition." *Goodridge*

The nature of marriage is that, through its enduring bond, two persons together can find other freedoms, such as expression, intimacy, and spirituality. This is true for all persons, whatever their sexual orientation. There is dignity in the bond between two men or two women who seek to marry and in their autonomy to make such profound choices.

A second principle in this Court's jurisprudence is that the right to marry is fundamental because it supports a two-person union unlike any other in its importance to the committed individuals. This point was central to *Griswold v. Connecticut*, which held the Constitution protects the right of married couples to use contraception. *Griswold* described marriage this way:

> Marriage is a coming together for better or for worse, hopefully enduring, and intimate to the degree of being sacred. It is an association that promotes a way of life, not causes; a harmony in living, not political faiths; a bilateral loyalty, not commercial or social projects. Yet it is an association for as noble a purpose as any involved in our prior decisions.
>
> *(Id., at 486.)*

And in *Turner*, the Court again acknowledged the intimate association protected by this right, holding prisoners could not be denied the right to marry because their committed relationships satisfied the basic reasons why marriage is a fundamental right. The right to marry thus dignifies couples who "wish to define themselves by their commitment to each other." Marriage responds to the universal fear that a lonely person might call out only to find no one there. It offers the hope of companionship and understanding and assurance that while both still live there will be someone to care for the other.

As this Court held in *Lawrence*, same-sex couples have the same right as opposite-sex couples to enjoy intimate association. *Lawrence* invalidated laws that made same-sex intimacy a criminal act. And it acknowledged that "[w]hen sexuality finds overt expression in intimate conduct with another person, the conduct can be but one element in a personal bond that is more enduring." 539 U. S., at 567. But while *Lawrence* confirmed a dimension of freedom that allows individuals to engage in intimate association without criminal liability, it does not follow that freedom stops there. Outlaw to outcast may be a step forward, but it does not achieve the full promise of liberty.

A third basis for protecting the right to marry is that it safeguards children and families and thus draws meaning from related rights of childrearing, procreation, and education. The Court has recognized these connections by describing the varied rights as a unified whole: "[T]he right to 'marry, establish a home and bring up children' is a central part of the liberty protected by the Due Process Clause." *Zablocki*. Under the laws of the several States, some of marriage's protections for children and families are material. But marriage also confers more profound benefits. By giving recognition and legal structure to their parents' relationship, marriage allows children "to understand the integrity and closeness of their own family and its concord with other families in their community and in their daily lives." *Windsor*. Marriage also affords the permanency and stability important to children's best interests.

As all parties agree, many same-sex couples provide loving and nurturing homes to their children, whether biological or adopted. And hundreds of thousands of children are presently being raised by such couples. Most States have allowed gays and lesbians to adopt, either as individuals or as couples, and many adopted and foster children have same-sex parents. This provides powerful confirmation from the law itself that gays and lesbians can create loving, supportive families.

Excluding same-sex couples from marriage thus conflicts with a central premise of the right to marry. Without the recognition, stability, and predictability marriage offers, their children suffer the stigma of knowing their families are somehow lesser. They also suffer the significant material costs of being raised by unmarried parents, relegated through no fault of their own to a more difficult and uncertain family life. The marriage laws at issue here thus harm and humiliate the children of same-sex couples.

That is not to say the right to marry is less meaningful for those who do not or cannot have children. An ability, desire, or promise to procreate is not and has not been a prerequisite for a valid marriage in any State. In light of precedent protecting the right of a married couple not to procreate, it cannot be said the Court or the States have conditioned the right to marry on the capacity or commitment to procreate. The constitutional marriage right has many aspects, of which childbearing is only one.

Fourth and finally, this Court's cases and the Nation's traditions make clear that marriage is a keystone of our social order. Alexis de Tocqueville recognized this truth on his travels through the United States almost two centuries ago:

> There is certainly no country in the world where the tie of marriage is so much respected as in America. . . . [W]hen the American retires from the turmoil of public life to the bosom of his family, he finds in it the image of order and of peace. . . . [H]e afterwards carries [that image] with him into public affairs.
>
> *(1 Democracy in America 309)*

In *Maynard*, the Court echoed de Tocqueville, explaining that marriage is "the foundation of the family and of society, without which there would be neither civilization nor progress." Marriage, the *Maynard* Court said, has long been " 'a great public institution, giving character to our whole civil polity.' " This idea has been reiterated even as the institution has evolved in substantial ways over time, superseding rules related to parental consent, gender, and race once thought by many to be essential. Marriage remains a building block of our national community.

For that reason, just as a couple vows to support each other, so does society pledge to support the couple, offering symbolic recognition and material benefits to protect and nourish the union. Indeed, while the States are in general free to vary the benefits they confer on all married couples, they have throughout our history made marriage the basis for an expanding list of governmental rights, benefits, and responsibilities. These aspects of marital status include: taxation; inheritance and property rights; rules of intestate succession; spousal privilege in the law of evidence; hospital access; medical decisionmaking authority; adoption rights; the rights and benefits of survivors; birth and death certificates; professional ethics rules; campaign finance restrictions; workers' compensation benefits; health insurance; and child custody, support, and visitation rules. Valid marriage under state law is also a significant status for over a thousand provisions of federal law. The States have contributed to the fundamental character of the marriage right by placing that institution at the center of so many facets of the legal and social order.

There is no difference between same- and opposite-sex couples with respect to this principle. Yet by virtue of their exclusion from that institution, same-sex couples are denied the constellation of benefits that the States have linked to marriage. This harm results in more than just material burdens. Same-sex couples are consigned to an instability many opposite-sex couples would deem intolerable in their own lives. As the State itself makes marriage all the more precious by the significance it attaches to it, exclusion from that status has the effect of teaching that gays and lesbians are unequal in important respects. It demeans gays and lesbians for the State to lock them out of a central institution of the Nation's society. Same-sex couples, too, may aspire to the transcendent purposes of marriage and seek fulfillment in its highest meaning.

The limitation of marriage to opposite-sex couples may long have seemed natural and just, but its inconsistency with the central meaning of the fundamental right to marry is now manifest. With that knowledge must come the recognition that laws excluding same-sex couples from the marriage right impose stigma and injury of the kind prohibited by our basic charter.

Objecting that this does not reflect an appropriate framing of the issue, which called for a "careful description" of fundamental rights. They assert the petitioners do not seek to exercise the right to marry but rather a new and non-existent "right to same-sex marriage." *Glucksberg* did insist that liberty under the Due Process Clause must be defined in a most circumscribed manner, with central reference to specific historical practices. Yet while that approach may have been appropriate for the asserted right there involved (physician-assisted suicide), it is inconsistent with the approach this Court has used in discussing other fundamental rights, including marriage and intimacy. *Loving* did not ask about a "right to interracial marriage"; *Turner* did not ask about a "right of inmates to marry"; and *Zablocki* did not ask about a "right of fathers with unpaid child support duties to marry." Rather, each case inquired about the right to marry in its comprehensive sense, asking if there was a sufficient justification for excluding the relevant class from the right.

That principle applies here. If rights were defined by who exercised them in the past, then received practices could serve as their own continued justification and new groups could not invoke rights once denied. This Court has rejected that approach, both with respect to the right to marry and the rights of gays and lesbians.

The right to marry is fundamental as a matter of history and tradition, but rights come not from ancient sources alone. They rise, too, from a better informed understanding of how constitutional imperatives define a liberty that remains urgent in our own era. Many who deem same-sex marriage to be wrong reach that conclusion based on decent and honorable religious or philosophical premises, and neither they nor their beliefs are disparaged here. But when that sincere, personal opposition becomes enacted law and public policy, the necessary consequence is to put the imprimatur of the State itself on an exclusion that soon demeans or stigmatizes those whose own liberty is then denied. Under the Constitution, same-sex couples seek in marriage the same legal treatment as opposite-sex couples, and it would disparage their choices and diminish their personhood to deny them this right.

The right of same-sex couples to marry that is part of the liberty promised by the Fourteenth Amendment is derived, too, from that Amendment's guarantee of the equal protection of the laws. The Due Process Clause and the Equal Protection Clause are connected in a profound way, though they set forth independent principles. Rights implicit in liberty and rights secured by equal protection may rest on different precepts and are not always co-extensive, yet in some instances each may be instructive as to the meaning and reach of the other. In any particular case one Clause may be thought to capture the essence of the right in a more accurate and comprehensive way, even as the two Clauses may converge in the identification and definition of the right. This interrelation of the two principles furthers our understanding of what freedom is and must become.

The Court's cases touching upon the right to marry reflect this dynamic. In *Loving* the Court invalidated a prohibition on interracial marriage under both the Equal Protection Clause and the Due Process Clause. The Court first declared the prohibition invalid because of its un-equal treatment of interracial couples. It stated: "There can be no doubt that restricting the freedom to marry solely because of racial classifications violates the central meaning of the Equal

Protection Clause." With this link to equal protection the Court proceeded to hold the prohibition offended central precepts of liberty:

> To deny this fundamental freedom on so unsupportable a basis as the racial classifications embodied in these statutes, classifications so directly subversive of the principle of equality at the heart of the Fourteenth Amendment, is surely to deprive all the State's citizens of liberty without due process of law.

The reasons why marriage is a fundamental right became more clear and compelling from a full awareness and understanding of the hurt that resulted from laws barring interracial unions.

The synergy between the two protections is illustrated further in *Zablocki*. There the Court invoked the Equal Protection Clause as its basis for invalidating the challenged law, which, as already noted, barred fathers who were behind on child-support payments from marrying without judicial approval. The equal protection analysis depended in central part on the Court's holding that the law burdened a right "of fundamental importance." It was the essential nature of the marriage right, discussed at length in *Zablocki*, that made apparent the law's incompatibility with requirements of equality. Each concept—liberty and equal protection—leads to a stronger understanding of the other.

Indeed, in interpreting the Equal Protection Clause, the Court has recognized that new insights and societal understandings can reveal unjustified inequality within our most fundamental institutions that once passed unnoticed and unchallenged. To take but one period, this occurred with respect to marriage in the 1970's and 1980's. Notwithstanding the gradual erosion of the doctrine of coverture, see *supra*, at 6, invidious sex-based classifications in marriage remained common through the mid-20th century. These classifications denied the equal dignity of men and women. One State's law, for example, provided in 1971 that

> the husband is the head of the family and the wife is subject to him; her legal civil existence is merged in the husband, except so far as the law recognizes her separately, either for her own protection, or for her benefit.

Responding to a new awareness, the Court invoked equal protection principles to invalidate laws imposing sex-based inequality on marriage. Like *Loving* and *Zablocki*, these precedents show the Equal Protection Clause can help to identify and correct inequalities in the institution of marriage, vindicating precepts of liberty and equality under the Constitution.

Other cases confirm this relation between liberty and equality. In *M. L. B. v. S. L. J.*, the Court invalidated under due process and equal protection principles a statute requiring indigent mothers to pay a fee in order to appeal the termination of their parental rights. In *Eisenstadt v. Baird*, the Court invoked both principles to invalidate a prohibition on the distribution of contraceptives to unmarried persons but not married persons.

In *Lawrence* the Court acknowledged the interlocking nature of these constitutional safeguards in the context of the legal treatment of gays and lesbians. Although *Lawrence* elaborated its holding under the Due Process Clause, it acknowledged, and sought to remedy, the continuing inequality that resulted from laws making intimacy in the lives of gays and lesbians a crime against the State. *Lawrence* therefore drew upon principles of liberty and equality to define and protect the rights of gays and lesbians, holding the State "cannot demean their existence or control their destiny by making their private sexual conduct a crime."

This dynamic also applies to same-sex marriage. It is now clear that the challenged laws burden the liberty of same-sex couples, and it must be further acknowledged that they abridge central precepts of equality. Here the marriage laws enforced by the respondents are in essence unequal: same-sex couples are denied all the benefits afforded to opposite-sex couples and are barred from exercising a fundamental right. Especially against a long history of disapproval of their relationships, this denial to same-sex couples of the right to marry works a grave and continuing harm. The imposition of this disability on gays and lesbians serves to disrespect and subordinate them. And the Equal Protection Clause, like the Due Process Clause, prohibits this unjustified infringement of the fundamental right to marry.

These considerations lead to the conclusion that the right to marry is a fundamental right inherent in the liberty of the person, and under the Due Process and Equal Protection Clauses of the Fourteenth Amendment couples of the same-sex may not be deprived of that right and that liberty. The Court now holds that same-sex couples may exercise the fundamental right to marry. No longer may this liberty be denied to them. *Baker v. Nelson* must be and now is overruled, and the State laws challenged by Petitioners in these cases are now held invalid to the extent they exclude same-sex couples from civil marriage on the same terms and conditions as opposite-sex couples.

IV

There may be an initial inclination in these cases to proceed with caution to await further legislation, litigation, and debate. The respondents warn there has been insufficient democratic discourse before deciding an issue so basic as the definition of marriage. In its ruling on the cases now before this Court, the majority opinion for the Court of Appeals made a cogent argument that it would be appropriate for the respondents' States to await further public discussion and political measures before licensing same-sex marriages.

Yet there has been far more deliberation than this argument acknowledges. There have been referenda, legislative debates, and grassroots campaigns, as well as countless studies, papers, books, and other popular and scholarly writings. There has been extensive litigation in state and federal courts. Judicial opinions addressing the issue have been informed by the contentions of parties and counsel, which, in turn, reflect the more general, societal discussion of same-sex marriage and its meaning that has occurred over the past decades. As more than 100 *amici* make clear in their filings, many of the central institutions in American life—state and local governments, the military, large and small businesses, labor unions, religious organizations, law enforcement, civic groups, professional organizations, and universities have devoted substantial attention to the question. This has led to an enhanced understanding of the issue—an understanding reflected in the arguments now presented for resolution as a matter of constitutional law.

Of course, the Constitution contemplates that democracy is the appropriate process for change, so long as that process does not abridge fundamental rights. Last Term, a plurality of this Court reaffirmed the importance of the democratic principle in *Schuette v. BAMN*, noting the "right of citizens to debate so they can learn and decide and then, through the political process, act in concert to try to shape the course of their own times." Indeed, it is most often through democracy that liberty is preserved and protected in our lives. But as *Schuette* also said,

> [t]he freedom secured by the Constitution consists, in one of its essential dimensions, of the right of the individual not to be injured by the unlawful exercise of governmental power.

Thus, when the rights of persons are violated, "the Constitution requires redress by the courts," notwithstanding the more general value of democratic decision making. This holds true even when protecting individual rights affects issues of the utmost importance and sensitivity.

The dynamic of our constitutional system is that individuals need not await legislative action before asserting a fundamental right. The Nation's courts are open to injured individuals who come to them to vindicate their own direct, personal stake in our basic charter. An individual can invoke a right to constitutional protection when he or she is harmed, even if the broader public disagrees and even if the legislature refuses to act. The idea of the Constitution "was to withdraw certain subjects from the vicissitudes of political controversy, to place them beyond the reach of majorities and officials and to establish them as legal principles to be applied by the courts." *West Virginia Bd. of Ed. v. Barnette*. This is why "fundamental rights may not be submitted to a vote; they depend on the outcome of no elections." It is of no moment whether advocates of same-sex marriage now enjoy or lack momentum in the democratic process. The issue before the Court here is the legal question whether the Constitution protects the right of same-sex couples to marry.

This is not the first time the Court has been asked to adopt a cautious approach to recognizing and protecting fundamental rights. In *Bowers*, a bare majority upheld a law criminalizing same-sex intimacy. That approach might have been viewed as a cautious endorsement of the democratic process, which had only just begun to consider the rights of gays and lesbians. Yet, in effect, *Bowers* upheld state action that denied gays and lesbians a fundamental right and caused them pain and humiliation. As evidenced by the dissents in that case, the facts and principles necessary to a correct holding were known to the *Bowers* Court. That is why *Lawrence* held *Bowers* was "not correct when it was decided." Although *Bowers* was eventually repudiated in *Lawrence*, men and women were harmed in the interim, and the substantial effects of these injuries no doubt lingered long after *Bowers* was overruled. Dignitary wounds cannot always be healed with the stroke of a pen.

A ruling against same-sex couples would have the same effect and, like *Bowers*, would be unjustified under the Fourteenth Amendment. The petitioners' stories make clear the urgency of the issue they present to the Court. James Obergefell now asks whether Ohio can erase his marriage to John Arthur for all time. April DeBoer and Jayne Rowse now ask whether Michigan may continue to deny them the certainty and stability all mothers desire to protect their children, and for them and their children the childhood years will pass all too soon. Ijpe DeKoe and Thomas Kostura now ask whether Tennessee can deny to one who has served this Nation the basic dignity of recognizing his New York marriage. Properly presented with the petitioners' cases, the Court has a duty to address these claims and answer these questions.

Indeed, faced with a disagreement among the Courts of Appeals a disagreement that caused impermissible geographic variation in the meaning of federal law the Court granted review to determine whether same-sex couples may exercise the right to marry. Were the Court to uphold the challenged laws as constitutional, it would teach the Nation that these laws are in accord with our society's most basic compact. Were the Court to stay its hand to allow slower, case-by-case determination of the required availability of specific public benefits to same-sex couples, it still would deny gays and lesbians many rights and responsibilities intertwined with marriage.

The respondents also argue allowing same-sex couples to wed will harm marriage as an institution by leading to fewer opposite-sex marriages. This may occur, the respondents contend, because licensing same-sex marriage severs the connection between natural procreation and marriage. That argument, however, rests on a counterintuitive view of opposite-sex couple's decisionmaking processes regarding marriage and parenthood. Decisions about whether to marry and raise children are based on many personal, romantic, and practical considerations; and it is unrealistic to conclude that an opposite-sex couple would choose not to marry simply because same-sex couples may do so. The respondents have not shown a foundation for the conclusion that allowing same-sex marriage will cause the harmful outcomes they describe. Indeed, with respect to this asserted basis for excluding same-sex couples from the right to marry, it is appropriate to observe these cases involve only the rights of two consenting adults whose marriages would pose no risk of harm to themselves or third parties.

Finally, it must be emphasized that religions, and those who adhere to religious doctrines, may continue to advocate with utmost, sincere conviction that, by divine precepts, same-sex marriage should not be condoned. The First Amendment ensures that religious organizations and persons are given proper protection as they seek to teach the principles that are so fulfilling and so central to their lives and faiths, and to their own deep aspirations to continue the family structure they have long revered. The same is true of those who oppose same-sex marriage for other reasons. In turn, those who believe allowing same-sex marriage is proper or indeed essential, whether as a matter of religious conviction or secular belief, may engage those who disagree with their view in an open and searching debate. The Constitution, however, does not permit the State to bar same-sex couples from marriage on the same terms as accorded to couples of the opposite sex.

V

These cases also present the question whether the Constitution requires States to recognize same-sex marriages validly performed out of State. As made clear by the case of Obergefell and Arthur, and by that of DeKoe and Kostura, the recognition bans inflict substantial and continuing harm on same-sex couples.

Being married in one State but having that valid marriage denied in another is one of "the most perplexing and distressing complication[s]" in the law of domestic relations. *Williams v. North Carolina*. Leaving the current state of affairs in place would maintain and promote instability and uncertainty. For some couples, even an ordinary drive into a neighboring State to visit family or friends risks causing severe hardship in the event of a spouse's hospitalization while across state lines. In light of the fact that many States already allow same-sex marriage and hundreds of thousands of these marriages already have occurred the disruption caused by the recognition bans is significant and ever-growing.

As counsel for the respondents acknowledged at argument, if States are required by the Constitution to issue marriage licenses to same-sex couples, the justifications for refusing to recognize those marriages performed elsewhere are undermined. The Court, in this decision, holds same-sex couples may exercise the fundamental right to marry in all States. It follows that the Court also must hold and it now does hold that there is no lawful basis for a State to refuse to recognize a lawful same-sex marriage performed in another State on the ground of its same-sex character.

* * *

No union is more profound than marriage, for it embodies the highest ideals of love, fidelity, devotion, sacrifice, and family. In forming a marital union, two people become something greater than once they were. As some of the petitioners in these cases demonstrate, marriage embodies a love that may endure even past death. It would misunderstand these men and women to say they disrespect the idea of marriage. Their plea is that they do respect it, respect it so deeply that they seek to find its fulfillment for themselves. Their hope is not to be condemned to live in loneliness, excluded from one of civilization's oldest institutions. They ask for equal dignity in the eyes of the law. The Constitution grants them that right.

The judgment of the Court of Appeals for the Sixth Circuit is reversed.

It is so ordered.

The Impact of *Obergefell v. Hodges* on the Institution of Family in the United States

In 2019–2020, one of the contenders for the Democratic presidential nomination was Mayor of South Bend, Indiana Pete Buttigieg: a Christian man who had served in the US military, and who was in a same-sex marriage to his husband, Chasten Buttigieg (Bailey, 2020). His campaign was considered groundbreaking, as it was the first time an openly gay candidate had run for president. He was able to secure victory at the Iowa caucus, in a state that had only legalized same-sex marriage ten years prior. Indeed, even the standard bearer for the Democratic Party, President Barack Obama, indicated he did not support gay marriage during his first term in office, until he stated having "evolved" on the position in 2012, and would endorse it. While Buttigieg was repeatedly questioned "Is America ready for a gay president," indicating that the matter was far from uncontroversial, his viability as a candidate suggests that support for same-sex marriage, and therefore, for a changed idea of what a family looks like in the United States, has expanded away from the **hegemonic** conception of the **nuclear**, **heteronormative** family consisting of a husband, wife, and their biological children. The conception of family is no longer exclusive of non-heterosexual marriages, particularly in the wake of *Obergefell v. Hodges* granting marriage equality. As 4.3 percent of adults in the United States identify as LGBTQ, this meant that almost 11 million people were immediately affected (FEC, 2017). Here, we look at the impact of *Obergefell* on marriage, same-sex families, and on American attitudes toward same-sex unions.[1]

Same-Sex Marriages

As with *Loving v. Virginia* not being the beginning of committed interracial relationships and families, it's important to state that *Obergefell* and related legal rulings were not the genesis of same-sex couples forming families, it merely conferred equal legal footing to those families and another degree of social "legitimacy." LGBTQ people held informal wedding ceremonies long before 2015, and in the United States began legally challenging their inability to be married legally beginning in the 1970s. **Domestic partnerships** emerged out of the 1970s, offering same-sex couples who wanted to make long-term commitments to each other a way to obtain benefits that were comparable—although not equal—to those of marriage, and stressed the importance of long-term commitments, as insurance companies would be otherwise resistant to offering coverage (NeJaime, 2014). Among the benefits that mimicked marriage, domestic partnerships allowed for hospital and jail visitations and bereavement leave.

With *Obergefell*, predictably, "alternatives" to marriage like domestic partnerships and civil unions have been declining, which can be seen as admission that such "separate but equal" options are not actually equal, and do not provide the same level of gravity as marriage, or communal recognition (Haddad, 2016). Feldblum argues:

> It is precisely because society believes that the married state is normatively better than the unmarried state that so many practical, economic, and social benefits have been attached to marriage . . . the belief that heterosexual marriage and the nuclear family form the cornerstones of a strong society is pronounced.
>
> *(2005)*

Marriage is widely viewed as the most significant way to publicly commit to a long-term relationship and to provide a stable environment for any potential offspring. It is such a dominant institution, most adults in the United States will marry (in 2009, among those 40–49, only 16.4 percent had never married) (Kreider & Ellis, 2011). Because there is so much societal approval for marriage, and also 1138 legal benefits, it has been found to provide psychological and social perks like lower rates of depression, better health, and more life satisfaction to couples than their cohabiting or single peers (Kennedy & Dalla, 2020). These benefits were denied to most same-sex couples until 2015. Indeed, it took up until 2013 for there to be federal marriage recognition (so, a couple married in a state that permitted same-sex marriage did not have to be recognized by a state which did not). Employer-sponsored health insurance is one such example. Coverage was 6 percent lower for those in same-sex relationships than heterosexual ones prior to marriage equality. Millions of adults gained this between 2008–2017, potentially because of policy changes that allow for coverage of same-sex partners (Downing & Cha, 2020).

To have one's relationship and family institutionally "affirmed" by the state and given the same legal and economic advantages has allowed the US conception of the family to change significantly, and in a relatively short amount of time, even though stigma, as we will see in the section on attitudes, still exists. Among same-sex couples, research has shown that marriage is perceived as protective. It positively impacts relationships, providing individuals with feelings of legitimacy, social recognition, and security (Kennedy & Dalla, 2020). Families often share health insurance, share last names, are entitled to bereavement, social security, tax advantages for filing jointly, and own property jointly. These were not guaranteed prior to legal marriage. The psychological benefits found in heterosexual marriage like commitment and emotional intimacy are found similarly with their same sex (Kennedy & Dalla, 2020). And, like their heterosexual counterparts, LGBTQ people cited similar reasons for choosing to get married, the primary among them being love and companionship (Masci, Brown, & Kiley, 2017).

Due to the lifting of legal barriers—including the Supreme Court decision in 2015—and wider social acceptance, same-sex marriages have been on the rise in the United States. In 2017, 10.2 percent of LGBT-identified Americans are married to a same-sex partner, up from 7.9 percent in the months before the decision was rendered. In 2017, remarkably, among those LGBTQ people who were cohabitating, almost two-thirds (61 percent) were married, compared to 38 percent prior to *Obergefell v. Hodges*. In 2019, the Williams Institute at UCLA reported that there were 646,500 total same-sex couples in the United States, about 54 percent of which were women–women households and 46 percent were male–male.

With the advent of same-sex marriage, same-sex divorce is now possible in all 50 states. Legally dissolving a marriage through divorce is common in the United States. In 2010, "almost one half of ever-married persons had been divorced or separated by the time they reached their late 50s," researchers noted (Kennedy & Ruggles, 2014). Because of the recentness of the *Obergefell* decision, there is not yet the kind of data that we have on heterosexual marriages to know how same-sex couples are faring in the longevity of their marriages. Some preliminary studies in states with same-sex civil unions or marriages found that same-sex divorce or dissolution was lower than among heterosexuals, with 1.1 percent of same-sex couples versus 1.6 percent of opposite-sex couples getting divorced per year (Smith, Rose, & Cosic, 2016).

Same-Sex Marriage and Parenting

In Congressional debates, opponents of same-sex marriage homed in the argument that without a "mom and a dad" at home, children were in suboptimal family environments that would not pass on the "right" values (Feldblum, 2005). Although heterosexual people are twice as likely to cite having children as a reason for marriage (Masci et al., 2017), more than 20 percent of same-sex couples cite this as one of the most important motivations for marriage. The *Obergefell* decision gives deference to this rationale for marital equality, in its emphasis on the central place of marriage in relation to parental roles and child-rearing. Queer theorists have written about this, highlighting how *Obergefell*, rather than changing radically the definition of the family, actually does the opposite—it upholds the normative idea of the nuclear family and **repronormativity**. Repronormativity calls attention to the way in which our society privileges and has made commonplace the idea that the family is created *through* biological reproduction and involvement in childrearing (Ghosh, 2018). In common usage in the United States, when one says "I wish to start a family," this means one thing: Having children. Thus, the idea of "family" is still very much narrowly defined. The general expectation has not changed that married couples will wish for, and try to have, biological children.

Because of structural limitations to fertility, same-sex couples can have biological children through a few limited options: donor insemination (in the case of female–female couples), assisted reproduction like surrogacy (in the case of male–male relationships), or from earlier heterosexual relationships. However, surrogacy can be preclusive in its expensiveness, with costs over $100,000 for medical, legal, and surrogacy fees. And in some states, surrogacy agreements are not legal or enforceable.

Adoption and providing homes for foster children has remained a popular option for same-sex spouses and couples. Yet, because same-sex marriage legalization in *Obergefell v. Hodges* did not lead to uniform protection of prospective LGBT adoptive and foster parents through state laws, and ten states have laws on the books which allow child placement agencies to deny LGBT parents on the basis of religion. Still, same-sex couples make up a sizeable percentage of adoptive parents or to raise foster children (especially older foster children and those with special needs), as they are seven times more likely than their heterosexual counterparts to do both (Bewkes et al., 2018). Contrary to the negative stereotypes and hesitancy of some of the child placement agencies,

> When the literature on family functioning of gay and lesbian parents and their children is reviewed, the results strongly suggest that lesbian mothers and gay fathers are capable of fostering warm, positive, and encouraging relationships . . . several studies of lesbian mothers revealed that they are as child-focused, loving, confident, nurturing, and responsive as their heterosexual counterparts . . . with regard to gay fathers and couples . . . gay fathers exhibit health intimate bonds with their children, motivation for their children, provision of recreational opportunities, encouragement of autonomy, and experience parental satisfaction as often as heterosexual fathers.

Sexual orientation itself has no negative effect on family functioning (Leung, Erich, & Kanenberg, 2005). The vast majorities of studies have shown that in spite the lack of non-discrimination protections that same-sex couples may experience during the adoption process, the outcomes on their physical, emotional, and social health are the same (Bewkes et al., 2018).

Attitudes Towards Same Sex Marriages

Opinions about same-sex marriage have changed dramatically in the United States over the past 20 years, suggesting more widespread acceptance of an expanded conception of family, rather than seeing same-sex marriage as an attack on a singular definition of what the family means. While parallels can be made with *Loving v. Virginia*'s changing attitudes toward interracial marriage, as McCarthy (2019) points out, support for same-sex marriage proceeded at a much quicker pace, becoming federally recognized 11 years after Massachusetts was the first state to legalize it. The trends in acceptance across all demographic categories and political groups began well before *Obergefell v. Hodges*, and continued after the ruling. In 1996, Gallup asked the question: "Do you think marriages between same-sex couples should or should not be recognized by the law as valid, with the same rights as traditional marriages?" Then, 27 percent of Americans supported same-sex marriage, during a time when only a few years earlier in 1991, American T.V. broadcast its first gay marriage on the Fox sitcom *Roc*. By 2015, when *Obergefell v. Hodges* was decided, that number had risen to 59 percent, and in 2019, was at 63 percent (McCarthy, 2019). This change was driven by a host of factors, including higher support from younger generations (a majority of young people across political party lines supported same-sex marriage after 2009), a decline in traditional religion, increasing educational levels, more contact with LGBT people, and perhaps higher exposure to LGBT characters via sitcoms like the popular *Will & Grace* (1998–2020) and *Ellen* (1994–1998) (Lee & Mutz, 2019; McCarthy, 2019).

Currently, demographic and partisan divides exist in support. Support is strongest among women vis-à-vis men, younger cohorts vis-à-vis older cohorts, Democrats and Independents vis-à-vis Republicans, those in regions other than the South, those who never attend religious services vis-à-vis those with weekly attendance, and Whites and Hispanics vis-à-vis Blacks (Pew, 2019; McCarthy, 2019). The fact that support has increased across the board for all groups, but that differences remain, point to broad cultural and societal shifts but variation in subcultural understandings of what family is. In the US currently, religious groups have sought for and obtained exemptions when they maintain that complying with laws against non-discrimination interfere with their beliefs that same-sex marriage or non-heterosexual relationships are wrong. At the same time, many religious organizations, such as the Episcopal Church, Quakers, Presbyterian Church, United Church of Christ, Reform Jewish Movement, Unitarian Universalists, and Evangelical Lutheran Church of the US support same-sex marriage and allow its clergy to perform services.

The LGBTQ Movement, Marriage, and New Models of the Family in the United States

While marriage equality between same-sex and heterosexual couples has been a central focus of LGBT rights' movements, there was not and is not a unified acceptance of marriage as an object worthy of pursuing. Debates existed about whether the goal of marriage excluded other types of more diverse, pluralistic family formations that bucked standard conceptions, and some activists insisted that marriage be eschewed (NeJaime, 2014). Marriage was furthermore linked to **patriarchy**—a social system in which power is predominantly held by men, with women holding subordinate roles within the marriage and to **heteronormativity**, meaning that heterosexuality is considered the primary model against which other sexualities are judged. Activist groups like the Gay Liberation Front and Radical Lesbians, in the 1970s, argued that women in marital relationships were oppressed, and the nuclear family worked against same-sex relationships.

As one queer theorist contends,

> The Court's opinion in *Obergefell* aggressively endorses a specific conception of the good intimate life—one that is firmly ensconced in the dominant culture's understanding of intimacy and family formation. Consequently, it ends up demeaning queer-identified and other non-assimilationist lesbian, gay, bisexual, and heterosexual individuals.
>
> *(Ghosh, 2018)*

Still, while the normative idea of what constitutes a "proper" family may still be a monogamous couple with children, it would have been hard to imagine even 20 years ago that same-sex marriage would be included in that normative vision. How will marriage and the family change and evolve in the future remains to be seen. "Marriage equality need not and should not be the end of innovation and experimentation around the issue of relationship recognition" (Murray quoted in Haddad, 2016, p. 33).

Review Questions

1. What is the backstory of the couple named in the *Loving v. Virginia* case?
2. What were the Constitutional reasons for the decision in the *Loving* case?
3. How has marriage and family in the United States been impacted by the *Loving* and *Obergefell* cases?
4. Discuss how attitudes within our society changed towards marriage through the decades.
5. How did the Due Process clause and Equal Protection clause impact the *Obergefell* decision?

Note

1. We specify same-sex marriages rather than marriages of LGBTQ people because for any number of reasons, LGBTQ people may be in heterosexual marriages: bisexual people may choose heterosexual partners, lesbian or gay people may be in "closeted" relationships, and the word transgender does not designate same-sex or opposite sex attraction or relationships.

References

Bailey, S. P. (2020, March 3). Buttigieg's candidacy made being openly gay and Christian normal, LGBT activists say. *The Washington Post*.

Bedley, C. (2018). *Multiracial families in television commercials: Diversifying notions of the family*. ProQuest Dissertations Publishing, Web. Retrieved from https://rucore.libraries.rutgers.edu/rutgers-lib/55976/

Bewkes, F., Mirza, S. A., Rooney, C., Durso, L. E., Kroll, J., & Wong, E. (2018). *Welcoming all families: Discrimination against LGBTQ foster and adoptive parents*. Center for American Progress. Retrieved from https://www.americanprogress.org/issues/lgbtq-rights/reports/2018/11/20/461199/welcoming-all-families/

Brown, C. C., Williams, Z., & Durtschi, J. A. (2019). Trajectories of interracial heterosexual couples: A longitudinal analysis of relationship quality and separation. *Journal of Marriage and Family Therapy*, *45*(4), 650–667.

Chito Childs, E. (2008). Listening to the interracial canary: Contemporary views on interracial relationships among Blacks and Whites. *Fordham Law Review*, *76*(6), 139–161.

de Guzman, N. S., & Nishina, A. (2017). 50 years of loving: Interracial romantic relationships and recommendations for future research. *Journal of Family Theory and Review*, *9*, 557–571.

Downing, J., & Cha, P. (2020). Same-sex marriage and gains in employer-sponsored insurance for US adults, 008–2017. *American Journal of Public Health*, *110*(4).

Edmonds, P. (2018). The many colors of matrimony. *National Geographic*, *233*(4), 71–72, 77.

Family Equality Council (FEC). (2017). *LGBTQ family factsheet*. Retrieved from https://www2.census.gov/cac/nac/meetings/2017-11/LGBTQ-families-factsheet.pdf

Feldblum, C. R. (2005). Gay is good: The moral case for marriage equality and more. *The Yale Journal of Law and Feminism*, *17*, 139–184.

Garcia, G. E., Lewis, R., & Ford-Robertson, J. (2015). Attitudes regarding laws limiting Black-White marriage: A longitudinal analysis of perceptions and related behaviors. *Journal of Black Studies*, *46*(2), 199–217.

Ghosh, C. (2018). Marriage equality and the injunction to assimilate: Romantic love, children, monogamy, and parenting in Obergefell v. Hodges. *Polity*, *50*(2), 275–299.

Haddad, J. J. (2016). The evolution of marriage: The role of dignity jurisprudence and marriage equality. *Boston University Law Review, 96*, 1489.

Kelly, H. (2016, November 2). We were married on the second day of June, and the police came after us the 14th of July. *Washingtonian*. Retrieved from www.washingtonian.com/2016/11/02/virginia-case-legalized-interracial-marriage-the-loving-story/

Kendall, D. (2011). *Sociology in our times*. Belmont, CA: Wadsworth.

Kennedy, H. R., & Dalla, R. L. (2020). "It may be legal, but it is not treated equally": Marriage equality and well-being implications for same-sex couples. *Journal of Gay & Lesbian Social Services, 32*(1), 67–98.

Kennedy, S., & Ruggles, S. (2014). Breaking up is hard to count: The rise of divorce in the United States, 1980–2010. *Demography, 51*(2), 587–598.

Kreider, R. M., & Ellis, R. (2011). *Number, timing, and duration of marriages and divorces: 2009*. US Census Bureau. Retrieved from www.U.S.census.gov

Lee, H., & Mutz, D. C. (2019). Changing attitudes toward same-sex marriage: A three-wave panel study. *Political Behavior, 41*, 701–722.

Leung, P., Erich, S., & Kanenberg, H. (2005). A comparison of family functioning in gay/lesbian, heterosexual and special needs adoptions. *Children & Youth Services Review, 27*(9), 1031–1044.

Livingston, G. (2017). *The rise of multiethnic and multiracial babies in the US*. Pew Research Center. Retrieved from www.pewresearch.org/fact-tank/2017/06/06/the-rise-of-multiracial-and-multiethnic-babies-in-the-u-s/

Livingston, G., & Brown, A. (2017). *Intermarriage in the US 50 years after Loving v. Virginia*. Pew Research Center. Retrieved from www.pewsocialtrends.org/2017/05/18/1-trends-and-patterns-in-intermarriage/

Lutz, M. (2017). The hidden cost of Brown v. Board: African American educators' resistance to desegregating schools. *Online Journal of Rural Research & Policy, 12*(4).

Masci, D., Brown, A., & Kiley, J. (2017). *5 facts about same-sex marriage*. Washington, DC: Pew Research Center.

McCarthy, J. (2019). US support for gay marriage stable, at 63%. *Gallup*. Retrieved from https://news.gallup.com/poll/257705/support-gay-marriage-stable.aspx

National Park Services. (2016a, March 22). *Civil rights act of 1964*. Retrieved from www.nps.gov/articles/civil-rights-act.htm

National Park Services. (2016b, September 7). *Voting rights act of 1965*. Retrieved from www.nps.gov/articles/votingrightsact.htm

NeJaime, D. (2014). Before marriage: The unexplored history of nonmarital recognition and its relationship to marriage. *California Law Review, 87*, 87–172.

Onwuachi-Willing, A., & Willig-Onwuachi, J. (2012). Finding a "loving" home. In K. N. Maillard & R. Cuison Villazor (Eds.), *Loving v. Virginia in a post-racial world: Rethinking race, sex, and marriage* (pp. 181–198). Cambridge: Cambridge University Press.

Parker, K., Menasce Horowitz, J., Morin, R., & Hugo Lopez, M. (2015). *Multiracial in America*. Pew Research Center. Retrieved from www.pewsocialtrends.org/2015/06/11/multiracial-in-america/

Pascoe, P. (1996). Miscegenation law, court cases and ideologies of "race" in twentieth-century America. *The Journal of American History, 83*(1), 44–69.

Perry, S. L., & Whitehead, A. L. (2015). Christian nationalism and White racial boundaries: Examining Whites' opposition to interracial marriage. *Ethnic and Racial Studies, 38*(10), 1671–1689.

Pew. (2014). *Record share of Americans have never married*. Retrieved from https://www.pewresearch.org/social-trends/2014/09/24/record-share-of-americans-have-never-married/

Pew. (2019). *Attitudes on same-sex marriage*. Pew Research Center. Retrieved from www.pewforum.org/fact-sheet/changing-attitudes-on-gay-marriage/

Pratt, C. (2012). Loving in Indian territory: Tribal miscegenation law in historical perspective. In K. N. Maillard & R. Cuison Villazor (Eds.), *Loving v. Virginia in a post-racial world: Rethinking race, sex, and marriage* (pp. 46–58). Cambridge: Cambridge University Press.

Rosenwald, Michael S. (2015). "How Jim Obergefell became the face of the Supreme Court gay marriage case," *The Washington Post* April 6, 2015, https://www.washingtonpost.com/local/how-jim-obergefell-became-the-face-of-thesupreme-court-gay-marriage-case/2015/04/06/3740433c-d958-11e4-b3f2- 607bd612aeac_story.html

Smith, K. E., Rose, S., & Cosic, D. (2016). *How might legal recognition of same-sex marriage affect retirement incomes and federal programs?* Urban Institute. Retrieved from https://www.urban.org/research/publication/how-might-legal-recognition-same-sex-marriage-affect-retirement-incomes-and-federal-programs

Syrett, N. L. (2018). Miscegenation law and the politics of mixed-race illegitimate children in the turn-of the century United States. *Journal of the History of Childhood and Youth*, 52–57.

Toosi, N. R., Babbitt, L. G., Ambady, N., & Sommers, S. R. (2012). Dyadic interracial interactions: a meta-analysis. *Psychological Bulletin, 138*(1), 1.

Volpp, L. (2005). Divesting citizenship: On Asian American history and the loss of citizenship through marriage. *UCLA Law Review, 53*, 405.

5

RELIGION

Learning Objectives

After reading this chapter, students should be able to:

- Evaluate the US Supreme Court case *Engel v. Vitale*
- Discuss the impact of the *Engel* decision on the institution of religion
- Explain societal attitudes towards religion in schools
- Report on the role of religion in the United States
- Provide an overview of the *Roe v. Wade* case
- Understand how the institution of religion was changed by the *Roe* ruling
- Summarize how individual attitudes were influenced by *Roe*
- Assess the impact of *Roe* on healthcare in America

Key Terms

Civil Religion
Engel v. Vitale
Refusal Clauses
Roe v. Wade
Sectarian

Engel v. Vitale Introduction

"Almighty God, we acknowledge our dependence upon Thee, and we beg Thy blessings upon us, our parents, our teachers and our Country." On July 8, 1958, Union Free School District No. 9 in New Hyde Park on Long Island adopted this 22-word prayer to be recited in their public schools daily, along with the Pledge of Allegiance. Mary Harte, a school board member and state regent, had fought hard to institute the prayer, which had been adopted by the New York State Board of Regents on November 30, 1951.

When school started in the fall of 1958, all schools belonging to the Union Free School District No. 9—which included five elementary schools with a total of over 5,000 students—adopted

DOI: 10.4324/9781003021438-6

the morning prayer that would be taught by a teacher. Words weren't the only thing taught though. Students were asked to bow their heads and clasp their hands in prayer. Although the prayer was said to be voluntary—meaning students had the chance to step outside of the classroom or simply wait in the classroom while other students who wanted to recite it did so—it did not take long for those students who were not comfortable with reciting the prayer to be singled out by their peers. It soon became easier for students of different faiths and beliefs to give into peer pressure and recite the prayer along with the majority of the other students, as a way for them to put a stop to being labeled different.

Michael Engel, who came from a Jewish family, was one of those students. One day, while at home, his father, Steven Engel witnessed his son bow his head and clasp his hands in prayer. Stunned, Steven Engel asked his son for an explanation and soon learned of the daily morning prayer ritual his son had been following in school. Steven Engel had to then explain to his son that Jewish people follow a different praying ritual, which does not include bowing heads or clasping hands.

It wasn't until he read an ad in the local newspaper that Mr. Engel realized he wasn't alone in his reaction to the daily prayer in public schools. The ad read: "Notice: To all Herrick's [sic] school district taxpayers: A taxpayers' suit will soon be started to challenge the legality of prayers in public schools. Counsel has been appointed." The person responsible for this ad was Lawrence Roth, another parent whose children had been subjected to the voluntary daily prayer. Although Roth did not practice religion, he still identified himself and his family as Jewish. Roth stated that, aside from the prayer, a third-grade teacher at his children's school had attempted to force the Christian faith onto them by keeping a statue of Jesus Christ in the classroom and telling students that if they were bad, Christ would punish them. As a result, Roth decided to take matters into his own hands after feeling that, "If the state could tell us what to pray and when to pray and how to pray, there was no stopping." So, he contacted the American Civil Liberties Union (ACLU), which had been founded in 1920, and brought up the issue that, in his opinion, violated the First Amendment of the US Constitution.

Many concerned parents contacted Roth after reading the ad in the newspaper, but many soon decided against it due to pressure from the school district or their religious connections, or because their children would soon be graduating from the schools and therefore this would no longer be an issue to them. As a result, only five parents remained in the group and agreed to serve as plaintiffs, with Steven Engel being the lead plaintiff in alphabetical order. The parents—who made up a diverse religious group that included atheists and Jewish people—asked the school board to stop the daily morning prayer, but the school board refused, claiming that the teacher-led prayer was voluntary and non-denominational, which meant that neither the teachers nor the school district were forcing a religion upon its students. As a result, the parents filed a petition in January 1959, asking the New York Supreme Court to discontinue the Regents' Prayer. The petition showed Willian J. Vitale, Jr., president of the school board, as the first name for the defense, hence the case is known as *Engel v. Vitale*.

The lawsuit against the school board argued that the morning prayer went against the Establishment Clause of the First Amendment. The Establishment Clause

> prohibits the government from making any law "respecting an establishment of religion." This clause not only forbids the government from establishing an official religion, but also prohibits government actions that unduly favor one religion over another. It also prohibits the government from unduly preferring religion over non-religion, or non-religion over religion.

The defendants argued that since the prayer had been deemed voluntary, it did not violate the Establishment Clause. The New York Supreme Court sided with the school board, declaring that "The state is not imposing a religious belief by using this prayer." The parents, unsatisfied with the result, took the lawsuit to the New York Court of Appeals, which again sided with the defendants and agreed with the New York Supreme Court that, since students were not forced to recite the prayer given its voluntary nature, it did not go against the First Amendment. Still, the parents did not give up and chose to take matters all the way to the United States Supreme Court, who agreed to hear the case on April 3, 1962.

The main question that the plaintiffs asked the Supreme Court was whether or not the teacher-led and school-sponsored voluntary and non-denominational prayer in public schools violated the Establishment Clause of the First Amendment of the US Constitution. The decision of the Supreme Court came on June 25, 1962. The six-to-one ruling—Justice White and Justice Frankfurter decided not to participate—was in favor of the parents. Justice Stewart, the only one who was in favor of the school board, stated that his fellow Justices "misapplied a great constitutional principle" and that he could not understand

> how an "official religion" is established by letting those who want to say a prayer say it. On the contrary, I think to deny the wish of these school children to join in reciting this prayer is to deny them the opportunity of sharing in the spiritual heritage of our Nation.

Justice Hugo Black wrote the Supreme Court's Opinion, which explained that the State of New York had indeed gone against the Establishment Clause by encouraging the Regents' Prayer through the public school system. Justice Black also explained that,

> The First Amendment was added to the Constitution to stand as a guarantee that neither the power nor the prestige of the Federal Government would be used to control, support or influence the kinds of prayer the American people can say. . . . Under that Amendment's prohibition against governmental establishment of religion, as reinforced by the provisions of the Fourteenth Amendment, government in this country, be it state or federal, is without power to prescribe by law any particular form of prayer which is to be used as an official prayer in carrying on any program of governmentally sponsored religious activity.

Although the Supreme Court ruled in favor of the parents, many parents across the United States did not agree with the decision. However, the ruling did not state that students across the country were forbidden from praying while in school. On the contrary, students still held the right and freedom to pray on public school grounds during their free time, as long as the prayer was not led by the public school system, as it had been in the case of the Regents' Prayer.

Engel v. Vitale Decision

ENGEL V. VITALE, 370 U.S. 421 (1962)

MR. JUSTICE BLACK delivered the opinion of the Court.

The respondent Board of Education of Union Free School District No. 9, New Hyde Park, New York, acting in its official capacity under state law, directed the School District's principal to cause the following prayer to be said aloud by each class in the presence of a teacher at the beginning of each school day:

> Almighty God, we acknowledge our dependence upon Thee, and we beg Thy blessings upon us, our parents, our teachers and our Country.

This daily procedure was adopted on the recommendation of the State Board of Regents, a governmental agency created by the State Constitution to which the New York Legislature has granted broad supervisory, executive, and legislative powers over the State's public school system. These state officials composed the prayer which they recommended and published as a part of their "Statement on Moral and Spiritual Training in the Schools," saying:

> We believe that this Statement will be subscribed to by all men and women of goodwill, and we call upon all of them to aid in giving life to our program.

Shortly after the practice of reciting the Regents' prayer was adopted by the School District, the parents of ten pupils brought this action in a New York State Court insisting that use of this official prayer in the public schools was contrary to the beliefs, religions, or religious practices of both themselves and their children. Among other things, these parents challenged the constitutionality of both the state law authorizing the School District to direct the use of prayer in public schools and the School District's regulation ordering the recitation of this particular prayer on the ground that these actions of official governmental agencies violate that part of the First Amendment of the Federal Constitution which commands that "Congress shall make no law respecting an establishment of religion"—a command which was "made applicable to the State of New York by the Fourteenth Amendment of the said Constitution." The New York Court of Appeals, over the dissents of Judges Dye and Fuld, sustained an order of the lower state courts which had upheld the power of New York to use the Regents' prayer as a part of the daily procedures of its public schools so long as the schools did not compel any pupil to join in the prayer over his or his parents' objection.

We granted certiorari to review this important decision involving rights protected by the First and Fourteenth Amendments.

We think that, by using its public school system to encourage recitation of the Regents' prayer, the State of New York has adopted a practice wholly inconsistent with the Establishment Clause. There can, of course, be no doubt that New York's program of daily classroom invocation of God's blessings as prescribed in the Regents' prayer is a religious activity. It is a solemn avowal of divine faith and supplication for the blessings of the Almighty. The nature of such a prayer has always been religious, none of the respondents has denied this, and the trial court expressly so found:

> The religious nature of prayer was recognized by Jefferson, and has been concurred in by theological writers, the United States Supreme Court, and State courts and administrative officials, including New York's Commissioner of Education. A committee of the New York Legislature has agreed.
>
> The Board of Regents as *amicus curiae*, the respondents, and intervenors all concede the religious nature of prayer, but seek to distinguish this prayer because it is based on our spiritual heritage.

The petitioners contend, among other things, that the state laws requiring or permitting use of the Regents' prayer must be struck down as a violation of the Establishment Clause because that prayer was composed by governmental officials as a part of a governmental program to further religious beliefs. For this reason, petitioners argue, the State's use of the Regents' prayer in its public school system breaches the constitutional wall of separation between Church and State. We agree with that contention, since we think that the constitutional prohibition against laws respecting an establishment of religion must at least mean that, in this country, it is no part of the business of government to compose official prayers for any group of the American people to recite as a part of a religious program carried on by government.

It is a matter of history that this very practice of establishing governmentally composed prayers for religious services was one of the reasons which caused many of our early colonists to leave England and seek religious freedom in America. The Book of Common Prayer, which was created under governmental direction and which was approved by Acts of Parliament in 1548 and 1549, set out in minute detail the accepted form and content of prayer and other religious ceremonies to be used in the established, tax supported Church of England. The controversies over the Book and what should be its content repeatedly threatened to disrupt the peace of that country as the accepted forms of prayer in the established church changed with the views of the particular ruler that happened to be in control at the time. Powerful groups representing some of the varying religious views of the people struggled among themselves to impress their particular views upon the Government and obtain amendments of the Book more suitable to their respective notions of how religious services should be conducted in order that the official religious establishment would advance their particular religious beliefs. Other groups, lacking the necessary political power to influence the Government on the matter, decided to leave England and its established church and seek freedom in America from England's governmentally ordained and supported religion.

It is an unfortunate fact of history that, when some of the very groups which had most strenuously opposed the established Church of England found themselves sufficiently in control of colonial governments in this country to write their own prayers into law, they passed laws making their own religion the official religion of their respective colonies. Indeed, as late as the time of the Revolutionary War, there were established churches in at least eight of the thirteen former colonies and established religions in at least four of the other five. But the successful Revolution against English political domination was shortly followed by intense opposition to the practice of establishing religion by law. This opposition crystallized rapidly into an effective political force in Virginia, where the minority religious groups such as Presbyterians, Lutherans, Quakers and Baptists had gained such strength that the adherents to the established Episcopal Church were actually a minority themselves. In 1785–1786, those opposed to the established Church, led by James Madison and Thomas Jefferson, who, though themselves not members of any of these dissenting religious groups, opposed all religious establishments by law on grounds of principle, obtained the enactment of the famous "Virginia Bill for Religious Liberty" by which all religious groups were placed on an equal footing so far as the State was concerned. Similar though less far-reaching legislation was being considered and passed in other states.

By the time of the adoption of the Constitution, our history shows that there was a widespread awareness among many Americans of the dangers of a union of Church and State. These people knew, some of them from bitter personal experience, that one of the greatest dangers to the freedom of the individual to worship in his own way lay in the Government's placing its official stamp of approval upon one particular kind of prayer or one particular form of religious services. They knew the anguish, hardship and bitter strife that could come when zealous religious groups struggled with one another to obtain the Government's stamp of approval from each King, Queen, or Protector that came to temporary power. The Constitution was intended to avert a part of this danger by leaving the government of this country in the hands of the people, rather than in the hands of any monarch. But this safeguard was not enough. Our Founders were no more willing to let the content of their prayers and their privilege of praying whenever they pleased be influenced by the ballot box than they were to let these vital matters of personal conscience depend upon the succession of monarchs. The First Amendment was added to the Constitution to stand as a guarantee that neither the power nor the prestige of the Federal Government would be used to control, support or influence the kinds of prayer the American people can say—that the people's religions must not be subjected to the pressures of government for change each time a new political administration is elected to office. Under that Amendment's prohibition against governmental establishment of religion, as reinforced by the provisions of the Fourteenth Amendment, government in this country, be it state or federal, is without power to prescribe by law any particular form of prayer which is to be used as an official prayer in carrying on any program of governmentally sponsored religious activity.

There can be no doubt that New York's state prayer program officially establishes the religious beliefs embodied in the Regents' prayer. The respondents' argument to the contrary, which is largely based upon the contention that the Regents' prayer is "non-denominational" and the fact that the program, as modified and approved by state courts, does not require all pupils to recite the prayer, but permits those who wish to do so to remain silent or be excused from the room, ignores the essential nature of the program's constitutional defects. Neither the fact that the prayer may be denominationally neutral nor the fact that its observance on the part of the students is voluntary can serve to free it from the limitations of the Establishment Clause, as it might from the Free Exercise Clause, of the First Amendment, both of which are operative against the States by virtue of the Fourteenth Amendment. Although these two clauses may, in certain instances, overlap, they forbid two quite different kinds of governmental encroachment upon religious freedom. The Establishment Clause, unlike the Free Exercise Clause, does not depend upon any showing of direct governmental compulsion and is violated by the enactment of laws which establish an official religion whether those laws operate directly to coerce non-observing individuals or not. This is not to say, of course, that laws officially prescribing a particular form of religious worship do not involve coercion of such individuals. When the power, prestige and financial support of government is placed behind a particular religious belief, the indirect coercive pressure upon religious minorities to conform to the prevailing officially approved religion is plain. But the purposes underlying the Establishment Clause go much further than that. Its first and most immediate purpose rested on the belief that a union of government and religion tends to destroy government and to degrade religion. The history of governmentally established religion, both in England and in this country, showed that whenever government had allied itself with one particular form of religion, the inevitable result had been that it had incurred the hatred, disrespect and even contempt of those who held contrary beliefs. That same history showed that many people had lost their respect for any religion that had relied upon the support of government to spread its faith. The Establishment Clause thus stands as an expression of principle on the part of the Founders of our Constitution that religion is too personal, too sacred, too holy, to permit its "unhallowed perversion" by a civil magistrate. Another purpose of the Establishment Clause rested upon an awareness of the historical fact that governmentally established religions and religious persecutions go hand in hand. The Founders knew that, only a few years after the Book of Common Prayer became the only accepted form of religious services in the established Church of England, an Act of Uniformity was passed to compel all Englishmen to attend those services and to make it a criminal offense to conduct or attend religious gatherings of any other kind—a law which was consistently flouted by dissenting religious groups in England and which contributed to widespread persecutions of people like John Bunyan who persisted in holding "unlawful [religious] meetings . . . to the great disturbance and distraction of the good subjects of this kingdom." And they knew that similar persecutions had received the sanction of law in several of the colonies in this country soon after the establishment of official religions in those colonies. It was in large part to get completely away from this sort of systematic religious persecution that the Founders brought into being our Nation, our Constitution, and our Bill of Rights, with its prohibition against any governmental establishment of religion. The New York laws officially prescribing the Regents' prayer are inconsistent both with the purposes of the Establishment Clause and with the Establishment Clause itself.

It has been argued that to apply the Constitution in such a way as to prohibit state laws respecting an establishment of religious services in public schools is to indicate a hostility toward religion or toward prayer. Nothing, of course, could be more wrong. The history of man is inseparable from the history of religion. And perhaps it is not too much to say that, since the beginning of that history, many people have devoutly believed that "More things are wrought by prayer than this world dreams of." It was doubtless largely due to men who believed this that there grew up a sentiment that caused men to leave the cross-currents of officially established state religions and religious persecution in Europe and come to this country filled with the hope that they could find a place in which they could pray when they pleased to the God of their faith in the language they chose. And there were men of this same faith in the power of prayer who led the fight for adoption of our Constitution and also for our Bill of Rights with the very guarantees of religious freedom that forbid the sort of governmental activity which New York has attempted here. These men knew that the First Amendment, which tried to put an end to governmental control of religion and of prayer, was not written to destroy either. They knew, rather, that it was written to quiet well justified fears which nearly all of them felt arising out of an awareness that governments of the past had shackled men's tongues to make them speak only the religious thoughts that government wanted them to speak and to pray only to the God that government wanted them to pray to. It is neither sacrilegious nor anti-religious to say that each separate government in this country should stay out of the business of writing or sanctioning official prayers and leave that purely religious function to the people themselves and to those the people choose to look to for religious guidance.

It is true that New York's establishment of its Regents' prayer as an officially approved religious doctrine of that State does not amount to a total establishment of one particular religious sect to the exclusion of all others—that, indeed, the governmental endorsement of that prayer seems relatively insignificant when compared to the governmental encroachments upon religion which were commonplace 200 years ago. To those who may subscribe to the view that, because the Regents' official prayer is so brief and general there can be no danger to religious freedom in its governmental establishment, however, it may be appropriate to say in the words of James Madison, the author of the First Amendment:

> [I]t is proper to take alarm at the first experiment on our liberties. . . . Who does not see that the same authority which can establish Christianity, in exclusion of all other Religions, may establish with the same ease any particular sect of Christians, in exclusion of all other Sects? That the same authority which can force a citizen to contribute three pence only of his property for the support of any one establishment may force him to conform to any other establishment in all cases whatsoever?

The judgment of the Court of Appeals of New York is reversed, and the cause remanded for further proceedings not inconsistent with this opinion.

The Impact of *Engel v. Vitale* on the Institution of Religion in the US

Following *Engel v. Vitale*, how was religion affected in the United States? As we think about this question, let's recall the definition of religion provided in Chapter 2 from foundational sociologist Emile Durkheim: "A unified system of beliefs and practices relative to sacred things, that is to say set apart and forbidden, beliefs and practices which unite into one single moral community, called a church, all those who adhere to them." Can the United States be said to have a singular "religion," that was affected through this landmark case? How were different institutionalized religions and those without belief in religion affected?

*Civil Religion and the United States Post-*Engel

Robert Bellah, an American sociologist of religion, argued that outside of formal organized religions in the United States, Americans have a **civil religion** in the sense described by Durkheim. For Bellah, **civil religion** is a "Collection of beliefs, symbols and rituals with respect to sacred things and institutionalized in a collectivity," since the beginning of the Republic, which, although sharing a lot in common with Christianity, is not specifically Christian and certainly not **sectarian.** For example, he mentions that although the Founding Fathers and first three presidents all used the word "God," in their inaugural addresses, none of them specifically mentioned Jesus Christ. Abraham Lincoln never joined a church, but Bellah considers him a representative of the civil religion of the United States (Bellah, 1967, 1992), embodying its ideals. In other words, Americans have general beliefs in shared values (such as in liberty, charity, freedom, justice). They have ritualized practices and traditions (singing the national anthem, reciting the pledge of allegiance) and days that affirm our commitment to civil religion, its primary figures and historical events (Memorial Day, Martin Luther King Jr. Day, Presidents' Day, the Fourth of July, Thanksgiving), symbols (the flag, the bald eagle), shared stories about the nation's origins and founders and historical 'heroes', objects, seminal events, and various practices that confer onto citizens a sense of shared identity and belonging. We ascribe a kind of religious importance to our nation and its history that transcends our personal meanings as individuals. As we watch Olympians tear up, for instance, while the flag is raised and the anthem played, we can understand the power of these constructions.

The presence of civil religion can rally feelings of patriotism in times of contentious international politics or war. In the period of the *Engel* decision, the United States was embroiled in the Cold War with the Soviet Union (U.S.S.R). Those wishing to keep prayers in public schools saw this as a way of creating a further level of distinction between the "enemy" U.S.S.R. and the United States. By constructing the United States as Christian/religious, this served during the time of the case to bolster a Cold War narrative against the Soviet Union, and to enhance collective feelings of shared values and solidarity. The Soviets, who had abolished the practice of religion, as a wholly atheist state, were the enemy. So, to keep showing that the United States was defined by a civil religion that included a God helped with the "us" versus "them" narrative (Kazin, 2009).

In thinking about *Engel v. Vitale*, does removing public school teachers' and other administrators' ability to lead a formal prayer before the start of the class mean that *civil* religion was diminished? Since one of the founding principles of the United States was "separation of church and state," and "Freedom of religion," the removal of 'coercive' religious practices like the Regents' prayer from taxpayer-funded schools might actually be supportive of US civil religious ideals. Certainly other practices and traditions related to civil religion remain as well (shared national celebrations, acknowledgment of the importance of historical figures and events, belief in American 'ideals').

On the other hand, arguments can be made that the prayer that was recited in the Herricks school district, the Regents prayer, which read "Almighty God, we acknowledge our dependence upon Thee, and we beg Thy blessings upon us, our parents, our teachers and our Country," was a prayer that demonstrated our civil religion. It was non-sectarian, and also affirming the importance of community, family, and the nation-state, and so therefore was a civil religious practice. Bellah declared "today, American civil religion is an empty and broken shell" (1992, p. 142), with a sense of the common good being eroded in favor of self-centeredness, rather than national ethical purpose. If we entertain his conclusion, though, the question becomes: can we attribute this to a lack of public school prayer? What other factors are implicated? And if we conclude that shared expressions of ethical values are important to the fabric of the nation, what might be done in lieu of school prayer to enhance these shared values?

*Institutionalized Religion Post-*Engel

Even if **civil religion** in the US was not greatly affected by removal of public school prayer, how did institutionalized religion fare and attitudes toward formal religion in general? Indeed, in the arguments to the Supreme Court, frequent references were made to the "traditions" that were a part of the country's fabric, which were, according to their narrative, enmeshed with Christianity so much so that to try to remove that would be to change the character of the United States itself, in essence, its civil religion. Did this happen? Certainly, there was a shift away from religion's embeddedness in public education and over the decades, more secularism, though not solely attributable of course to this single case involving public school prayer. The pervasiveness of the Christian religion in American life was noted by de Tocqueville in the 19th century, as we described in Chapter 2. The United States, the first secular government, was established by the Founders without a formal state-sanctioned religion to avoid the persistent problems of religious fighting that they had witnessed on the European continent. However, it had a cultural rooting nevertheless in Protestant Christianity, with the English settlers who arrived seeking religious liberty. Most British colonies in what would become the United States had a government-sponsored church (Dierenfield, 2007). Even so, it was not atheists who insisted, shortly after the founding of the Republic, that freedom in religious issues be addressed in state and federal constitutions: it was Christian evangelical dissenters from two dominant churches of the time, the Congregational Church and Episcopal Church (Laycock, 2006). The question of religion's role in school would not become a matter of public concern for several decades after the founding of the Republic, though, as most schooling, if there were any, was performed in the home. Once public schools were developed beginning in the 1830s, though, Protestantism was an underpinning of instruction. Horace Mann, who we previously described as the leader of the Common School movement, wanted a "pan-Protestant foundation in public education" and held a favorable attitude toward religious instruction in schools. Many schools, indeed, were founded for the purpose of instilling religion in children (Dierenfield, 2007).

Protestant Christian theological ideas and the Bible were therefore widely taught in the 19th and first half of the 20th century. For instance, The National Teacher's Association supported the Bible's veneration and inculcation in public schools in 1869, and during this period, 75 percent of New York State's enrolled students were in schools that had religious exercises. In some states there were harsh consequences for *not* teaching from the Bible. For example, in Arkansas, teachers could be fined and dismissed for not reading Biblical passages daily, and in Delaware teachers could have their teaching credentials revoked for not doing so. Although sometimes the inclusion of 'non-sectarian' Biblical material was done with the intention of not getting into sectarian or theological arguments among various Christian groups, heated conflicts erupted across the country. Interestingly, the push to keep religion in schools at the time was fueled less by a fear about secularism or atheism or non-Christian religions, than by anti-Catholic discrimination, which was associated with 'undesirable' immigrants from Ireland, Germany, and elsewhere. Catholicism held a tiny position in the United States during colonial times (Laycock, 2006) and a historical aversion to Catholics can be seen in the history of the United States, notably, out of 46 presidents, only two has been Catholic—president John Fitzgerland Kennedy and Joseph Biden. Catholic children were beaten for not reciting Protestant versions of the ten commandments, textbooks denounced Irish Catholic immigrants and even suggested the Pope was the Anti-Christ (Dierenfield, 2007). Catholics were understandably then generally dissatisfied with what they saw as public school teaching of "Protestant" ways of practicing Christianity and anti-Catholicism, and as time wore on and Jewish migration to the US increased, Jewish parents and students were similarly unhappy. Unless they wanted to break off and start schools of their own—which many did, leading to the parochial Catholic school systems, which would cost parents tuition dollars, as the state would not pay for private religion school, they pushed for secularized schools (Laycock, 2006).

There were challenges to the inclusion of religion generally and prayer specifically in public schools into the 20th century. Yet, in 1960, just prior to the *Engel v. Vitale* case, 87.9 percent of public schools had a Christmas celebration, 57.8 percent had an Easter celebration, 41.8 percent had Bible readings, 42.7 percent had a Gideon Bible distribution, and 27.4 percent had a lunch-time prayer. And 5.4 percent had a Hanukkah celebration (Dierenfield, 1962).

Clearly, *Engels v. Vitale* and the four subsequent decisions on school prayer would modify institutionalized religion's role in public school during the regular school day (although children can congregate afterwards on their own to pray after school has ended, per the Equal Access Act), and are not prohibited from praying or discussing religion among themselves (Dierenfield, 2007). Prayers—denominational or not—cannot be recited by teachers in public schools, public schools cannot distribute Bibles (or any other religious texts) or celebrate religious holidays. But scholars argue that it is *because* of separation of church and state, including through decisions such as *Engel v. Vitale*, that the United States continues to be a country where religion plays a dominant role in individuals' lives. "Many Americans believe that separation is one important reason why religious faith persists in the US to a far greater extent than most other industrialized democracies . . . separation need not lead to secularism" Laycock states (2006, p. 505). Similarly, Dierenfield (2007) notes

> [a] continuing pattern of religiosity prevails because Jefferson, Madison, and other Founding Fathers devised a recipe for freedom . . . that allows religion to flourish by removing its dependence on the state . . . arguably, the most important reason that school prayer has receded from US public life is that *Engel* has not impaired the ability of Americans to worship freely.
>
> *(212, 217)*

This may seem counterintuitive—that removing the nexus between government and religion could actually help keep religiosity in the United States. But what if government were to interject itself into the religious affairs of its citizenry? We might feel that it is a kind of unwanted interference. Additionally, it allows for minority religious groups and sects (such as Catholics were) to flourish. Thomas Jefferson was quoted as saying, in his Bill for Establishing Religious Freedom, he "Sought to protect all religions, including 'the Jew and the Gentile, the Christian and Mahometan, the Hindoo, and infidel of every denomination" (Gottschalk, 2013, p. 176). By removing school prayer, it became possible for children of all religions or none to pray (or not pray) as they chose without a teacher as a representative of the government mandating it. We turn now to look at American attitudes toward religion in school.

American Attitudes About Religion in Schools

The United States is the most religiously diverse country in the world, with 1500 religions/sects (Dierenfield, 2007). Still, 78 percent of Americans now say that religion is losing influence in American life. More debate exists about whether this perceived reality is good for the country or not. About 42 percent say this is a bad thing; 55 percent of people in the US see religion as a force for good, 53 percent say it strengthens morality in society, and 50 percent say it mostly brings people together, but one in five say it does more harm than good and mostly pushes people apart (Pew Research Center, 2019b).

Despite the passage of decades and the beliefs evinced earlier that religion is losing influence in American life—and perhaps because of it—most Americans when polled disagree with the *Engels v. Vitale* ruling. A majority of Americans support allowing daily prayer in school. In 2014, Gallup reported that 61 percent favored prayer in school, and 37 percent opposed. In 1999, 70 percent favored and 28 percent opposed. Rather unsurprisingly, frequent churchgoers are much more likely to support daily classroom prayers, prayers at graduation ceremonies and allowing public school facilities to host religious groups after hours (Pew Research Center, 2019a). Yet, this number has declined since the time Pew began polling, suggesting that the rise of secularism has had an influence, and perhaps the legacy of *Engel v. Vitale* normalizing the lack of religious instruction/proselytizing in the school. Digging a little deeper gives a more complex reality "Even if Americans could obtain a prayer amendment, 69% favor a moment of silence, not a spoken prayer" (Dierenfield, 2007), but there is substantial subset of Republican voters who would like to establish Christianity as a national religion—57 percent (Bruenig, 2015).

Roe v. Wade Introduction

"Hi. I'm Norma McCorvey." This is how the woman behind the pseudonym Jane Roe of the landmark case *Jane Roe v. Henry Wade* introduced herself in February 1970 to Linda Coffee and Sarah Weddington, two lawyers who had been waiting for her. Sitting at a corner table of Columbo's Italian Restaurant in Dallas, Texas, Coffee and Weddington greeted the 21-year-old woman who wore a pair of jeans and a shirt. What caught their attention though was the bandana McCorvey wore tied to her left leg. An odd style choice, which McCorvey would later explain as a symbol that gay women use to say they do not have a girlfriend. Two months pregnant, her third pregnancy overall—the first resulting in the birth of her daughter Melissa who was being raised by McCorvey's mother and the second in the birth of a child she placed for adoption—McCorvey was poor, homeless, and determined to have an abortion. To the two lawyers, she was the perfect plaintiff for their lawsuit against the abortion statute in the state of Texas—where abortion was only allowed if the mother's life was at risk, which wasn't McCorvey's case.

At the time, there were only six states that allowed women to get a legal abortion: Alaska, California, Hawaii, New York, Oregon, and Washington. If McCorvey wanted to terminate the pregnancy and couldn't afford to travel to one of those six states, her only choice was an illegal abortion, performed by a questionable person in a squalid location with filthy tools and less-than-ideal equipment. It was not surprising that many women who underwent an illegal abortion died because of the irreparable damage done to them during the procedure. But those women were desperate. And so was McCorvey when, in late 1969, she went to talk to her doctor Richard Lane about getting an abortion. When Lane proposed she meet Henry McCluskey, an adoption lawyer in Dallas, McCorvey was clear that she had already placed a baby for adoption and did not want to go through the experience again. She was firm on her decision, but still agreed to meet with McCluskey who eventually referred her to Coffee and Weddington.

Sitting at the table, which featured a classic red and white checkered tablecloth, the three women got to know one another over pizza and beer. McCorvey (née Nelson) told them about her unhappy childhood made up of an abusive mother, an absent father, and a brother who was mentally ill. At 16, she married Elwood "Woody" McCorvey—six years her senior—who was so abusive toward her that she divorced him soon after, before their daughter Melissa was born. After placing her second child for adoption at the age of 19, McCorvey told the two lawyers that, although she only had girlfriends since then, she had recently been raped, and the abuse resulted in this third and unwanted pregnancy—years later, she admitted that she had lied to Coffee and Weddington about being raped, a detail that didn't affect the case since it was never made known in the actual suit. When the meeting was over, Norma McCorvey walked out of Columbo's with a new name: Jane Roe.

A few weeks later, Coffee and Weddington filed a lawsuit against Henry Wade, Dallas district attorney. The *Roe v. Wade* case had been officially presented to the Dallas federal district courthouse. A three-judge panel soon delivered their decision in favor of Jane Roe—who by now was in her third trimester. However, the victory was short-lived for Coffee and Weddington—who had turned the lawsuit into a class action so that the decision would affect every woman in the state of Texas—because the state appealed the decision and brought the case directly to the United States Supreme Court. When McCorvey expressed her hope that the appeal wouldn't take too long so she could still get the abortion, her two lawyers informed her that, regardless of when the nine justices would deliver their opinion, it was already too late for her to legally terminate the pregnancy. McCorvey became so irate that she "got drunk, and pounded my fists into my [pregnant] belly in frustration."

Feeling lost and desperate, McCorvey was faced with the reality that she would indeed have to carry this baby against her will. Her due date quickly approaching, McCorvey did what she could to find shelter and earn an income. Her father allowed her to live with him, but nobody wanted to hire a woman who was seven months pregnant. Aware that she would never be able to support this baby, she called Henry McCluskey for help and he soon found her a couple who not only adopted her child but also paid all of her hospital fees.

The Supreme Court agreed to hear the case in December 1971. Jay Floyd—attorney on behalf of appellee—opened his argument with, "Mr. Chief Justice and may it please the Court. It's an old joke, but when a man argues against two beautiful ladies like this, they are going to have the last word." Regarded as the worst joke in legal history—especially because the case focused on women's rights—Floyd's statement was met with deafening silence from the courtroom and a visibly upset Chief Justice Warren Burger. After arguments had been heard, the justices decided that the case had to be reargued because the opinion that Justice Harry Blackmun had been tasked to write did not accurately mirror the liberal views of his fellow justices. A year later, in October 1972, *Roe v. Wade* was reargued and this time there were not only two new justices—William Rehnquist and Lewis Powell, Jr., who had replaced Hugo Black and John Harlan II—but also a new attorney, Robert Flowers who had replaced Floyd.

The main question presented to the Supreme Court was, "Does the Constitution recognize a woman's right to terminate her pregnancy by abortion?" But the justices had another question to answer first: Since McCorvey had already given birth to her child, did her non-pregnant status make the entire case moot? While the justices debated on the decision, outside the Supreme Court pro-choice crowds argued against pro-life supporters, a debate that had also claimed media attention nationwide. In January 1973, the Supreme Court voted 7–2 in favor of Jane Roe, claiming that the case was not moot. The seven justices based their decision on the First, Fourth, Ninth, and Fourteenth Amendments, explaining that the Constitution protects a person's zone of privacy and that this zone was "broad enough to encompass a woman's decision whether or not to terminate her pregnancy." However, the justices also specified that just because a woman had the right to receive a legal abortion, this didn't mean that there were no limits—for example, they declared that an abortion in the third trimester could be regulated or prohibited by the state unless the procedure was deemed necessary to save the mother's life. As a result, the justices asserted that the abortion statute of Texas violated the Due Process Clause of the Fourteenth Amendment (see Box 5.1).

BOX 5.1 FOURTEENTH AMENDMENT AND THE DUE PROCESS CLAUSE

The Due Process Clause that is part of the Fourteenth Amendment is the only law that is repeated twice in the US Constitution. Due Process was first highlighted in the Fifth Amendment, which instructed the federal government that nobody shall be "deprived of life, liberty or property without due process of law." The Fourteenth Amendment extends the same command—actually using the same exact 11 words—put forth by the Fifth to each and every state, thus no longer limiting the Due Process to the federal government.

But what exactly does Due Process mean? This clause was first issued by King John of England in 1215 in the Magna Carta Libertatum, which is Latin for "Great Charter of Freedoms," a proclamation made by the monarch to ensure to noblemen—who had been rebelling against the king—that he would be committed to acting only according to the law. Due Process, therefore, ensures citizens of a country that before the government deprives them of life, liberty, or property, the government—whether state of federal—must follow the law and apply fair procedures.

The *Barron v. Mayor of Baltimore* case of 1833 shows the reason why it was pivotal to extend the Due Process clause to the state government and not limit it to the federal government. When John Barron, owner of the Baltimore wharf, suffered significant loss of profit after the city diverted the stream in the harbor—which resulted in the formation of shallow waters that could no longer properly host boats—he sued the city for taking his property and turning it to public use without properly compensating him, thus violating the Fifth Amendment. However, after the state appellate sided with the city of Baltimore, Barron took the case to the US Supreme Court. Chief Justice Marshall, on behalf of a unanimous court, said that the Fifth Amendment only applied to the federal government and, as a result, the city of Baltimore was not responsible for compensating Barron for his loss.

Once Congress, after the American Civil War (1861–1865), agreed upon the Fourteenth Amendment, the Supreme Court focused on the Due Process clause and elaborated it further, dividing it into three classifications: procedural due process, incorporation of the Bill of Rights against the states, and substantive due process.

The procedural due process ensures that government officials notify the person before depriving the individual of life, liberty, or property, allow the person to be heard on the case, and ensure that the decision will be made by a neutral decision maker. In the *Goldberg v. Kelly* case (1970), the Supreme Court agreed that John Kelly, whose financial aid had been terminated by the state of New York, had the right to a pre-termination hearing.

With the incorporation of the Bill of Rights against the states, the Fourteenth Amendment mandates that most basic human rights highlighted in the first ten amendments of the Constitution are to be incorporated against the states, meaning that the state and federal government must grant these rights. The only non-incorporated amendments were the Third, Fifth, Seventh, and Eighth.

The substantive due process protects those rights that, even though they are not listed in the Constitution, are so important that they cannot be denied—although there is not a specific list of such rights. For example, in *Griswold v. Connecticut* (1965), the Warren Court agreed that the right to privacy was protected by the Constitution against state governments that deemed married couples law breakers when they opted to use contraception.

After the Supreme Court's decision, Norma McCorvey revealed her real identity to the public, forever shedding herself from the anonymity of Jane Roe. Appearing next to women's rights attorney Gloria Allred in interviews, publishing a book titled *I Am Roe*, and becoming the face of pro-choice supporters, she shocked the nation when in 1995 she declared to have accepted Jesus as her savior and had become a born-again Christian. She vocally opposed her previous pro-choice stand and published another book titled *Won by Love*. However, with yet another shocking confession, in a documentary titled "AKA Jane Roe" that aired in 2020 but was filmed before her death in 2017, McCorvey revealed that her pro-life stand was simply a way for her to make money—hundreds of thousands of dollars. "I took their money and they took me out in front of the cameras and told me what to say," stated 69-year-old McCorvey who, in what she referred to as her deathbed confession, described herself as a good actress and specified she had always been pro-choice.

Roe v. Wade Decision

ROE V. WADE, 410 U.S. 113 (1973)

MR. JUSTICE BLACKMUN delivered the opinion of the Court.

This Texas federal appeal and its Georgia companion, Doe v. Bolton, present constitutional challenges to state criminal abortion legislation. The Texas statutes under attack here are typical of those that have been in effect in many States for approximately a century. The Georgia statutes, in contrast, have a modern cast, and are a legislative product that, to an extent at least, obviously reflects the influences of recent attitudinal change, of advancing medical knowledge and techniques, and of new thinking about an old issue.

We forthwith acknowledge our awareness of the sensitive and emotional nature of the abortion controversy, of the vigorous opposing views, even among physicians, and of the deep and seemingly absolute convictions that the subject inspires. One's philosophy, one's experiences, one's exposure to the raw edges of human existence, one's religious training, one's attitudes toward life and family and their values, and the moral standards one establishes and seeks to observe, are all likely to influence and to color one's thinking and conclusions about abortion.

In addition, population growth, pollution, poverty, and racial overtones tend to complicate and not to simplify the problem.

Our task, of course, is to resolve the issue by constitutional measurement, free of emotion and of predilection. We seek earnestly to do this, and, because we do, we have inquired into, and in this opinion place some emphasis upon, medical and medical-legal history and what that history reveals about man's attitudes toward the abortion procedure over the centuries. We bear in mind, too, Mr. Justice Holmes' admonition in his now-vindicated dissent in *Lochner v. New York*:

> [The Constitution] is made for people of fundamentally differing views, and the accident of our finding certain opinions natural and familiar or novel and even shocking ought not to conclude our judgment upon the question whether statutes embodying them conflict with the Constitution of the United States.

I

The Texas statutes that concern us here are Arts. 1191–1194 and 1196 of the State's Penal Code. These make it a crime to "procure an abortion," as therein defined, or to attempt one, except with respect to "an abortion procured or attempted by medical advice for the purpose of saving the life of the mother." Similar statutes are in existence in a majority of the States.

Texas first enacted a criminal abortion statute in 1854. Texas Laws 1854, c. 49, § 1, set forth in 3 H. Gammel, Laws of Texas 1502 (1898). This was soon modified into language that has remained substantially unchanged to the present time. The final article in each of these compilations provided the same exception, as does the present Article 1196, for an abortion by "medical advice for the purpose of saving the life of the mother."

II

Jane Roe, a single woman who was residing in Dallas County, Texas, instituted this federal action in March 1970 against the District Attorney of the county. She sought a declaratory judgment that the Texas criminal abortion statutes were unconstitutional on their face, and an injunction restraining the defendant from enforcing the statutes.

Roe alleged that she was unmarried and pregnant; that she wished to terminate her pregnancy by an abortion "performed by a competent, licensed physician, under safe, clinical conditions"; that she was unable to get a "legal" abortion in Texas because her life did not appear to be threatened by the continuation of her pregnancy; and that she could not afford to travel to another jurisdiction in order to secure a legal abortion under safe conditions. She claimed that the Texas statutes were unconstitutionally vague and that they abridged her right of personal privacy, protected by the First, Fourth, Fifth, Ninth, and Fourteenth Amendments. By an amendment to her complaint, Roe purported to sue "on behalf of herself and all other women" similarly situated.

James Hubert Hallford, a licensed physician, sought and was granted leave to intervene in Roe's action. In his complaint, he alleged that he had been arrested previously for violations of the Texas abortion statutes, and that two such prosecutions were pending against him. He described conditions of patients who came to him seeking abortions, and he claimed that for many cases he, as a physician, was unable to determine whether they fell within or outside the exception recognized by Article 1196. He alleged that, as a consequence, the statutes were vague and uncertain, in violation of the Fourteenth Amendment, and that they violated his own and his patients' rights to privacy in the doctor-patient relationship and his own right to practice medicine, rights he claimed were guaranteed by the First, Fourth, Fifth, Ninth, and Fourteenth Amendments.

John and Mary Doe, a married couple, filed a companion complaint to that of Roe. They also named the District Attorney as defendant, claimed like constitutional deprivations, and sought declaratory and injunctive relief. The Does alleged that they were a childless couple; that Mrs. Doe was suffering from a "neural-chemical" disorder; that her physician had "advised her to avoid pregnancy until such time as her condition has materially improved" (although a pregnancy at the present time would not present "a serious risk" to her life); that, pursuant to medical advice, she had discontinued use of birth control pills; and that, if she should become pregnant, she would want to terminate the pregnancy by an abortion performed by a competent, licensed physician under safe, clinical conditions. By an amendment to their complaint, the Does purported to sue "on behalf of themselves and all couples similarly situated."

The principal thrust of appellant's attack on the Texas statutes is that they improperly invade a right, said to be possessed by the pregnant woman, to choose to terminate her pregnancy. Appellant would discover this right in the concept of personal "liberty" embodied in the Fourteenth Amendment's Due Process Clause; or in personal, marital, familial, and sexual privacy said to be protected by the Bill of Rights. Before addressing this claim, we feel it desirable briefly to survey, in several aspects, the history of abortion, for such insight as that history may afford us, and then to examine the state purposes and interests behind the criminal abortion laws.

Three reasons have been advanced to explain historically the enactment of criminal abortion laws in the 19th century and to justify their continued existence.

It has been argued occasionally that these laws were the product of a Victorian social concern to discourage illicit sexual conduct. Texas, however, does not advance this justification in the present case, and it appears that no court or commentator has taken the argument seriously. The appellants and amici contend, moreover, that this is not a proper state purpose, at all and suggest that, if it were, the Texas statutes are overbroad in protecting it, since the law fails to distinguish between married and unwed mothers.

A second reason is concerned with abortion as a medical procedure. When most criminal abortion laws were first enacted, the procedure was a hazardous one for the woman. This was particularly true prior to the development of antisepsis. Antiseptic techniques, of course, were based on discoveries by Lister, Pasteur, and others first announced in 1867, but were not generally accepted and employed until about the turn of the century. Abortion mortality was high. Even after 1900, and perhaps until as late as the development of antibiotics in the 1940's, standard modern techniques such as dilation and curettage were not nearly so safe as they are today. Thus, it has been argued that a State's real concern in enacting a criminal abortion law was to protect the pregnant woman, that is, to restrain her from submitting to a procedure that placed her life in serious jeopardy.

Modern medical techniques have altered this situation. Appellants and various amici refer to medical data indicating that abortion in early pregnancy, that is, prior to the end of the first trimester, although not without its risk, is now relatively safe. Mortality rates for women undergoing early abortions, where the procedure is legal, appear to be as low as or lower than the rates for normal childbirth. Consequently, any interest of the State in protecting the woman from an inherently hazardous procedure, except when it would be equally dangerous for her to forgo it, has largely disappeared. Of course, important state interests in the areas of health and medical standards do remain.

The State has a legitimate interest in seeing to it that abortion, like any other medical procedure, is performed under circumstances that insure maximum safety for the patient. This interest obviously extends at least to the performing physician and his staff, to the facilities involved, to the availability of after-care, and to adequate provision for any complication or emergency that might arise. The prevalence of high mortality rates at illegal "abortion mills" strengthens, rather than weakens, the State's interest in regulating the conditions under which abortions are performed. Moreover, the risk to the woman increases as her pregnancy continues. Thus, the State retains a definite interest in protecting the woman's own health and safety when an abortion is proposed at a late stage of pregnancy.

The third reason is the State's interest—some phrase it in terms of duty—in protecting prenatal life. Some of the argument for this justification rests on the theory that a new human life is present from the moment of conception. The State's interest and general obligation to protect life then extends, it is argued, to prenatal life. Only when the life of the pregnant mother herself is at stake, balanced against the life she carries within her, should the interest of the embryo or fetus not prevail. Logically, of course, a legitimate state interest in this area need not stand or fall on acceptance of the belief that life begins at conception or at some other point prior to live birth. In assessing the State's interest, recognition may be given to the less rigid claim that as long as at least potential life is involved, the State may assert interests beyond the protection of the pregnant woman alone.

Parties challenging state abortion laws have sharply disputed in some courts the contention that a purpose of these laws, when enacted, was to protect prenatal life. Pointing to the absence of legislative history to support the contention, they claim that most state laws were designed solely to protect the woman. Because medical advances have lessened this concern, at least with respect to abortion in early pregnancy, they argue that with respect to such abortions the laws can no longer be justified by any state interest. There is some scholarly support for this view of original purpose. The few state courts called upon to interpret their laws in the late 19th and early 20th centuries did focus on the State's interest in protecting the woman's health, rather than in preserving the embryo and fetus. Proponents of this view point out that in many States, including Texas, by statute or judicial interpretation, the pregnant woman herself could not be prosecuted for self-abortion or for cooperating in an abortion performed upon her by another. They claim that adoption of the "quickening" distinction through received common law and state statutes tacitly recognizes the greater health hazards inherent in late abortion and impliedly repudiates the theory that life begins at conception.

It is with these interests, and the eight to be attached to them, that this case is concerned.

The Constitution does not explicitly mention any right of privacy. In a line of decisions, however, going back perhaps as far as *Union Pacific R. Co. v. Botsford*, the Court has recognized that a right of personal privacy, or a guarantee of certain areas or zones of privacy, does exist under the Constitution.

This right of privacy, whether it be founded in the Fourteenth Amendment's concept of personal liberty and restrictions upon state action, as we feel it is, or, as the District Court determined, in the Ninth Amendment's reservation of rights to the people, is broad enough to encompass a woman's decision whether or not to terminate her pregnancy. The detriment that the State would impose upon the pregnant woman by denying this choice altogether is apparent. Specific and direct harm medically diagnosable even in early pregnancy may be involved. Maternity, or additional offspring, may force upon the woman a distressful life and future. Psychological harm may be imminent. Mental and physical health may be taxed by child care. There is also the distress, for all concerned, associated with the unwanted child, and there is the problem of bringing a child into a family already unable, psychologically and otherwise, to care for it. In other cases, as in this one, the additional difficulties and continuing stigma of unwed motherhood may be involved. All these are factors the woman and her responsible physician necessarily will consider in consultation.

On the basis of elements such as these, appellant and some amici argue that the woman's right is absolute and that she is entitled to terminate her pregnancy at whatever time, in whatever way, and for whatever reason she alone chooses. With this we do not agree. Appellant's arguments that Texas either has no valid interest at all in regulating the abortion decision, or no interest strong enough to support any limitation upon the woman's sole determination, are unpersuasive. The Court's decisions recognizing a right of privacy also acknowledge that some state regulation in areas protected by that right is appropriate. As noted above, a State may properly assert important interests in safeguarding health, in maintaining medical standards, and in protecting potential life. At some point in pregnancy, these respective interests become sufficiently compelling to sustain regulation of the factors that govern the abortion decision. The privacy right involved, therefore, cannot be said to be absolute. In fact, it is not clear to us that the claim asserted by some amici that one has an unlimited right to do with one's body as one pleases bears a close relationship to the right of privacy previously articulated in the Court's decisions. The Court has refused to recognize an unlimited right of this kind in the past.

We, therefore, conclude that the right of personal privacy includes the abortion decision, but that this right is not unqualified, and must be considered against important state interests in regulation.

We note that those federal and state courts that have recently considered abortion law challenges have reached the same conclusion. A majority, in addition to the District Court in the present case, have held state laws unconstitutional, at least in part, because of vagueness or because of overbreadth and abridgment of rights.

Although the results are divided, most of these courts have agreed that the right of privacy, however based, is broad enough to cover the abortion decision; that the right, nonetheless, is not absolute, and is subject to some limitations; and that, at some point, the state interests as to protection of health, medical standards, and prenatal life, become dominant. We agree with this approach.

Where certain "fundamental rights" are involved, the Court has held that regulation limiting these rights may be justified only by a "compelling state interest."

In the recent abortion cases, courts have recognized these principles. Those striking down state laws have generally scrutinized the State's interests in protecting health and potential life, and have concluded that neither interest justified broad limitations on the reasons for which a physician and his pregnant patient might decide that she should have an abortion in the early stages of pregnancy. Courts sustaining state laws have held that the State's determinations to protect health or prenatal life are dominant and constitutionally justifiable.

The appellee and certain amici argue that the fetus is a "person" within the language and meaning of the Fourteenth Amendment. In support of this, they outline at length and in detail the well known facts of fetal development. If this suggestion of personhood is established, the appellant's case, of course, collapses, for the fetus' right to life would then be guaranteed specifically by the Amendment. The appellant conceded as much on reargument. On the other hand, the appellee conceded on reargument that no case could be cited that holds that a fetus is a person within the meaning of the Fourteenth Amendment.

The Constitution does not define "person" in so many words. Section 1 of the Fourteenth Amendment contains three references to "person." The first, in defining "citizens," speaks of "persons born or naturalized in the United States." The word also appears both in the Due

Process Clause and in the Equal Protection Clause. "Person" is used in other places in the Constitution: in the listing of qualifications for Representatives and Senators, Art. I, § 2, cl. 2, and § 3, cl. 3; in the Apportionment Clause, Art. I, § 2, cl. 3; in the Migration and Importation provision, Art. I, § 9, cl. 1; in the Emolument Clause, Art. I, § 9, cl. 8; in the Electors provisions, Art. II, § 1, cl. 2, and the superseded cl. 3; in the provision outlining qualifications for the office of President, Art. II, § 1, cl. 5; in the Extradition provisions, Art. IV, § 2, cl. 2, and the superseded Fugitive Slave Clause 3; and in the Fifth, Twelfth, and Twenty-second Amendments, as well as in §§ 2 and 3 of the Fourteenth Amendment. But in nearly all these instances, the use of the word is such that it has application only post-natally. None indicates, with any assurance, that it has any possible pre-natal application.

All this, together with our observation, supra, that, throughout the major portion of the 19th century, prevailing legal abortion practices were far freer than they are today, persuades us that the word "person," as used in the Fourteenth Amendment, does not include the unborn. This is in accord with the results reached in those few cases where the issue has been squarely presented.

This conclusion, however, does not of itself fully answer the contentions raised by Texas, and we pass on to other considerations. The pregnant woman cannot be isolated in her privacy. She carries an embryo and, later, a fetus, if one accepts the medical definitions of the developing young in the human uterus. The situation therefore is inherently different from marital intimacy, or bedroom possession of obscene material, or marriage, or procreation, or education, with which Eisenstadt and Griswold, Stanley, Loving, Skinner, and Pierce and Meyer were respectively concerned. As we have intimated above, it is reasonable and appropriate for a State to decide that, at some point in time another interest, that of health of the mother or that of potential human life, becomes significantly involved. The woman's privacy is no longer sole and any right of privacy she possesses must be measured accordingly.

Texas urges that, apart from the Fourteenth Amendment, life begins at conception and is present throughout pregnancy, and that, therefore, the State has a compelling interest in protecting that life from and after conception. We need not resolve the difficult question of when life begins.

When those trained in the respective disciplines of medicine, philosophy, and theology are unable to arrive at any consensus, the judiciary, at this point in the development of man's knowledge, is not in a position to speculate as to the answer.

It should be sufficient to note briefly the wide divergence of thinking on this most sensitive and difficult question. Substantial problems for precise definition of this view are posed, however, by new embryological data that purport to indicate that conception is a "process" over time, rather than an event, and by new medical techniques such as menstrual extraction, the "morning-after" pill, implantation of embryos, artificial insemination, and even artificial wombs.

In areas other than criminal abortion, the law has been reluctant to endorse any theory that life, as we recognize it, begins before live birth, or to accord legal rights to the unborn except in narrowly defined situations and except when the rights are contingent upon live birth. For example, the traditional rule of tort law denied recovery for prenatal injuries even though the child was born alive. That rule has been changed in almost every jurisdiction. In most States, recovery is said to be permitted only if the fetus was viable, or at least quick, when the injuries were sustained, though few courts have squarely so held. In a recent development, generally opposed by the commentators, some States permit the parents of a stillborn child to maintain an action for wrongful death because of prenatal injuries. Such an action, however, would appear to be one to vindicate the parents' interest and is thus consistent with the view that the fetus, at most, represents only the potentiality of life. Similarly, unborn children have been recognized as acquiring rights or interests by way of inheritance or other devolution of property, and have been represented by guardians ad litem. Perfection of the interests involved, again, has generally been contingent upon live birth. In short, the unborn have never been recognized in the law as persons in the whole sense.

In view of all this, we do not agree that, by adopting one theory of life, Texas may override the rights of the pregnant woman that are at stake. We repeat, however, that the State does have an important and legitimate interest in preserving and protecting the health of the pregnant woman, whether she be a resident of the State or a non-resident who seeks medical consultation and treatment there, and that it has still another important and legitimate interest in protecting the potentiality of human life. These interests are separate and distinct. Each grows in substantiality as the woman approaches term and, at a point during pregnancy, each becomes "compelling."

With respect to the State's important and legitimate interest in the health of the mother, the "compelling" point, in the light of present medical knowledge, is at approximately the end of the first trimester. This is so because of the now-established medical fact, referred to above at 149, that, until the end of the first trimester mortality in abortion may be less than mortality in normal childbirth. It follows that, from and after this point, a State may regulate the abortion procedure to the extent that the regulation reasonably relates to the preservation and protection of maternal health. Examples of permissible state regulation in this area are requirements as to the qualifications of the person who is to perform the abortion; as to the licensure of that person; as to the facility in which the procedure is to be performed, that is, whether it must be a hospital or maybe a clinic or some other place of less-than-hospital status; as to the licensing of the facility; and the like.

This means, on the other hand, that, for the period of pregnancy prior to this "compelling" point, the attending physician, in consultation with his patient, is free to determine, without regulation by the State, that, in his medical judgment, the patient's pregnancy should be terminated. If that decision is reached, the judgment may be effectuated by an abortion free of interference by the State.

With respect to the State's important and legitimate interest in potential life, the "compelling" point is at viability. This is so because the fetus then presumably has the capability of meaningful life outside the mother's womb. State regulation protective of fetal life after viability thus has both logical and biological justifications. If the State is interested in protecting fetal life after viability, it may go so far as to proscribe abortion during that period, except when it is necessary to preserve the life or health of the mother.

This conclusion makes it unnecessary for us to consider the additional challenge to the Texas statute asserted on grounds of vagueness.

To summarize and to repeat:

1. A state criminal abortion statute of the current Texas type, that excepts from criminality only a lifesaving procedure on behalf of the mother, without regard to pregnancy stage and without recognition of the other interests involved, is violative of the Due Process Clause of the Fourteenth Amendment.

    (a) For the stage prior to approximately the end of the first trimester, the abortion decision and its effectuation must be left to the medical judgment of the pregnant woman's attending physician.
    (b) For the stage subsequent to approximately the end of the first trimester, the State, in promoting its interest in the health of the mother, may, if it chooses, regulate the abortion procedure in ways that are reasonably related to maternal health.

   (c) For the stage subsequent to viability, the State in promoting its interest in the potentiality of human life may, if it chooses, regulate, and even proscribe, abortion except where it is necessary, in appropriate medical judgment, for the preservation of the life or health of the mother.

2. The State may define the term "physician," as it has been employed in the preceding paragraphs of this Part XI of this opinion, to mean only a physician currently licensed by the State, and may proscribe any abortion by a person who is not a physician as so defined.

In *Doe v. Bolton*, post, p. 179, procedural requirements contained in one of the modern abortion statutes are considered. That opinion and this one, of course, are to be read together.

This holding, we feel, is consistent with the relative weights of the respective interests involved, with the lessons and examples of medical and legal history, with the lenity of the common law, and with the demands of the profound problems of the present day. The decision leaves the State free to place increasing restrictions on abortion as the period of pregnancy lengthens, so long as those restrictions are tailored to the recognized state interests. The decision vindicates the right of the physician to administer medical treatment according to his professional judgment up to the points where important state interests provide compelling justifications for intervention. Up to those points, the abortion decision in all its aspects is inherently, and primarily, a medical decision, and basic responsibility for it must rest with the physician. If an individual practitioner abuses the privilege of exercising proper medical judgment, the usual remedies, judicial and intra-professional, are available.

Our conclusion that Art. 1196 is unconstitutional means, of course, that the Texas abortion statutes, as a unit, must fall. The exception of Art. 1196 cannot be struck down separately, for then the State would be left with a statute proscribing all abortion procedures no matter how medically urgent the case.

Although the District Court granted appellant Roe declaratory relief, it stopped short of issuing an injunction against enforcement of the Texas statutes. The Court has recognized that different considerations enter into a federal court's decision as to declaratory relief, on the one hand, and injunctive relief, on the other. We are not dealing with a statute that, on its face, appears to abridge free expression, an area of particular concern under Dombrowski and refined in *Younger v. Harris*.

We find it unnecessary to decide whether the District Court erred in withholding injunctive relief, for we assume the Texas prosecutorial authorities will give full credence to this decision that the present criminal abortion statutes of that State are unconstitutional.

The judgment of the District Court as to intervenor Hallford is reversed, and Dr. Hallford's complaint in intervention is dismissed. In all other respects, the judgment of the District Court is affirmed. Costs are allowed to the appellee.

It is so ordered.

The Impact of *Roe v. Wade* on Religion in the United States

The *Roe v. Wade* decision was not made based on the Constitutional guarantee of religious freedom, but rather, on a Constitutional right to privacy. Nevertheless, the abortion issue in the United States has been intimately intertwined with the institution of religion in the United States, and affected this institution. "The fight over abortion is not just a fight about the role of women in our society, but also the role of religion" Nye states (2017). Religions have played an important role in the continuing debates about abortion and the controversy of *Roe*, but the social and political context of that debate has been shaped also in reciprocal fashion by the *Roe v. Wade* decision. *Roe* has had an impact on the way in which religion has, for instance, become imbricated in politics and healthcare, as well as in affirming or challenging personal religious beliefs, issues which we discuss in the following sections of this chapter.

Roe v. Wade, *Religion and Politics*

Although church and state have been separated in the United States and the First Amendment guarantees freedom of religion, this does not mean that religion has ever been or is absent currently from political life. One of the key impacts of *Roe v. Wade* on religion in the United States was the greater direct involvement of organized religions (especially conservative Protestant sects and Catholicism) in political issues not immediately related to the practice of that religion. Protestant fundamentalists first entered national politics, for example, after the *Roe* decision (Hoffman & Johnson, 2005). Before *Roe*, too, Catholic bishops in the United States generally avoided getting involved in politics unless it had direct bearing on the Catholic Church. This all changed post *Roe*, which gave an enormous push in general to the anti-abortion movement and the involvement of religious groups—the Catholic bishops at first notably—in that movement. The bishops post-*Roe* took a more outspoken role almost immediately, criticizing the Supreme Court's decision in a statement. They wrote:

> Although as a result of the Court decision, abortion may be legally permissible, it is still morally wrong . . . as religious leaders we cannot accept the Court's judgment and we urge people not to follow its reasoning or conclusions.
>
> *(Parsons, 2011, p. 1)*

Roe brought the Bishops much more influence in the political process itself, with an outsized focus of their politics being on abortion. They became essential figures in the landscape with the power to exert pressure on the votes of their congregants to abide by Catholic teachings, with the local organizational infrastructure (through **parishes**) to achieve this.

Primarily, the bishops exerted this power to influence political candidates when it came to matters related to abortion. Although they issued statements about political questions that connected to Catholic teachings (such as opposition to euthanasia or capital punishment), decisions to support a political candidate or not were largely based on that person's stance on abortion. It was a single issue of paramount importance. By the presidential election of 1976, only a few years after *Roe v. Wade*, candidates had to contend with the fact that Catholic voters were a formidable voting bloc, and to ignore the abortion issue and not court the bishops' support was politically risky. Catholic presidential candidate John Kerry, for example, would be denied communion by the bishops because of his pro-choice stance almost 40 years after *Roe*, in 2004 (Parsons, 2011, p. 6).

Many individual Catholics and Catholic groups were influenced by the *Roe* decision to enter into politics and came to dominate what was to be known as the Right-to-Life or anti-abortion movement. This movement grew quickly, as Catholics mobilized across the country. And, since the 1970s and 1980s, conservative evangelical Protestant groups also became successfully organized around the issue, entering into politics under an anti-abortion banner and continue to do so to this day. This was a move away from their pre-*Roe* positions, when even conservative Protestants stayed generally out of politics or even sanctioned therapeutic abortion. They helped push anti-abortion political initiatives and legislation (Adamczyk & Valdimarsdottir, 2018), and brought the movement to prominence and political heft (Cassidy, 1990) with resources capable of influencing legislation and policy.

Roe's impact of centering of religion in the political debates about abortion continues to the present, and anti-abortion stances of candidates can indeed sway conservative Protestants and Catholics in elections (Adamczyk & Valdimarsdottir, 2018), as well as the obverse: anti-abortion stances sway those in religions that consider abortion morally admissible, or those without religion, away from these candidates. Religion has also been impacted in that religious adherents may feel that according to their institutions' beliefs about abortion, that they are more welcomed in a political party. Political affiliations were reconfigured around abortion—whereas Republicans were more pro-choice than Democrats until the 1980s, the party is now associated with a pro-life/anti-abortion position becoming increasingly allied with the Republican party, after Republicans began to seek support from Catholic groups traditionally associated with the Democratic Party (Greenhouse & Siegel, 2011; Hoffman & Johnson, 2005).

Roe v. Wade*'s Impact on Religion and Healthcare*

The discussion of the impact of *Roe v. Wade* on religion necessarily requires thinking also about its intersection with, and impact on the institution of healthcare in the US (see box 5.2 "Healthcare in the US"). While healthcare as a concept encompasses any activities meant to improve health (Kendall, 2011), when we speak of healthcare in the US, we are typically referring to the formal system that provides medical and health services to individuals and the way in which that is paid for. Personal religious beliefs and institutionalized religious affect both personal health and healthcare. Abortion was legal in the United States until 1821—the establishment of the American Medical Association led to a campaign to criminalize abortion except for when a woman's life was in danger. Even this push was indirectly related to religion, among other factors, namely, anti-Catholicism. Native-born Protestants were seeing declining birthrates, whereas immigrant Catholics had much higher birthrates, so to oppose abortion became a way of promoting fertility among the native-born Protestant population (Greenhouse & Siegel, 2011; Pollitt, 1997). By the end of the 19th century, the practice was largely criminalized until a wave of liberalizing reforms took hold in the 1960s, ending ultimately in the *Roe* decision (Greenhouse & Siegel, 2011). For those individuals and religious organizations that opposed the decision, how has this affected healthcare?

BOX 5.2 HEALTH AND HEALTHCARE IN THE UNITED STATES

We expect that the institution of health and healthcare define, diagnose, and manage **disease** and **disability**. Although it may seem straightforward to define what a disease is—commonly thought of as a biological abnormality—and disability—described by the WHO as "impairments, activity limitations, and participation restriction," but none of these exist independent of the social meaning we ascribe to them. The social basis of the institution of health and healthcare is made clearer if we consider the following examples: In the mid-nineteenth century, a surgeon published a report about the 'disease' of drapetomania that 'caused' slaves to run away from their masters (Eakin, 2000). And up until 1973 the American Psychiatric Association had "homosexuality" included as a mental disorder in its Diagnostic and Statistical Manual (DSM). These cases illustrate the degree to which our notions of "disease" and "health" are culturally and historically conditioned. Who we think is responsible for treating/caring for these concerns and the 'health' of society, what we consider to be 'disease,' how we 'treat' disease, and inequalities in systems that act as purveyors of health—these are all part of the institution of health/healthcare.

As with the other institutions we have covered, health and healthcare depend on norms, behaviors, and laws that structure human interactions. In the US today, we expect that **health** (a state of complete physical, mental, and social well-being) is provided for by, for the most part, licensed doctors who have attended medical school. This was not always the case, but the rise of **professionalization** at the end of the 19th century meant the consolidation of power among medical school graduates in cornering the market on medical care (Kendall, 2011). Until the 20th century, for example, the majority of child births occurred in the home, with midwives rather than doctors.

While healthcare as a concept encompasses any activities meant to improve health (Kendall, 2011), when we speak of healthcare in the US, we are typically referring to the institutionalized, formal system that provides medical and health services to individuals and the way in which that is paid for. This system is enormously complex, but below, we offer a brief description of major characteristics.

The US does not have a universal healthcare system, found in, as of 2020, 32 countries which offer some form of universal health coverage for their citizens (NYDOH, 2020). The system is characterized by a private industry with a fee-for-service model of insurance, meaning that all services are paid for separately (lab work, visits, prescriptions, band-aids, and so forth). A problem with fee-for service comes about as doctors may have a financial incentive to perform tests or see patients more than necessary. Some forms of public healthcare are available for those with the most limited incomes, like Medicare, which covers seniors and some people with disabilities. Medicare is a single-payer system, meaning there is only one entity (e.g. the government) that reimburses the cost of care. Medicaid provides medical care to the poor, and State Children's Health Insurance Program (SCHIP), provides for children whose families make too much to qualify for Medicaid, but who cannot afford private insurance. The Veterans Administration (VA) is also a federally administered program to provide for veterans of the military in government-owned hospitals and clinics.

Most Americans, however, are covered through employer-sponsored insurance, thus making the system a 'multipayer system.' This insurance is administered through both for profit and non-profit insurance companies. Employers typically pay part of the premium, or monthly cost of the insurance, for their employees. In addition to the premiums, healthcare coverage also involves deductibles, amounts that the insured must pay towards their plan before the insurance coverage kicks in, as well as copays, which is the amount that a patient owes for a service after the deductible has been met. Americans cannot always keep up with these costs. Medical bills are implicated in 67 percent of all bankruptcies (over 500,000 per year) (Konish, 2019).

Sociologists point to the way in which demographic variables like gender, race, or class can have a profound impact on the way one experiences health or illness. For example, Blacks, in the US, for example, live six years fewer years than Whites and have more chronic health problems and women's health concerns may be downplayed by doctors vis-à-vis their male counterparts, resulting in their being prescribed less pain medication after surgery, or their pain being dismissed as being 'in their head' (Noe Pagan, 2018).

Many religions prohibit various kinds of medical procedures, and so for medical institutions affiliated with religions that oppose abortion, the *Roe* decision created a divide between what was constitutionally legal and what was morally legal. Religiously affiliated hospitals are no small part of the US healthcare landscape, and have seen an expansion in their size and importance in the decades after *Roe*—5 of 10 largest healthcare systems in the US are Catholic, with 18 percent of all hospitals and 20 percent of hospital beds controlled by Catholic systems (Fogel & Rivera, 2004, p. 730), which impose a large amount of restrictions on particularly reproductive services. Their decisions are governed by Ethical and Religious Directives for Health Care services from US Conference of Catholic Bishops, which prohibits abortion, including that sought for rape, incest, or the health of the mother.

If the religion prohibits a procedure (in this case we are discussing abortion, but other practices from contraception to AIDS testing to infertility treatment are also potentially banned), the services offered by the healthcare facility are limited to what is permitted by the religion, "even if religious principles are in conflict with accepted standards of medical practice and patients' rights to self-determination" (Fogel & Rivera, 2004, p. 727). If there is a public–private partnership (for example, if a non-sectarian private insurance plan or Medicaid contracts with religiously controlled hospitals), conflicts may arise between the personal religious beliefs of the individual seeking abortion and the hospital or clinic, as the patient can be declined the legally permissible procedure.

Post-*Roe*, one of the ways in which anti-abortion religious organizations mobilized to prevent their healthcare systems from engaging in such procedures was through **refusal clauses. Refusal clauses** and **medical conscience clauses** have since proliferated at the state and federal level, and allow religious-sponsored health organizations and individual medical professionals to opt out of complying with the law to provide or pay for services based on moral objections. For example, Congress enacted the Church Amendment, so that healthcare entities receiving certain federal funds may "refuse to provide abortion or sterilization if such services are contrary to their religious or moral beliefs." Pharmacist right of refusal laws were also passed with political engagement from religious groups, which allows pharmacists to refuse to fill prescriptions that may induce abortions or birth control if it interferes with their religious beliefs (Marshall, 2013).

Personal Religious Beliefs and Abortion

"Individuals' attitudes toward abortion continue to be closely entangled with religious belief post *Roe v. Wade*." The number of those seeking an abortion has fallen over the past 40 years (13.5/100,000 women had an abortion in 2017, this number was 29.3 in 1981) but almost 20 percent of pregnancies end in abortion today, and so this issue affected a large swath of the American population (Jerman, Jones, & Onda, 2016). Since *Roe*, overall, supportive attitudes towards the right to have an abortion have not changed dramatically. In 1975 22 percent of women and 20 percent of men thought abortion should be legal under any circumstances. By 2019, that number had risen only a few percentages points, with 25 percent of women agreeing and 24 percent of men agreeing (Gallup, 2020). This stands in contrast to other opinions that evince a cultural shift (such as towards gay marriage, which we discussed in Chapter 4), that have seen a dramatic shift in support over a shorter period of time since the Supreme Court legalized the practice. This evenness may be partially explained by the relatively consistent positions of religious organizations and leaders on abortion, as Americans who most routinely attend religious services are the most likely to disapprove.

Of the major religious groups, the Roman Catholic Church, African Methodist Episcopal Church, Church of Jesus Christ of Latter-Day Saints, Hinduism, the Lutheran Church-Missouri

Synod, and Southern Baptist Convention have not been affected by *Roe* in their strong opposition to abortion with few or no exceptions (Masci, 2016). In fact, the Southern Baptist convention in the decade following *Roe* decided to use more 'hard' language against abortion (Hoffman & Johnson, 2005). The Episcopal Church, Evangelical Lutheran Church, and Methodist Church support abortion with some limitations—in fact these religious organizations issued policy statements arguing against government intrusion in providing abortion, and the Methodist Church issued a resolution supporting the Supreme Court's decision. Conservative and Reform Judaism, the Presbyterian Church, United Church of Christ, and Unitarians support it with few or no limits (other religious groups such as Buddhists and Muslims have no clear public position on the issue) (Masci, 2016). Yet, almost all of the groups that allow for abortion in some cases distinguish among ethically permissible situations and those which are not morally permissible, which is in line with the *Roe* decision, "that relied on the timing of abortion by establishing trimesters during which the strength of government interest engages at increasing levels" (Hoffman & Johnson, 2005).

Still, there is disagreement between official doctrine and the beliefs of practitioners. The issue has had the impact of contentious debate and division *within* religious groups, as sizeable percentages of adherents disagree with dogma. In spite of Catholicism's official stance, 48 percent of Catholics think abortion should be legal in all or most cases, a number that has increased since *Roe*. About 33 percent of Evangelical Protestants think it should be legal, and among mainline Protestants, 60 percent. The lowest support comes from Jehovah's witnesses (18 percent) and Mormon's (27 percent), while the highest support is seen among those who are Buddhist (82 percent), Jewish (83 percent), or those who do not indicate any religion (73 percent). Of those who said that they think abortion should be illegal in all cases, they are also the most likely to indicate absolute belief in God, to indicate that religion is very important in their lives, to attend religious services at least once a week, to pray at least once daily, attend religious education, to say they seek religion as a source of guidance when looking to what is right and wrong, to read scripture, to think scripture is the literal word of God, and to believe in heaven and hell (PRC, 2020).

Personal religious belief has the ability to transcend the individual and influence the community, as shared bonds can create shared understanding, practices, and values. Local religious contexts (such as within counties) have been found to be powerful in shaping abortion attitudes. The degree to which a county, for example, is engaged religiously is not only predictive of individual levels of disapproval, but in fact can shape attitudes even among other individuals who do not share the same faith or who may not have any faith at all. These areas with high levels of religious engagement versus those with lower engagement predict whether abortion clinics will be found there. Even states' abortion rates can differ because of religious influence (Adamczyk & Valdimarsdottir, 2018; Hansen, 1980).

While public opinion may not have changed much since *Roe*, how have religious beliefs actually affected likelihood of having an abortion at the individual level for a religious practitioner? Religion can obviously affect the likelihood of obtaining an abortion if access is restricted, it can also provide either the support for or against a decision. Some scholars have noted that the causal link between religiosity and abortion *behavior* as opposed to opinion, is not straightforward (Henshaw, 2006). Abortion rates were found to increase with the percentage of population who identified as Catholic, whereas the percentage of Mormons had a negative relationship—"many states' abortion rates are substantially higher or lower than one might predict on the basis of . . . religious preference" (Hansen, 1980). Of those women who obtained an abortion and noted belonging to a religious group, 17 percent identified as mainline Protestant, 13 percent as Evangelical Protestant, 25 percent as Catholic, and 8 percent reported some other religious affiliation (Jerman et al., 2016).

Review Questions

1. Why did the families in *Engel v. Vitale* sue their children's school district?
2. What reasons did the Court provide for their decision?
3. How has religion in America and in schools changed due to this case?
4. Discuss the influence of *Roe v. Wade* on our society. Be certain to include religion and politics in your answer.
5. What are refusal clauses and how do they interact with the *Roe* ruling?

References

Adamczyk, A., & Valdimarsdottir, M. (2018). Understanding Americans' abortion attitudes: The role of local religious context. *Social Science Research*, *71*, 129–144.

Bellah, R. (1967). Religion in America. *Journal of the American Academy of Arts and Sciences*, *96*(1), 1–21.

Bellah, R. (1992). *The broken covenant: American civil religion in a time of trial*. Chicago: University of Chicago Press.

Bruenig, E. (2015, February 26). Making Christianity our national religion would be terrible for Christianity. *The New Republic*. Retrieved from https://newrepublic.com/article/121153/poll-republican-majority-wants-christianity-be-national-religion

Cassidy, K. M. (1990). Right to life. In D. G. Reid (Ed.), *Dictionary of Christianity in America* (pp. 1017–1018). Downers Grove, IL: Intervarsity Press.

Dierenfield, B. J. (2007). *The battle over school prayer: How Engel v. Vitale changed America*. Lawrence, KS: University Press of Kansas.

Dierenfield, R. (1962). *Religion in American public schools*. Washington, DC: Public Affairs Press.

Eakin, E. (2000, January 15). Bigotry as mental illness or just another norm. *New York Times*.

Fain, P. (2019, May 23). Wealth's influence on enrollment and completion. *Inside HigherEd*.

Fogel, S., & Rivera, L. A. (2004). Saving Roe is not enough: When religion controls healthcare. *Fordham Urban Law Journal*, *31*(3), 725–750.

Gallup. (2020). Abortion trends by gender. *Gallup*. Retrieved from https://news.gallup.com/poll/245618/abortion-trends-gender.aspx

Gottschalk, P. (2013). *American heretics: Catholics, Jews, Muslims, and the history of religious intolerance*. New York: St. Martin's Press.

Greenhouse, L., & Siegel, R. B. (2011). Before (and after) Roe v. Wade: New questions about backlash. *The Yale Law Journal*, 2028–2087.

Hansen, S. B. (1980). State implementation of supreme court decisions: Abortion rates since Roe v. Wade. *The Journal of Politics*, *42*(2), 372–395.

Henshaw, S. K. (2006, October 13). *Fédération internationale des associés professionels de l'avortement et de la contraception*. Presentation of FIAPAC Conference, Rome, Italy.

Hoffmann, J. P., & Johnson, S. M. (2005). Attitudes toward abortion among religious traditions in the United States: Change or continuity? *Sociology of Religion*, *66*(2), 161–182.

Retrieved from https://www.law.cornell.edu/supremecourt/text/410/113

Jerman, J., Jones, R. K., & Onda, T. (2016). *Characteristics of US abortion patients in 2014 and changes since 2008*. New York: Guttmacher Institute.

Kazin, M. (Ed.). (2009). *The Princeton encyclopedia of American political history*. Princeton, NJ: Princeton University Press.

Kendall, D. (2011). *Sociology in our times*. Belmont, CA: Wadsworth.

Konish, L. (2019). *This is the real reason most Americans file for bankruptcy*. Retrieved from www.cnbc.com/2019/02/11/this-is-the-real-reason-most-americans-file-for-bankruptcy.html

Laycock, D. L. (2006). Church and state in the United States: Competing conceptions and historic changes. *Indiana Journal of Global Legal Studies*, *13*, 503–516.

Marshall, C. (2013). The spread of conscience clause legislation. *Human Rights Magazine*, *39*(2). American Bar Association. Retrieved from www.americanbar.org/groups/crsj/publications/human_rights_magazine_home/2013_vol_39/january_2013_no_2_religious_freedom/the_spread_of_conscience_clause_legislation/

Masci, D. (2016). *Where major religious groups stand on abortion*. Washington, DC: Pew Research Center.
Noe Pagan, 2018. https://www.nytimes.com/2018/05/03/well/live/when-doctors-downplay-womens-health-concerns.html
New York State Department of Health (NYDOH). 2020. Foreign Countries with Universal Health Care. Retrieved: https://www.health.ny.gov/regulations/hcra/univ_hlth_care.htm
Nye, J. (2017). Abortion is not just about the role of women in society, but also the role of religion. *American Journal of Public*, *107*(11), 1690–1691. Retrieved from www.ncbi.nlm.nih.gov/pmc/articles/PMC5637668/
Parsons, M. S. (2011). *Abortion and religion: The politics of the American Catholic bishops* (Dissertation). The Catholic University of America, Washington, DC.
Pew Research Center (PRC). (2019a). *Religion in the public schools*. Retrieved from www.pewforum.org/2019/10/03/religion-in-the-public-schools-2019-update/
Pew Research Center (PRC). (2019b). *Americans have positive views about religion's role in society but want it out of politics*. Pew Research Center. Retrieved from www.pewforum.org/2019/11/15/americans-have-positive-views-about-religions-role-in-society-but-want-it-out-of-politics/
Pew Research Center (PRC). (2020). *Religious landscape study*. Pew Research Center. Retrieved from www.pewforum.org/religious-landscape-study/#religions
Pollitt, K. (1997, May). Abortion in American history. *The Atlantic*. Retrieved from www.theatlantic.com/magazine/archive/1997/05/abortion-in-american-history/376851/

6

GOVERNMENT

Learning Objectives

After reading this chapter, students should be able to:

- Analyze the US Supreme Court case *Scott v. Sandford*
- Describe the impact of the *Scott* case on the institution of Government
- Provide an overview of race, power, and citizenship in the US
- Discuss connections between slavery and the Criminal Justice System
- Summarize the *Citizens United v. FEC* case
- Understand how government and politics were changed by the *Citizens United* ruling
- Expound on the role of Super PACs on elections
- Paraphrase the links between money, organizations, and elections

Key Terms

Bribe
Citizens United v. FEC
Citizenship
Dark Money
Domination
Enfranchisement
Ideology
Independent Expenditure
Institutional Racism
Jim Crow
Lobby
Politics
Power
Quid Pro Quo
Scott v. Sandford
Subalterns
White Supremacy

Dred Scott v. Sandford Introduction

Was Dred Scott a free man or enslaved? This was the question that the United States Supreme Court, under the Taney Court, was tasked to answer when the case *Dred Scott v. John F. A. Sandford* was presented to them in 1857. Chief Justice Roger Taney's opinion became one of the most publicly and eloquently criticized opinions in the history of the US Supreme Court. When Taney died in 1864, Charles Sumner, a Republican, opposed the request to include a bust of the late Chief Justice in the hall, asserting that,

DOI: 10.4324/9781003021438-7

FIGURE 6.1 "Dred Scott"

"I declare that the opinion of the chief justice in the case of Dred Scott was more thoroughly abominable than anything of the kind in the history of courts. Judicial baseness reached its lowest point on that occasion."

Dred Scott was born into slavery in 1799. His enslaver, Peter Blow, owned an 860-acre farm in Southampton County, Virginia. Scott was still a teenager when Blow moved the family to Alabama, where they ran an unsuccessful farm. In 1830, Blow moved the family to Missouri, where he sold Scott to Dr. John Emerson. The physician, who had graduated with a medical degree from the University of Pennsylvania in 1824, had his sights set on a career in the army, which he was able to fulfill in 1832, and a year later he was assigned to Fort Armstrong, in Mississippi. Scott followed his enslaver.

Unhappy with the assignment, Emerson had to wait three more years until he was able to transfer to Fort Snelling, located in the Wisconsin Territory, part of the land that the United States had acquired from France with the Louisiana Purchase. Although Scott followed Emerson, slavery was prohibited in this territory, as it followed the terms of the Missouri Compromise. When in 1803 the United States acquired territories via the Louisiana Purchase, southern states wanted the newly assimilated territories to become slave states, while the northern states wanted them to be free states. To solve the dispute, in 1820 the United States Congress came to an agreement—the Missouri Compromise—which consisted of the clause that the newly formed state of Missouri was to be a slave state, while all the other territories north of the 36°30′ north parallel were to be free states.

It was while living at Fort Snelling that Dred Scott met Harriet Robinson, also enslaved as well. Her enslaver Major Lawrence Taliaferro was also a justice of the peace and he presided over the civil ceremony during which Scott and Robinson got married. Even though slave marriage was not recognized under the law, Scott and Robinson's marriage was official given that it had been performed in a free state. Soon after the civil ceremony, Taliaferro sold Robinson to Emerson, who decided, however, to lease out those enslaved to him in Fort Snelling when he moved to Missouri on army duty. By gaining profit from leasing out the labor of those he enslaved through leases in a free state, Emerson was going against the Missouri Compromise. In 1838, however, Emerson, who had then moved to Louisiana and married Eliza Sandford, called for Scott and his wife to go work for him again. While on their way to Louisiana, Harriet gave birth to their daughter, Eliza, on a boat on the Missouri River—between what would eventually become the state of Iowa and Illinois. Technically, Scott's daughter was born in free territory, which meant that she was born free and not into slavery, like her parents. Although Scott and his wife could have sued to gain their freedom as soon as they entered Louisiana, they chose not to and went back to work as slaves for Emerson and his wife, until Emerson died in 1843 and his wife inherited his properties, which included those enslaved to him.

In 1846, Scott tried to buy his freedom—as well as his family's freedom—but Emerson's widow refused. Although both Scott and his wife could read or write, they successfully sued Mrs. Emerson when, with the help of abolitionists, they filed legal action against her, claiming that not only she had beaten, bruised, and even imprisoned him for 12 hours, but that he and his family were free people held into slavery and they were seeking $10,000 in damages. The documents were filed to the Missouri state circuit court. Unfortunately, Scott lost the trial by a technicality—he had not proven that he had been enslaved by Emerson's wife. A judge granted Scott a new trial, in which the jury sided with Scott and his family. Emerson, however, didn't want to lose four enslaved people so she appealed the decision to the Missouri Supreme Court, while also transferring ownership of Scott and his family to her brother, John F. A. Sanford.

In 1852, the Missouri Supreme Court reversed the previous decision that had granted freedom to Scott and his family, and stated that they were still legally enslaved:

> Times are not now as they were when the former decisions on this subject were made. Since then not only individuals but States have been possessed with a dark and fell spirit in relation to slavery, whose gratification is sought in the pursuit of measures, whose inevitable consequences must be the overthrow and destruction of our government. Under such circumstances it does not behoove the State of Missouri to show the least countenance to any measure which might gratify this spirit. She is willing to assume her full responsibility for the existence of slavery within her limits, nor does she seek to share or divide it with others.

Scott and his family had been defeated yet again, but now the situation looked even more hopeless because the Blow family—Scott's first enslavers—who had been helping Scott financially with his legal fees during the trials, could no longer afford Scott's legal representation. Scott was hired as janitor in a legal office, which had agreed to take on the case pro bono and in 1853 sued Scott's current enslaver John Sanford. The court, however, sided with the decision of the Missouri Supreme Court, which led Scott to appeal his case to the United States Supreme Court.

The Court agreed to hear the case of *Dred Scott v. John F. A. Sandford* in 1856—the last name's correct spelling is Sanford, but due to a clerical error it was registered as Sandford. In a 7–2 vote, the Taney Court agreed with the decision of the Missouri Supreme Court. Chief Justice Taney began his opinion by addressing the main question presented to the Court:

> The question is simply this: Can a negro, whose ancestors were imported into this country, and sold as slaves, become a member of the political community formed and brought into existence by the Constitution of the United States, and as such become entitled to all of the rights, and privileges, and immunities, guarantied [sic] by that instrument to the citizen?

The Taney Court's answer was an astounding no, because

> [black people] are not included, and were not intended to be included, under the word "citizens" in the Constitution, and can therefore claim none of the rights and privileges which that instrument provides for and secures to citizens of the United States. On the contrary, they were at that time [of America's founding] considered as a subordinate and inferior class of beings who had been subjugated by the dominant race, and, whether emancipated or not, yet remained subject to their authority, and had no rights or privileges but such as those who held the power and the Government might choose to grant them.

Taney's decision went on to be publicly criticized by many, including an up-and-coming Republican in Illinois named Abraham Lincoln, who viewed this decision as a way

BOX 6.1 HISTORY OF THE FOURTEENTH AMENDMENT

The Fourteenth Amendment is one of three amendments—along with the Thirteenth and Fifteenth, —passed during the Reconstruction era (1865–1877), the historical period that followed the Civil War. The War had left the American people struggling to find answers to two of the most important questions of the time: How to reintegrate into the Union those states that seceded. And should African Americans—who had been previously enslaved and considered to be only three-fifths of a person after the Three/Fifths Compromise reached during the 1787 US Constitutional Convention—be granted citizenship?

President Andrew Johnson, who had succeeded President Abraham Lincoln after he was assassinated in 1865, opposed the passing of the Fourteenth Amendment, but both the House and the Senate vetoed his opposition—thanks to the Congressional elections of 1866, which had given Republicans majority of the Legislative Branch. Johnson, a Democratic senator from Tennessee and former enslaver had not been well received by northerners, who viewed him as too much of a southerner, especially when he supported the enactment of a series of laws aimed at limiting free labor ideology for African Americans. Known as black codes, these laws allowed former enslaved people to marry legally and own property but restricted the freedom of the African American population and, as a result, effectively kept them under the control of the White population. For example, in South Carolina, freed African Americans only had two job options—servant or farmer—unless they paid an annual tax that would cost between $10 to $100. Eventually, black codes turned into Jim Crow laws in the southern states—and it would take close to one hundred years for Jim Crow laws to be abolished by the 1964 Civil Rights Act.

With the Fourteenth Amendment, legislators aimed at ensuring citizenship for all people born or naturalized in the United States of America, thus going against Chief Justice Roger Taney who, in the *Dred Scott v. Sanford* Supreme Court case of 1857, decided—along with six other Justices—that Dred Scott, could not be recognized as an American citizen. The equal protection clause detailed in the Fourteenth Amendment, guaranteed that every American citizen was equally protected by laws—a clause that would come up often in civil rights cases, especially when state governments tried to discriminate against African Americans.

The Fourteenth Amendment also guaranteed protections to American citizens of their legal and civil rights against state infringement and expanded the due process—which was a clause in the Fifth Amendment—from just the federal government to each state. The clause of the due process, in particular, would later on be interpreted as a way to guarantee basic rights outlined in the Bill of Rights—such as free exercise of religion and freedom of speech. The Fourteenth Amendment repealed the three/fifth rule, thus appointing each citizen, regardless of their race, as a whole person. Male citizens aged 21 years and over were also granted the right to vote regardless of race—however, Jim Crow laws in southern states found ways to deny this right to African American men.

Since its ratification in 1868, the Fourteenth Amendment—and especially its equal protection clause and due process clause—has been referenced often in some of the most famous cases argued by the Supreme Court, including *Brown v. Board of Education of Topeka* (1954) that ended racial segregation in schools and *Obergefell v. Hodges* (2015), which ruled that the ban on same-sex marriage by state governments was unconstitutional.

for the Supreme Court to eventually legalize slavery in every state. A few months after the US Supreme Court had denied the Scott's family their right to freedom, their owner transferred them to Taylor Blow—son of Scott's former enslaver—who freed them from slavery by filing for manumission. Scott died of tuberculosis in 1858, only 18 months after finally gaining his freedom.

Dred Scott v. Sandford Decision

DRED SCOTT V. SANDFORD, 60 U.S. 393 (1856)

The case, as he himself states it, on the record brought here by his writ of error, is this:

> The plaintiff was a negro slave, belonging to Dr. Emerson, who was a surgeon in the army of the United States. In the year 1834, he took the plaintiff from the State of Missouri to the military post at Rock Island, in the State of Illinois, and held him there as a slave until the month of April or May, 1836. At the time last mentioned, said Dr. Emerson removed the plaintiff from said military post at Rock Island to the military post at Fort Snelling, situate on the west bank of the Mississippi river, in the Territory known as Upper Louisiana, acquired by the United States of France, and situate north of the latitude of thirty-six degrees thirty minutes north, and north of the State of Missouri. Said

> Dr. Emerson held the plaintiff in slavery at said Fort Snelling from said last-mentioned date until the year 1838.

In the year 1835, Harriet, who is named in the second count of the plaintiff's declaration, was the negro slave of Major Taliaferro, who belonged to the army of the United States. In that year, 1835, said Major Taliaferro took said Harriet to said Fort Snelling, a military post, situated as hereinbefore stated, and kept her there as a slave until the year 1836, and then sold and delivered her as a slave, at said Fort Snelling, unto the said Dr. Emerson hereinbefore named. Said Dr Emerson held said Harriet in slavery at said Fort Snelling until the year 1838.

In the year 1836, the plaintiff and Harriet intermarried, at Fort Snelling, with the consent of Dr. Emerson, who then claimed to be their master and owner. Eliza and Lizzie, named in the third count of the plaintiff's declaration, are the fruit of that marriage. Eliza is about fourteen years old, and was born on board the steamboat *Gipsey*, north of the north line of the State of Missouri, and upon the river Mississippi. Lizzie is about seven years old, and was born in the State of Missouri, at the military post called Jefferson Barracks.

In the year 1838, said Dr. Emerson removed the plaintiff and said Harriet and their said daughter Eliza from said Fort Snelling to the State of Missouri, where they have ever since resided.

Before the commencement of this suit, said Dr. Emerson sold and conveyed the plaintiff, and Harriet, Eliza, and Lizzie, to the defendant, as slaves, and the defendant has ever since claimed to hold them, and each of them, as slaves.

In considering this part of the controversy, two questions arise: 1. Was he, together with his family, free in Missouri by reason of the stay in the territory of the United States hereinbefore mentioned? And 2. If they were not, is Scott himself free by reason of his removal to Rock Island, in the State of Illinois, as stated in the above admissions?

We proceed to examine the first question.

The act of Congress upon which the plaintiff relies declares that slavery and involuntary servitude, except as a punishment for crime, shall be forever prohibited in all that part of the territory ceded by France, under the name of Louisiana, which lies north of thirty-six degrees thirty minutes north latitude, and not included within the limits of Missouri. And the difficulty which meets us at the threshold of this part of the inquiry is whether Congress was authorized to pass this law under any of the powers granted to it by the Constitution; for if the authority is not given by that instrument, it is the duty of this court to declare it void and inoperative, and incapable of conferring freedom upon anyone who is held as a slave under the have of anyone of the States.

The counsel for the plaintiff has laid much stress upon that article in the Constitution which confers on Congress the power "to dispose of and make all needful rules and regulations respecting the territory or other property belonging to the United States," but, in the judgment of the court, that provision has no bearing on the present controversy, and the power there given, whatever it may be, is confined, and was intended to be confined, to the territory which at that time belonged to, or was claimed by, the United States, and was within their boundaries as settled by the treaty with Great Britain, and can have no influence upon a territory afterwards acquired from a foreign Government. It was a special provision for a known and particular territory, and to meet a present emergency, and nothing more.

Whether, therefore, we take the particular clause in question, by itself, or in connection with the other provisions of the Constitution, we think it clear that it applies only to the particular territory of which we have spoken, and cannot, by any just rule of interpretation, be extended to territory which the new Government might afterwards obtain from a foreign nation. Consequently, the power which Congress may have lawfully exercised in this Territory, while it remained under a Territorial Government, and which may have been sanctioned by judicial decision, can furnish no justification and no argument to support a similar exercise of power over territory afterwards acquired by the Federal Government. We put aside, therefore, any argument, drawn from precedents, showing the extent of the power which the General Government exercised over slavery in this Territory, as altogether inapplicable to the case before us.

Thus it will be seen by these quotations from the opinion that the court, after stating the question it was about to decide in a manner too plain to be misunderstood, proceeded to decide it, and announced, as the opinion of the tribunal, that in organizing the judicial department of the Government in a Territory of the United States, Congress does not act under, and is not restricted by, the third article in the Constitution, and is not bound, in a Territory, to ordain and establish courts in which the judges hold their offices during good behaviour, but may exercise the discretionary power which a State exercises in establishing its judicial department and regulating the jurisdiction of its courts, and may authorize the Territorial Government to establish, or may itself establish, courts in which the judges hold their offices for a term of years only, and may vest in them judicial power upon subjects confided to the judiciary of the United States. And in doing this, Congress undoubtedly exercises the combined power of the General and a State Government. It exercises the discretionary power of a State Government in authorizing the establishment of a court in which the judges hold their appointments for a term of years only, and not during good behaviour, and it exercises the power of the General Government in investing that court with admiralty jurisdiction, over which the General Government had exclusive jurisdiction in the Territory.

Taking this rule to guide us, it may be safely assumed that citizens of the United States who migrate to a Territory belonging to the people of the United States cannot be ruled as mere colonists, dependent upon the will of the General Government and to be governed by any laws it may think proper to impose. The principle upon which our Governments rest and upon which alone they continue to exist, is the union of States, sovereign and independent within their own limits in their internal and domestic concerns, and bound together as one people by a General Government, possessing certain enumerated and restricted powers delegated to it by the people of the several States, and exercising supreme authority within the scope of the powers granted to it throughout the dominion of the United States. A power, therefore, in the General Government to obtain and hold colonies and dependent territories over which they might legislate without restriction would be inconsistent with its own existence in its present form. Whatever it acquires, it acquires for the benefit of the people of the several States who created it. It is their trustee acting for them, and charged with the duty of promoting the interests of the whole people of the Union in the exercise of the powers specifically granted.

At the time when the Territory in question was obtained by cession from France, it contained no population fit to be associated together and admitted as a State, and it therefore was absolutely necessary to hold possession of it, as a Territory belonging to the United States, until it was settled and inhabited by a civilized community capable of self-government, and in a condition to be admitted on equal terms with the other States as a member of the Union. But, as we have before said, it was acquired by the General Government as the representative and trustee of the people of the United States, and it must therefore be held in that character for their common and equal benefit, for it was the people of the several States, acting through their agent and representative, the Federal Government, who in fact acquired the Territory in question, and the Government holds it for their common use until it shall be associated with the other States as a member of the Union.

But, until that time arrives, it is undoubtedly necessary that some Government should be established in order to organize society and to protect the inhabitants in their persons and property, and as the people of the United States could act in this matter only through the Government which represented them and through which they spoke and acted when the Territory was obtained, it was not only within the scope of its powers, but it was its duty, to pass such laws and establish such a Government as would enable those by whose authority they acted to reap the advantages anticipated from its acquisition and to gather there a population which would enable it to assume the position to which it was destined among the States of the Union. The power to acquire necessarily carries with it the power to preserve and apply to the purposes for which it was acquired. The form of government to be established necessarily rested in the discretion of Congress. It was their duty to establish the one that would be best suited for the protection and security of the citizens of the United States and other inhabitants who might be authorized to take up their abode there, and that must always depend upon the existing condition of the Territory as to the number and character of its inhabitants and their situation in the Territory. In some cases, a Government consisting of persons appointed by the Federal Government would best subserve the interests of the Territory when the inhabitants were few and scattered, and new to one another. In other instances, it would be more advisable to commit the powers of self-government to the people who had settled in the Territory, as being the most competent to determine what was best for their own interests. But some form of civil authority would be absolutely necessary to organize and preserve civilized society and prepare it to become a State, and what is the best form must always depend on the condition of the Territory at the time, and the choice of the mode must depend upon the exercise of a discretionary power by Congress, acting within the scope of its constitutional authority, and not infringing upon the rights of person or rights of property of the citizen who might go there to reside, or for any other lawful purpose. It was acquired by the exercise of this discretion, and it must be held and governed in like manner until it is fitted to be a State.

But the power of Congress over the person or property of a citizen can never be a mere discretionary power under our Constitution and form of Government. The powers of the Government and the rights and privileges of the citizen are regulated and plainly defined by the Constitution itself. And when the Territory becomes a part of the United States, the Federal Government enters into possession in the character impressed upon it by those who created it. It enters upon it with its powers over the citizen strictly defined, and limited by the Constitution, from which it derives its own existence and by virtue of which alone it continues to exist and act as a Government and sovereignty. It has no power of any kind beyond it, and it cannot, when it enters a Territory of the United States, put off its character and assume discretionary or despotic powers which the Constitution has denied to it. It cannot create for itself a new character separated from the citizens of the United States and the duties it owes them under the provisions of the Constitution. The Territory being a part of the United States, the Government and the citizen both enter it under the authority of the Constitution, with their respective rights defined and marked out, and the Federal Government can exercise no power over his person or property beyond what that instrument confers, nor lawfully deny any right which it has reserved.

These powers, and others in relation to rights of person which it is not necessary here to enumerate, are, in express and positive terms, denied to the General Government, and the rights of private property have been guarded with equal care. Thus, the rights of property are united with the rights of person, and placed on the same ground by the Fifth Amendment to the Constitution, which provides that no person shall be deprived of life, liberty, and property, without due process of law. And an act of Congress which deprives a citizen of the United States of his liberty or property merely because he came himself or brought his property into a particular Territory of the United States, and who had committed no offence against the laws, could hardly be dignified with the name of due process of law.

But, in considering the question before us, it must be borne in mind that there is no law of nations standing between the people of the United States and their Government and interfering with their relation to each other. The powers of the Government and the rights of the citizen under it are positive and practical regulations plainly written down. The people of the United States have delegated to it certain enumerated powers and forbidden it to exercise others. It has no power over the person or property of a citizen but what the citizens of the United States have granted. And no laws or usages of other nations, or reasoning of statesmen or jurists upon the relations of master and slave, can enlarge the powers of the Government or take from the citizens the rights they have reserved. And if the Constitution recognizes the right of property of the master in a slave, and makes no distinction between that description of property and other property owned by a citizen, no tribunal, acting under the authority of the United States, whether it be legislative, executive, or judicial, has a right to draw such a distinction or deny to it the benefit of the provisions and guarantees which have been provided for the protection of private property against the encroachments of the Government.

Now, as we have already said in an earlier part of this opinion upon a different point, the right of property in a slave is distinctly and expressly affirmed in the Constitution. The right to traffic in it, like an ordinary article of merchandise and property, was guaranteed to the citizens of the United States in every State that might desire it for twenty years. And the Government in express terms is pledged to protect it in all future time if the slave escapes from his owner. This is done in plain words—too plain to be misunderstood. And no word can be found in the Constitution which gives Congress a greater power over slave property or which entitles property of that kind to less protection that property of any other description. The only power conferred is the power coupled with the duty of guarding and protecting the owner in his rights.

Upon these considerations, it is the opinion of the court that the act of Congress which prohibited a citizen from holding and owning property of this kind in the territory of the United States north of the line therein mentioned is not warranted by the Constitution, and is therefore void, and that neither Dred Scott himself nor any of his family were made free by being carried into this territory, even if they had been carried there by the owner with the intention of becoming a permanent resident.

We have so far examined the case, as it stands under the Constitution of the United States, and the powers thereby delegated to the Federal Government.

But there is another point in the case which depends on State power and State law. And it is contended, on the part of the plaintiff, that he is made free by being taken to Rock Island, in the State of Illinois, independently of his residence in the territory of the United States, and being so made free, he was not again reduced to a state of slavery by being brought back to Missouri.

Our notice of this part of the case will be very brief, for the principle on which it depends was decided in this court, upon much consideration, in the case of *Strader et al. v. Graham,* reported in 10th Howard 82. In that case, the slaves had been taken from Kentucky to Ohio, with the consent of the owner, and afterwards brought back to Kentucky. And this court held that their status or condition as free or slave depended upon the laws of Kentucky when they were brought back into that State, and not of Ohio, and that this court had no jurisdiction to revise the judgment of a State court upon its own laws. This was the point directly before the court, and the decision that this court had not jurisdiction turned upon it, as will be seen by the report of the case.

So in this case. As Scott was a slave when taken into the State of Illinois by his owner, and was there held as such, and brought back in that character, his status as free or slave depended on the laws of Missouri, and not of Illinois.

It has, however, been urged in the argument that, by the laws of Missouri, he was free on his return, and that this case therefore cannot be governed by the case of *Strader et al. v. Graham*, where it appeared, by the laws of Kentucky, that the plaintiffs continued to be slaves on their return from Ohio. But whatever doubts or opinions may at one time have been entertained upon this subject, we are satisfied, upon a careful examination of all the cases decided in the State courts of Missouri referred to, that it is now firmly settled by the decisions of the highest court in the State that Scott and his family upon their return were not free, but were, by the laws of Missouri, the property of the defendant, and that the Circuit Court of the United States had no jurisdiction when, by the laws of the State, the plaintiff was a slave and not a citizen.

Moreover, the plaintiff, it appears, brought a similar action against the defendant in the State court of Missouri, claiming the freedom of himself and his family upon the same grounds and the same evidence upon which he relies in the case before the court. The case was carried before the Supreme Court of the State, was fully argued there, and that court decided that neither the plaintiff nor his family were entitled to freedom, and were still the slaves of the defendant, and reversed the judgment of the inferior State court, which had given a different decision. If the plaintiff supposed that this judgment of the Supreme Court of the State was erroneous, and that this court had jurisdiction to revise and reverse it, the only mode by which he could legally bring it before this court was by writ of error directed to the Supreme Court of the State, requiring it to transmit the record to this court. If this had been done, it is too plain for argument that the writ must have been dismissed for want of jurisdiction in this court. The case of *Strader and others v. Graham* is directly in point, and, indeed, independent of any decision, the language of the 25th section of the act of 1789 is too clear and precise to admit of controversy.

But the plaintiff did not pursue the mode prescribed by law for bringing the judgment of a State court before this court for revision, but suffered the case to be remanded to the inferior State court, where it is still continued, and is, by agreement of parties, to await the judgment of this court on the point. All of this appears on the record before us, and by the printed report of the case.

And while the case is yet open and pending in the inferior State court, the plaintiff goes into the Circuit Court of the United States, upon the same case and the same evidence and against the same party, and proceeds to judgment, and then brings here the same case from the Circuit Court, which the law would not have permitted him to bring directly from the State court. And if this court takes jurisdiction in this form, the result, so far as the rights of the respective parties are concerned, is in every respect substantially the same as if it had, in open violation of law, entertained jurisdiction over the judgment of the State court upon a writ of error, and revised and reversed its judgment upon the ground that its opinion upon the question of law was erroneous. It would ill become this court to sanction such an attempt to evade the law, or to exercise an appellate power in this circuitous way which it is forbidden to exercise in the direct and regular and invariable forms of judicial proceedings.

Upon the whole, therefore, it is the judgment of this court that it appears by the record before us that the plaintiff in error is not a citizen of Missouri in the sense in which that word is used in the Constitution, and that the Circuit Court of the United States, for that reason, had no jurisdiction in the case, and could give no judgment in it. Its judgment for the defendant must, consequently, be reversed, and a mandate issued directing the suit to be dismissed for want of jurisdiction.

Dred Scott vs. Sandford

Impact on the Institution of Politics and Government

Dred Scott v. Sandford, which some have argued was among the worst decisions ever rendered by the Supreme Court since its establishment, had a major impact on the trajectory of US politics and history itself. By invalidating the Missouri Compromise, opening new US territories to the possibility of having slavery, and declaring that Blacks could *never* be citizens, it added fire to the anti-slavery movement, and the divide between northern "Free" states and southern slaveholding states. The case inspired Abraham Lincoln to run for Senate, and is seen as one of the precipitating factors for southern secession and the Civil War (Blight, 2008). Here, we will not concentrate on the specifics of historical events that transpired and their linkage to the decision. Rather, we show how the sociological institutions of politics and government were broadly affected, particularly in regard to race and citizenship rights, the central concerns of *Scott v. Sandford*.

Race, Power, and Citizenship

If we consider that **politics** from a sociological perspective refers to power relations among people at the governmental level and interpersonal level (Conley, 2013), *Scott v. Sandford* affected this institution in multiple ways. Most profoundly, it attempted to, even in a time when slavery was legal in many states, further entrench **power** in the United States in the hands of White slaveowners, while disempowering Black enslaved people and freemen. Sociologist Max Weber defines power as "the probability that a command with a given specific content will be obeyed by a given group of people," including through **coercion** and force. Certainly, as we read in the text of the decision, stripping Black people of the ability to become citizens of the US federal government, avowing their inferiority *vis-à vis* Whites, and classifying them as property created the conditions that would allow for complete **domination.** The decision gave the force of the nation's highest court to a highly rigid hierarchy on the basis of **race,** placing Black people on the bottom of the social order (Austin, 2004). While racial definitions and categories are historically contingent and culturally situated, meaning they are not fixed and vary according to time and place, **race** refers to a group of people who share a set of characteristics—typically, but not always physical ones—and are said to share a common bloodline. In the case of *Scott v. Sandford*, the decision referred to Dred Scott's "being a negro of African descent, whose ancestors were of pure African blood," as a reason for establishing his inability to be a citizen of the US, and thus also unable to bring suit. This demonstrated the prevalent **racism** in place that allowed for slavery's existence: a belief that separate races possess different and unequal traits (Conley, 2013). Chief Justice Taney and his contemporaries considered dark-skinned people (and women) to be inferior to White males, but in this case singled out Black people for the specific exclusion from the right to citizenship (Austin, 2004)

Citizenship is a "legal relationship in which purportedly free individuals give allegiance to a sovereign community in exchange for the protection of a shifting bundle of rights" (Allen, 2004, p. 230). It is of the utmost importance in terms of the rights it confers upon individuals in a nation-state. By excluding Blacks from ever obtaining citizenship, the Court dealt a blow to the political power of Blacks in the US, their ability to be incorporated at any level into the government, their civil and human rights. Citizenship was equated with Whiteness, thus solidifying a racist conception of the polity of the United States which barred Blacks (but not necessarily other groups like Native Americans or Mexicans, although citizenship challenges existed for these groups as well) forever from civic belonging and from legal recourse in the courtroom (Pelmas, 1998). Legal effects of the ruling were indeed dramatic. Blacks who had earned their freedom and/or were residing in non-slave states were no longer citizens of the United States. "This aspect was applied in criminal and civil cases as well as having other legal applications in both the North and the South." For example, a free Black man who applied for a passport to travel abroad for business was denied in 1857 because only citizens were eligible for passports.

Black people, according to *Scott v. Sandford* were not legally "people," but chattel, property. Such **ideology,** that is, systems of ideas, which posits Whites as superior to other racial groups is **White supremacy**. Chief Justice Taney dedicated a full 24 pages in the decision to the question of black citizenship, referring 21 times within that text to so-called White superiority compared to Blacks, and citing allegedly widespread public opinion that supported his claims. As Michelle Alexander describes in her book *The New Jim Crow,*

> White supremacy, over time, became a religion of sorts. Faith in the idea that the people of the African race were bestial . . . justified an economic and political system in which plantation owners acquired land and great wealth through brutality, torture, and coercion of other human beings.
>
> *(Alexander, 2010, p. 26)*

Blacks' status as enslaved people devoid of rights positioned them as **subalterns**: individuals or groups of individuals that are excluded from the dominant, **hegemonic** power structure.

The *Scott v. Sandford* decision and the kind of racist thinking that excluded and discriminated against Blacks in the United States did not end with the death of slavery following the Civil War and the ratification of the Thirteenth Amendment in 1865.

> The Dred Scott decision would still continue to play a role in American politics and society long after it was supposed to have been made ineffective by the Thirteenth, Fourteenth, and Fifteenth Amendments. It remains a factor in American politics and society. Although by law Blacks were free citizens of the United States, they [are] still repressed and treated as inferior to Whites in American society.

One way in which the legacy of *Scott v. Sandford* can be seen in the current moment is in the criminal justice system, part of the institution of government.

The Criminal Justice System, Slavery, and Disenfranchisement

The Thirteenth and Fourteenth Amendments overturned parts of the *Dred Scott* ruling by ending slavery. However, there was one exception to the ban on slavery in the Thirteenth Amendment's Punishment Clause, which allowed for citizens to be enslaved as a punishment for crime. There was objection to the inclusion of this clause by slavery abolitionists, who wanted to use "involuntary servitude" rather than "slavery" in the punishment clause. However, a former slave-owner co-authored the draft which ultimately was adopted (Goodwin, 2019). Slavery, not involuntary servitude, was associated almost exclusively with Blacks in the United States, and so the language used in the Amendment carried symbolic and social significance.

Slavery's continued existence in the Thirteenth Amendment entailed the use of the criminal justice system, which includes law enforcement, the court system, and corrections system. Even before the end of the Civil War and emancipation of slaves, slavery and the criminal justice system had not been independent of each other. For example, enslavers could send Blacks to prisons for correction (Goodwin, 2019). "A legally sanctioned law enforcement system existed in America before the Civil War for the express purpose of controlling the slave population and protecting the interests of slave owners" (Turner, Giacopassi, & Vandiver, 2006). The origins of modern police can be found in the slave patrols that assisted enslavers and attempted to control the Black population, further evidence of the enmeshment of criminal justice with slavery. In a kind of cruel paradox, furthermore, even though Blacks were deprived of civil and legal rights as "property," they were still considered people for the purpose of being punished under criminal law (Pelmas, 1998).

The *Scott v. Sandford* decision meant Blacks were incapable of relying on the law for recourse. It also meant that there were two separate systems of "justice," and laws according to whether one was black or not. The racist beliefs espoused in the ruling embedded and institutionalized discriminatory practices that have endured in different forms to the current moment in the criminal justice system. Michelle Alexander in her book *The New Jim Crow* (2010) and other scholars have argued that we can find the persistence of the racist ideology and practices linked to slavery through the punishment clause and the criminal justice system broadly. In essence, one form of slavery and rigid race-based **caste** system was ruled unconstitutional, and so another (penal slavery) was adopted instead, as southern Whites feared losing control over millions of former slaves and therefore their power in the country at large—a concern Chief Justice Taney had expressed in the *Scott v. Sandford* opinion.

There is evidence of this dynamic, as after the adoption of the Thirteenth Amendment, the Punishment clause was used to "systematically criminalize and incarcerate Blacks" (Goodwin, 2019). So-called Black Codes and Penal Codes were passed through a political process in which Blacks had no power. They were enacted with the purpose of keeping control over the Black population (Alexander, 2010, p. 28). These far-ranging Black Codes offered only limited legal freedoms (such as the right to marry and own property) but criminalized far more behavior. They made it a punishable crime for free Blacks to congregate in "disorderly" fashion. Blacks under these codes couldn't vote, bring law suits against rights, or possess weapons. Penalties were excessive, and if they couldn't pay, they were hired out to work in the plantations where they may have been previously enslaved. Prisons engaged in a "convict leasing" system which lasted into the 20th century, the majority—90 percent—of whom were Black (Goodwin, 2019; Robinson, 2019).

Convict leasing and laws specifying differential treatment of Blacks and Whites have been abandoned for decades (in the case of **Jim Crow** laws, segregation, and laws against miscegenation, as we saw in *Brown v. Board of Ed* and *Loving v. Virginia* in this book, the Supreme Court would play a role in that dismantlement). The *Scott v. Sandford* decision's ideological underpinnings have proven harder to expel. **Institutional racism**—institutions and dynamics that might seem race-neutral but actually disadvantage minority groups (Conley, 2013, p. 365), persists in the institution of politics and government in the United States. We can trace the origin points back to the social order that made racist thinking normative, and decisions like *Scott v. Sandford*. For example, in the criminal justice system today, sentencing laws for drug offenses have seen huge racial disparities that on the surface may not appear discriminatory. The Anti-Drug Abuse Act of 1986 decreed that possession of 1 gram of crack cocaine was equal to 100 grams of powdered cocaine. However, because crack cocaine was more inexpensive and found in urban Black communities this led to Black people serving much more time for crack, a drug pharmacologically the same as cocaine. Fear of losing power and control has also led to Blacks being more heavily surveilled through invasive policing practices.

Citizenship and Disenfranchisement Through the Criminal Justice System

There is a strong link between citizenship, **enfranchisement** (the ability to vote), and political influence. (Of course, that link is not a perfect one: women citizens of the United States were barred from the vote until 1920, and citizens who are children also cannot vote.) "Casting a vote is demonstrative of the power an individual has," Bassett writes (2011). The denial of citizenship and its accompanying basket of rights and privileges to even free Blacks on the basis of the

Scott decision kept power concentrated in the hands of Whites as Blacks not only did not have the ability to vote but also to run for office. *Dred Scott v. Sandford's* hindering of black people from voting did not stop, however, with the Fifteenth Amendment, which states: "The right of citizens of the United States to vote shall not be denied or abridged by the United States or by any State on account of race, color, or previous condition of servitude." Poll taxes that charged people to be able to vote and literacy tests disproportionately kept Blacks from voting. The criminal justice system also functions to continue to disproportionately keep Black citizens from political power.

The punishment clause of the ThirteenthAmendment described earlier, which made it possible to enslave those who are incarcerated, also led to the systematic and disproportionate deprivation of the right to vote among Black people. Prior to the Civil War, enfranchisement was not linked to having a conviction. But between 1865 and 1880, a third of the US enacted felony disenfranchisement laws with the explicitly stated purpose of suppressing Black political power (Robinson, 2019). Incarceration or having a record, depending on which state one lives in, can mean that one can be barred from voting for life. In 2020, only incarcerated people in Maine and New Hampshire can vote. In Iowa, Kentucky, and Virginia, a felony record leads to permanent disenfranchisement. Blacks are overrepresented in jails and prisons, with Black males sentenced to prison at twice the rate of Hispanics and six times that of White males (DOJ, 2019). These percentages have a large impact on the institution of politics and government in the US. In the present day, 1 in 13 Black people of voting age does not have the right to vote on the basis of either current or prior incarceration. This means that over 7 percent of Blacks do not have the right to vote. This percentage is notably high among former slave-holding states: for example, in Kentucky, the percentage is 26 percent, in Tennessee, 21 percent, and in Virginia, 22 percent. This is over four times higher than disenfranchisement rates among the other racial groups that reside in the United States (Uggen, Larson, & Shannon, 2016).

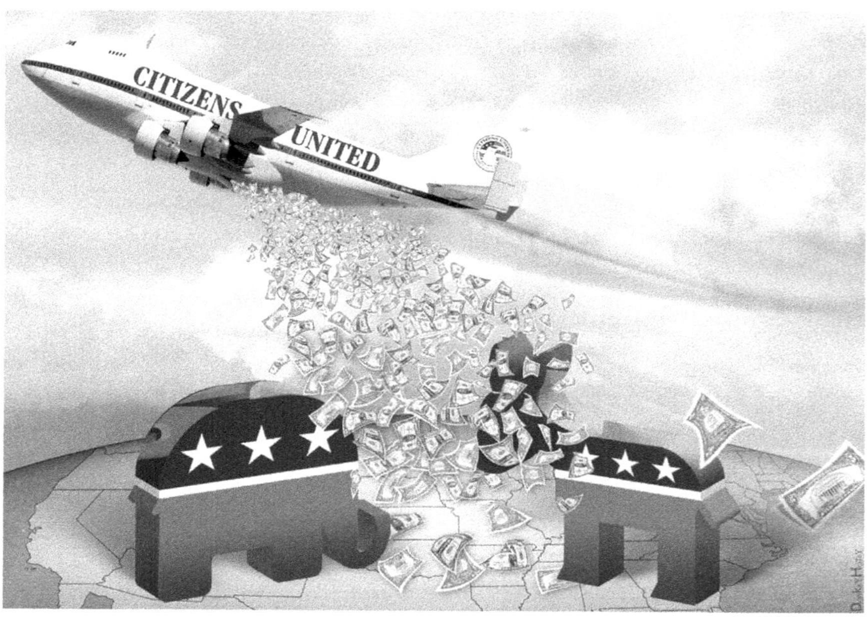

FIGURE 6.2 "CITIZENS UNITED CARPET BOMBING DEMOCRACY"

Citizens United v. Federal Election Commission Introduction

"Last week the Supreme Court reversed a century of law that I believe will open the floodgates for special interests—including foreign corporations—to spend without limit in our elections. I don't think American elections should be bankrolled by America's most powerful interests, or worse, by foreign entities. They should be decided by the American people. And I'd urge Democrats and Republicans to pass a bill that helps to correct some of these problems."

President Barack Obama made this statement during his first State of the Union address in January 2010, referring to the recent decision made by the United States Supreme Court in the *Citizens United v. Federal Election Commission* case. Justice Samuel A. Alito Jr. was in attendance and when he heard President Obama's comment, he broke decorum by shaking his head and visibly mouthing the words "not true." The decision Obama was referring to related to a case that saw its beginning two years prior—in 2008.

Citizens United is a conservative non-profit organization founded in 1988. Its mission is to restore "our government to citizens' control. Through a combination of education, advocacy, and grassroots organization" that "seek to reassert the traditional American values of limited government, freedom of enterprise, strong families, and national sovereignty and security." Before the Democratic presidential primary elections—whose nominees were Senator Barack Obama of Illinois and Senator Hillary Clinton of New York—the organization wanted to release a documentary through a video-on-demand option available to subscribers of cable television, as well as air advertisements in three televised commercials. The documentary, titled *Hillary: The Movie*, was a highly critical representation of the Democratic presidential candidate.

With commentary by Ann Coulter, who called her a liar, Dick Morris, who stated "she's the closest thing we have in America to a European socialist," and then-Senator Barack Obama who stated, "Hillary Clinton is claiming basically the entire eight years of the Clinton Presidency as her own, except for the stuff that didn't work out, in which case she says she has nothing to do with it," Hillary Clinton was presented as a vindictive, ruthless, and highly incompetent for the responsibilities and duties that the president of the United States of America would be called to uphold. A deep look into her life as first lady during her husband Bill Clinton's presidential term (1993–2001), the documentary conveys a life plagued by scandal and controversy. When paired with the documentary's representation of the Senator of New York as a potential presidential candidate, the version that mainly comes across is of a power-hungry woman who often goes back on statements she's made through the years. As a result, the documentary successfully fulfils its main goal of diminishing the authority and legitimacy of Hillary Clinton as a potential commander-in-chief.

While the documentary had been completed and edited by the end of 2007, it was not going to air until beginning of 2008. Since it was going to be released shortly before the primaries and it would be classified as electioneering communication, the Citizens United documentary violated the Bipartisan Campaign Reform Act (BCRA) of 2002, a legislation signed into federal law by President Richard Nixon in 1972.

The BRCA, which amended the Federal Election Commission (FEC), regulated spending and fundraising for political campaign purposes and applied restrictions to "an electioneering communication," which "is any broadcast, cable or satellite communication that refers to a clearly identified federal candidate, is publicly distributed within 30 days of a primary or 60 days of a general election and is targeted to the relevant electorate." Also known as the

McCain–Feingold Act, a name given after Senator John McCain and Russell Feingold were successful in reforming the way money was raised during political campaigns, the BRCA restricted or banned altogether soft money donations by unions, corporations, and also wealthy individuals, as long as they were made directly to specific political parties or solicited by elected officials.

The Act had already been at the center of another case presented to the US Supreme Court when in 2003, Mitch McConnell, Senator of Kentucky and lead plaintiff of the *McConnell v. Federal Election Commission* case, pointed at the BRCA as unconstitutional for going against the First Amendment. However, in a 5–4 majority, the Supreme Court upheld the key provisions of the McCain–Feingold Act.

The producers of *Hillary: The Movie* decided to file a case with the United States District Court of the District of Columbia, in the hopes of receiving permission to air the documentary, even though it went against the BRCA and, as a result, it was classified as "electioneering communication." Citizens United argued that since "Section 203 of the BCRA prevents corporations or labor unions from funding such communication from their general treasuries," it went against the First Amendment of the United States Constitution and, as a result, it violated their rights. Moreover, the non-profit organization argued that since "Sections 201 and 311 require the disclosure of donors to such communication and a disclaimer when the communication is not authorized by the candidate it intends to support"; this too is unconstitutional when applied to the documentary.

The three-judge court, however, found that the documentary was indeed electioneering communication because there was "no reasonable interpretation [of the movie] other than as an appeal to vote against Senator Clinton."

Since the BRCA dictated that constitutional appeals from the District of Columbia had to immediately be presented to the United States Supreme Court—thus bypassing the common federal judicial process—the producers decided to quickly proceed by presenting the case *Citizens United v. Federal Election Commission* to the Court, which heard the case in March, 2009.

In January 2010, 5 out of 4 Supreme Court Justices of the Roberts Court found that the BRCA indeed was unconstitutional and violated the First Amendment, thus reversing part of the *McConnell v. FED* case of 2003. According to Justice Anthony Kennedy, who wrote the majority opinion, freedom of speech, especially in a political situation, is pivotal to a democracy and that *Hillary: The Movie* simply revealed information warranted by "government interest" in providing the "electorate with information" regarding election-related financial resources.

Justice Paul Stevens wrote the dissenting opinion, in which he states that,

> the Court's opinion is thus a rejection of the common sense of the American people, who have recognized a need to prevent corporations from undermining self-government since the founding, and who have fought against the distinctive corrupting potential of corporate electioneering since the days of Theodore Roosevelt. . . . While American democracy is imperfect, few outside the majority of this Court would have thought its flaws included a dearth of corporate money in politics.

During the presidential elections of 2016, people questioned if this decision had opened the doors for Russia to influence the election results that titled Donald Trump the 45th President of the United States of America.

Citizen United v. Federal Election Commission Decision

CITIZEN UNITED V. FEDERAL ELECTION COMMISSION, 558 U. S. (2010)

Justice Kennedy delivered the opinion of the Court.

Federal law prohibits corporations and unions from using their general treasury funds to make independent expenditures for speech defined as an "electioneering communication" or for speech expressly advocating the election or defeat of a candidate. 2 U. S. C. §441b. Limits on electioneering communications were upheld in *McConnell v. Federal Election Comm'n*, 540 U. S. 93, 203–209 (2003). The holding of *McConnell* rested to a large extent on an earlier case, *Austin v. Michigan Chamber of Commerce*, 494 U. S. 652 (1990). Austin had held that political speech may be banned based on the speaker's corporate identity.

The Government may regulate corporate political speech through disclaimer and disclosure requirements, but it may not suppress that speech altogether. We turn to the case now before us.

I

A

Citizens United is a non-profit corporation. It brought this action in the United States District Court for the District of Columbia. A three-judge court later convened to hear the cause. The resulting judgment gives rise to this appeal.

Citizens United has an annual budget of about $12 million. Most of its funds are from donations by individuals; but, in addition, it accepts a small portion of its funds from for-profit corporations.

In January 2008, Citizens United released a film entitled *Hillary: The Movie*. We refer to the film as *Hillary*. It is a 90-minute documentary about then-Senator Hillary Clinton, who was a candidate in the Democratic Party's 2008 Presidential primary elections. *Hillary* mentions Senator Clinton by name and depicts interviews with political commentators and other persons, most of them quite critical of Senator Clinton. *Hillary* was released in theaters and on DVD, but Citizens United wanted to increase distribution by making it available through video-on-demand.

Video-on-demand allows digital cable subscribers to select programming from various menus, including movies, television shows, sports, news, and music. The viewer can watch the program at any time and can elect to rewind or pause the program. In December 2007, a cable company offered, for a payment of $1.2 million, to make *Hillary* available on a video-on-demand channel called "Elections'08." App. 255a–257a. Some video-on-demand services require viewers to pay a small fee to view a selected program, but here the proposal was to make *Hillary* available to viewers free of charge.

To implement the proposal, Citizens United was prepared to pay for the video-on-demand; and to promote the film, it produced two 10-second ads and one 30-second ad for *Hillary*. Each ad includes a short (and, in our view, pejorative) statement about Senator Clinton, followed by the name of the movie and the movie's Website address. Id., at 26a–27a. Citizens United desired to promote the video-on-demand offering by running advertisements on broadcast and cable television.

B

Before the Bipartisan Campaign Reform Act of 2002 (BCRA), federal law prohibited—and still does prohibit—corporations and unions from using general treasury funds to make direct contributions to candidates or independent expenditures that expressly advocate the election or defeat of a candidate, through any form of media, in connection with certain qualified federal elections. An electioneering communication is defined as "any broadcast, cable, or satellite communication" that "refers to a clearly identified candidate for Federal office" and is made within 30 days of a primary or 60 days of a general election. The Federal Election Commission's (FEC) regulations further define an electioneering communication as a communication that is "publicly distributed." "In the case of a candidate for nomination for President . . . publicly distributed means" that the communication "[c]an be received by 50,000 or more persons in a State where a primary election . . . is being held within 30 days." Corporations and unions are barred from using their general treasury funds for express advocacy or electioneering communications. They may establish, however, a "separate segregated fund" (known as a political action committee, or PAC) for these purposes. The moneys received by the segregated fund are limited to donations from stockholders and employees of the corporation or, in the case of unions, members of the union. Ibid.

C

Citizens United wanted to make *Hillary* available through video-on-demand within 30 days of the 2008 primary elections. It feared, however, that both the film and the ads would be covered by §441b's ban on corporate-funded independent expenditures, thus subjecting the corporation to civil and criminal penalties. In December 2007, Citizens United sought declaratory and injunctive relief against the FEC. It argued that (1) §441b is unconstitutional as applied to *Hillary*; and (2) are unconstitutional as applied to *Hillary* and to the three ads for the movie.

The court held that §441b was facially constitutional and that §441b was constitutional as applied to *Hillary* because it was "susceptible of no other interpretation than to inform the electorate that Senator Clinton is unfit for office, that the United States would be a dangerous place in a President Hillary Clinton world, and that viewers should vote against her." The court also rejected Citizens United's challenge to BCRA's disclaimer and disclosure requirements. It noted that "the Supreme Court has written approvingly of disclosure provisions triggered by political speech even though the speech itself was constitutionally protected under the First Amendment." Id., at 281.

We noted probable jurisdiction. The case was reargued in this Court after the Court asked the parties to file supplemental briefs addressing.

III

The First Amendment provides that "Congress shall make no law . . . abridging the freedom of speech." Laws enacted to control or suppress speech may operate at different points in the speech process. The following are just a few examples of restrictions that have been attempted at different stages of the speech process—all laws found to be invalid: restrictions requiring a permit at the outset, *Watchtower Bible & Tract Soc. of N. Y., Inc. v. Village of Stratton*, 536 U. S. 150, 153 (2002); imposing a burden by impounding proceeds on receipts or royalties, *Simon & Schuster, Inc. v. Members of N. Y. State Crime Victims Bd.*, 502 U. S. 105, 108, 123 (1991); seeking to exact a cost after the speech occurs, *New York Times Co. v. Sullivan*, 376 U. S., at 267; and subjecting the speaker to criminal penalties, *Brandenburg v. Ohio*, 395 U. S. 444, 445 (1969) (per curiam).

The law before us is an outright ban, backed by criminal sanctions. Section 441b makes it a felony for all corporations—including non-profit advocacy corporations—either to expressly advocate the election or defeat of candidates or to broadcast electioneering communications within 30 days of a primary election and 60 days of a general election. Thus, the following acts would all be felonies under §441b: The Sierra Club runs an ad, within the crucial phase of 60 days before the general election, that exhorts the public to disapprove of a Congressman who favors logging in national forests; the National Rifle Association publishes a book urging the public to vote for the challenger because the incumbent U. S. Senator supports a handgun ban; and the American Civil Liberties Union creates a Web site telling the public to vote for a Presidential candidate in light of that candidate's defense of free speech. These prohibitions are classic examples of censorship.

Section 441b is a ban on corporate speech notwithstanding the fact that a PAC created by a corporation can still speak. See *McConnell*, 540 U. S., at 330–333 (opinion of Kennedy, J.). A PAC is a separate association from the corporation. So the PAC exemption from §441b's expenditure ban, §441b(b)(2), does not allow corporations to speak. Even if a PAC could somehow allow a corporation to speak—and it does not—the option to form PACs does not alleviate the First Amendment problems with §441b. PACs are burdensome alternatives; they are expensive to administer and subject to extensive regulations. For example, every PAC must appoint a treasurer, forward donations to the treasurer promptly, keep detailed records of the identities of the persons making donations, preserve receipts for three years, and file an organization statement and report changes to this information within 10 days.

And that is just the beginning. PACs must file detailed monthly reports with the FEC, which are due at different times depending on the type of election that is about to occur:

> (Government could repress speech by "attacking all levels of the production and dissemination of ideas," for "effective public communication requires the speaker to make use of the services of others"). If §441b applied to individuals, no one would believe that it is merely a time, place, or manner restriction on speech. Its purpose and effect are to silence entities whose voices the Government deems to be suspect.

Speech is an essential mechanism of democracy, for it is the means to hold officials accountable to the people. See Buckley, supra, at 14–15 ("In a republic where the people are sovereign, the ability of the citizenry to make informed choices among candidates for office is essential"). The right of citizens to inquire, to hear, to speak, and to use information to reach consensus is a precondition to enlightened self-government and a necessary means to protect it. The First Amendment "'has its fullest and most urgent application' to speech uttered during a campaign for political office."

For these reasons, political speech must prevail against laws that would suppress it, whether by design or inadvertence. Laws that burden political speech are "subject to strict scrutiny," which requires the Government to prove that the restriction "furthers a compelling interest and is narrowly tailored to achieve that interest."

Premised on mistrust of governmental power, the First Amendment stands against attempts to disfavor certain subjects or viewpoints. Prohibited, too, are restrictions distinguishing among different speakers, allowing speech by some but not others. As instruments to censor, these categories are interrelated: Speech restrictions based on the identity of the speaker are all too often simply a means to control content.

Quite apart from the purpose or effect of regulating content, moreover, the Government may commit a constitutional wrong when by law it identifies certain preferred speakers. By taking the right to speak from some and giving it to others, the Government deprives the disadvantaged person or class of the right to use speech to strive to establish worth, standing, and respect for the speaker's voice. The Government may not by these means deprive the public of the right and privilege to determine for itself what speech and speakers are worthy of consideration. The First Amendment protects speech and speaker, and the ideas that flow from each.

The Court has upheld a narrow class of speech restrictions that operate to the disadvantage of certain persons, but these rulings were based on an interest in allowing governmental entities to perform their functions. The corporate independent expenditures at issue in this case, however, would not interfere with governmental functions, so these cases are inapposite. These precedents stand only for the proposition that there are certain governmental functions that cannot operate without some restrictions on particular kinds of speech. By contrast, it is inherent in the nature of the political process that voters must be free to obtain information from diverse sources in order to determine how to cast their votes. At least before Austin, the Court had not allowed the exclusion of a class of speakers from the general public dialogue.

We find no basis for the proposition that, in the context of political speech, the Government may impose restrictions on certain disfavored speakers. Both history and logic lead us to this conclusion.

A

1

The Court has recognized that First Amendment protection extends to corporations.

This protection has been extended by explicit holdings to the context of political speech.

At least since the latter part of the 19th century, the laws of some States and of the United States imposed a ban on corporate direct contributions to candidates.

For almost three decades thereafter, the Court did not reach the question whether restrictions on corporate and union expenditures are constitutional.

If the First Amendment has any force, it prohibits Congress from fining or jailing citizens, or associations of citizens, for simply engaging in political speech. If the antidistortion rationale were to be accepted, however, it would permit Government to ban political speech simply because the speaker is an association that has taken on the corporate form.

Political speech is "indispensable to decisionmaking in a democracy, and this is no less true because the speech comes from a corporation rather than an individual."

It is irrelevant for purposes of the First Amendment that corporate funds may "have little or no correlation to the public's support for the corporation's political ideas." All speakers, including individuals and the media, use money amassed from the economic marketplace to fund their speech. The First Amendment protects the resulting speech, even if it was enabled by economic transactions with persons or entities who disagree with the speaker's ideas.

Rapid changes in technology—and the creative dynamic inherent in the concept of free expression—counsel against upholding a law that restricts political speech in certain media or by certain speakers. Today, 30-second television ads may be the most effective way to convey a political message.

V

When word concerning the plot of the movie *Mr. Smith Goes to Washington* reached the circles of Government, some officials sought, by persuasion, to discourage its distribution. See Smoodin, "Compulsory" Viewing for Every Citizen: Mr. Smith and the Rhetoric of Reception, 35 Cinema Journal 3, 19, and n. 52 (Winter 1996) (citing Mr. Smith Riles Washington, Time, October 30, 1939, p. 49); Nugent, Capra's Capitol Offense, N. Y. Times, October 29, 1939, p. X5. Under Austin, though, officials could have done more than discourage its distribution—they could have banned the film. After all, it, like *Hillary*, was speech funded by a corporation that was critical of Members of Congress. *Mr. Smith Goes to Washington* may be fiction and caricature; but fiction and caricature can be a powerful force.

Modern day movies, television comedies, or skits on YouTube.com might portray public officials or public policies in unflattering ways. Yet if a covered transmission during the blackout period creates the background for candidate endorsement or opposition, a felony occurs solely because a corporation, other than an exempt media corporation, has made the "purchase, payment, distribution, loan, advance, deposit, or gift of money or anything of value" in order to engage in political speech. 2 U. S. C. §431(9)(A)(i). Speech would be suppressed in the realm where its necessity is most evident: in the public dialogue preceding a real election.

Governments are often hostile to speech, but under our law and our tradition it seems stranger than fiction for our Government to make this political speech a crime. Yet this is the statute's purpose and design.

Some members of the public might consider *Hillary* to be insightful and instructive; some might find it to be neither high art nor a fair discussion on how to set the Nation's course; still others simply might suspend judgment on these points but decide to think more about issues and candidates. Those choices and assessments, however, are not for the Government to make.

> The First Amendment underwrites the freedom to experiment and to create in the realm of thought and speech. Citizens must be free to use new forms, and new forums, for the expression of ideas. The civic discourse belongs to the people, and the Government may not prescribe the means used to conduct it.
>
> *McConnell, supra, at 341 (opinion of Kennedy, J.)*

The judgment of the District Court is reversed with respect to the constitutionality of 2 U. S. C. §441b's restrictions on corporate independent expenditures. The judgment is affirmed with respect to BCRA's disclaimer and disclosure requirements. The case is remanded for further proceedings consistent with this opinion.

It is so ordered.

The Influence of *Citizens United v. FEC* on the Institution of Politics and Government in the United States

The institution of politics is that which structures how power is gained and exercised by individuals, governments, and other social groups/actors. In Chapter 2, we described how beyond individual citizens' votes and ability to run for office, other legal routes of obtaining political power in the United States include forming interest groups or organizations that can mobilize around an issue, get out the vote, **lobby**, or protest. *Citizens United v. FEC* gave corporations, unions, and individuals the right to give "voice" to their political preferences via unlimited independent expenditures. An independent expenditure is money donated "for a communication that expressly advocates the election or defeat of a clearly identified candidate and which is not made in coordination with any candidate, [their] authorized committees or agents, or a political party committee or its agents" (FEC, 2020). For example, a pharmaceutical company may give a million dollars to a Super PAC (which we will explain later), to run ads advocating for Candidate A, who is against affordable drug pricing. How did this actually affect the dynamic of power in the United States? Here we look at the impact of the landmark decision on the **power** of individuals and groups to have their interests represented and policies benefiting them enacted in **government.** Because the government has the authority to regulate our lives and, as sociologist Max Weber noted, has a monopoly on the use of force, this is of immense importance.

American Attitudes on Money and Politics Post Citizens United

Citizens United and its effects on campaign financing cannot be said to have been the sole factor in the outsized role money plays in politics in the United States, nor the attitudes Americans have about that role. However, the case has received wide attention and, coupled with the ability of more wealthy and powerful individuals and organizations to directly lobby politicians, has impacted Americans' attitudes about the fairness of the electoral process. Simply put, Americans have drawn a strong connection between money, power, politics and democracy itself. Indeed, the top issue concerning voters in the 2016 presidential election was that "wealthy individuals and corporations will have too much influence over who wins" ("Influence of Money in Politics", 2015).

In the post-*Citizens United v. FEC* era, across political party lines, the vast majority—84 percent—of Americans thought that money has too much influence in political campaigns, and candidates who win office will promote policies to help their donors. (Of course, if there is the *direct* promise of doing so in exchange for money and other support—a quid pro quo—this rises to the level of illegality, as it is a **bribe**.) About 66 percent of Americans thought that the wealthy had more influence on the outcome of the electoral process than those with less. Also, a vast majority thought that to remedy this imbalance, changes were needed to campaign financing, with 46 percent saying that there were so many changes needed that the system had to be fundamentally rebuilt from the ground up. Directly related to the *Citizens United* decision, 77 percent of Americans thought that there should be more limiting of the amount of money individuals can contribute to political campaigns, with only 21 percent agreeing with the Supreme Court that unlimited resources should be able to be given to political campaigns. Furthermore, Americans by a margin of three to one thought that groups not affiliated with a candidate should be required to publicly disclose their contributors, rather than be able to keep this information private. A slight majority of Americans (54 percent) disagreed with the idea that donating money to candidates is a form of free speech, one of the bedrock notions undergirding campaign financing in the United States currently ("Americans Views on Money in Politics", 2015).

Why might Americans hold these very cynical views about money, power, and politics? For one, coupled with the loosened regulation on how much money can be given by individuals and corporations/unions and a lack of transparency about the source of funds, there is growing inequality of wealth generally in the United States. If access and influence can increasingly be bought through large sums by the very wealthy and corporations/organizations, and the inequality of distribution of wealth is also increasing, it stands to reason that power will be perceived of as lying in the hands of the few.

Changes Post Citizens United v. FEC

Traditional **Political Action Committees (PACs)** had been in existence for almost 70 years before *Citizens United v. FEC*, after a labor union, the Congress of Industrial Organizations (CIO) formed a committee to try to re-elect President Franklin Roosevelt, and raised funds from contributions of union members. These organizations are regulated by the Federal Election Commission, and cannot coordinate with candidates or be created by candidates. They are limited in their power to raise and distribute money to candidates in several ways: they cannot take money or contributions directly from corporations or unions' general funds. There are also donation caps, where individuals can give $5000 to each PAC. Each PAC, in turn, can give $5000 directly to candidates, and any extra money can be used on indirect expenses related to candidates. Although PACs cannot be created by divisions of foreign companies abroad, they can be created by American divisions of these companies and collect contributions from employees.

After *Citizens United*, an even more powerful entity was created. **Super PACs** did not exist prior to the 2010 decision. The difference between the two is that they can raise unlimited funds from corporations, unions, and individuals, and spend these in an unlimited manner, but only be used for independent expenditures—in other words they cannot be given directly to a candidate or his/her campaign. This was a big rule change, allowing also for corporations, unions, and other organizations to air ads in support or opposition to a candidate, regardless of the timing of those ads or the medium.

This was a big shift in the law that could dramatically change the political landscape. But what did happen in terms of spending in elections post *Citizens United*? Did corporations take advantage of the new Super PACs to try to influence elections and policies?

Impact of Citizens United *on Money in Politics*

Before we look at how *Citizens United* affected the influx and influence of money in politics, some history about campaign finance should be noted. Campaign finance (in other words, how campaigns can be funded, by whom, how much, and with what transparency) was not always strictly regulated. The earliest ban on corporate contributions did come in 1907, but there was no working enforcement mechanism. Generally, someone could contribute whatever he or she wished. It was under that system that presidents from Franklin Roosevelt to John F. Kennedy were elected (Smith, 2018, p. 143). It was only in 1974 in the aftermath of the Watergate scandal, when Congress passed amendments to the Federal Election Campaign Act, that campaign finance regulation had "teeth." In 2002, further restrictions were made after the passage of the McCain-Feingold Act, including banning political ads paid for by corporations or unions (known as electioneering communications) if made in a period of time close to an election (Smith, 2018).

Citizens United v. FEC, which removed some of those limitations put in place since the 1970s and through the McCain–Feingold act for independent expenditures, did have an impact on power and politics, but not in a way most had anticipated. It did indeed increase the amount of spending on elections. For example, the 2012 presidential election saw an almost 600 percent increase in independent expenditures, up to one billion dollars. However, even with more options of how to spend on politics open to them, corporations were not the source of this dramatic increase in spending. Their spending largely remained the same. They did not use the Super PACs as were predicted, but rather kept using "regular" PACs. In fact, only 10 of the Fortune 500 firms gave to Super PACs. "Simply stated, Citizens United did not open the floodgates to corporate spending in federal elections. . . [it] amounted to a relative trickle" (Hansen et al., 2015). So if corporations did not cause the increase in money coming into our presidential elections, who did? The answer lies in wealthy individuals, including billionaires from across the political spectrum, who now without limitations on giving, donated to Super PACs, infusing millions into the political landscape. About 60 percent of super PAC donations, in fact, came from individuals such as billionaires Michael Bloomberg, Tom Steyer, and David Koch (Hansen et al., 2015; Shribman, 2020). Therefore, even though these donors' large donations were made through Super PACS indirectly to campaigns, they were able to exert more influence over the political process than previously. The more money one has at one's disposal, the more one has to give to these entities to sway public opinion and policy.

There was also dramatically increased spending on campaigns after *Citizens United* by individuals through mechanisms that enable the donor to hide his/her identity (Gordon,

2016/2017; Shribman, 2020). This kind of anonymous spending is also known as **dark money.** By hiding the identity of the donors, voters are unable to "see" who is behind campaign-related ads and materials, and transparency in elections is diminishing. Without limits on giving to PACs and Super PACs, this exacerbates the problem as powerful interests have much more ability to amplify their political voice—and without anyone knowing they are doing so.

Gaining Power: The Link Between Money, Organizations, and Winning Elections

Just because individuals and organizations have had their ability to give money to organizations that advocate for the election of a candidate, does this necessarily mean that there is a direct causal link between money and an election outcome? If so this would mean that having one's interests represented is completely a matter of having resources, that money alone is political power in the United States. Because ultimately in our democracy, citizens have to be convinced to cast votes to have a candidate elected, even with the most well-funded campaign money can buy, the outcome is not 100 percent guaranteed. People can read materials, watch ads, and be canvassed in their homes by well-funded politicians and still, ultimately, decide not to vote for them. One prominent example over the past ten years of a less well-funded campaign ultimately winning the presidency was the election of Donald Trump. Clinton raised 1 billion dollars, whereas Trump raised 600 million (Peters & Shorey, 2016). But as the 1.6 billion together raised for the presidential campaign of 2016 indicate, there is a link between money and the ability to have an influence on the political process.

One link is that it is taking larger and larger amounts of money to get elected in the United States, ruling out the possibility of campaigns by well-qualified citizens who do not have access to such funds. It is very uncommon for Congressional candidates without much funding to defeat heavily funded candidates, for a number of reasons. For example, your campaign might be able to pay for more ads that lead to name-recognition, which is key for elections. The average cost of getting elected to Congress is extremely high: 1.6 million to be elected to Congress, and 10.5 million to be elected to the Senate (Prokop, 2014). Because fundraising requires a good amount of time and also experience, who can run for office becomes limited. Most candidates are professionals from affluent backgrounds that may allow them time off to work on their campaigns or even leave their jobs to focus full-time on their campaign. The Senate, for example, is majority comprised of millionaires. Average citizens are much less represented among the ranks of elected politicians, especially low-wage workers.

A second link is that a small percentage of the US population is donating the kind of sums that would, in an era where politics can be awash in cash, persuade politicians to listen more carefully to their concerns. Less than one percent—0.25 percent—of the entire US population gives away 68 percent of the money (Prokop, 2014). It is unsurprising, then, that even if there is no overt bribery or **corruption** involved—if everything is done completely legally and in accordance with campaign finance regulation—the interests of those with more money are more likely to be represented. Policies that favor those at the top of the economic ladder pass more frequently (Garcia, 2016). Research has also shown a relationship between political contributions and the amount of government regulation affecting a business (Hansen et al., 2015). If there were no benefit to come to the individual or business or labor union, after all, it would make little sense for them to donate. There is something expected (although not explicitly stated) in return for their financial commitments.

The power of money to sway politics, then, is one that existed before *Citizens United*. As we saw, most corporations did not change their spending in response to the eased regulations on independent expenditures. They choose to use their regular PACs and continue their lobbying efforts, building and maintaining their relationships with politicians over time. However, *Citizens United v. FEC* provided yet another way for money to "talk" in democracy through massive independent expenditures primarily from the very wealthy, to talk over the interests of those unable to pay. They are much better represented in government accordingly.

Review Questions

1. Who was Dred Scott and what was the constitutional issue raised in *Dred Scott v. Sandford*?
2. How was race, power and citizenship impacted by the *Scott* case?
3. What role does the criminal justice system play today with racial injustice in America?
4. What facts serve as the background to the *Citizens United v. FEC* case?
5. How have elections been altered due to this case?

References

Allen, A. (2004). The political economy of blackness: citizenship, corporations, and race in Dred Scott. Civil War History, *50*(3), 229–260.

Alexander, M. (2010). *The new Jim Crow: Mass incarceration in an age of colorblindness*. New York: New Press.

Americans' Views on Money in Politics. (2015, June 2). *New York Times*. Retrieved from www.nytimes.com/interactive/2015/06/02/us/politics/money-in-politics-poll.html

Bassett, J. (2011). *Restricted citizenship: The struggle for Native American voting rights in Arizona* (Master's Thesis). Arizona State University, Tempe, AZ.

Blight, D. (2008, November 21). *Dred Scott, bleeding Kansas, and the impending crisis of the union, 1855–58*. Yale University Lecture, the Civil War and Reconstruction (HIST 119). Retrieved from www.youtube.com/watch?v=aVFlkEonxhs

Citizens United v. Federal Election Commission. (n.d.a). *Oyez*. Retrieved June 18, 2020, from www.oyez.org/cases/2008/08-205

Conley, D. (2013). *You may ask yourself* (3rd ed.). New York: W.W. Norton.

Department of Justice (DOJ). (2019). *Prison and jail incarceration rates decreased by more than 10% from 2007 to 2017*. Department of Justice Office of Justice Programs. Retrieved from https://content.govdelivery.com/accounts/USDOJOJP/bulletins/240cf09

Garcia, R. J. (2016). Politics at work after citizens united. *Loyola of Los Angeles Law Review*, *49*(1), 1–37.

Goodwin, M. (2019). The Thirteenth Amendment: Modern slavery, capitalism, and mass incarceration. *Cornell Law Review*, *104*, 899–990.

Gordon, N. A. (2016/2017). Options for continued reform of money in politics: "Citizens united" is not the end. *Albany Law Review*, *80*(10), 83–160.

Hansen, W. L., Rocca, M. S., & Ortiz, B. L. (2015). The effects of Citizens United on corporate spending in the 2012 presidential election. The Journal of Politics, 77(2), 535–545.

The Influence of "Citizens United" v. FEC on the Institution of Politics and Government in the United States. Retrieved from https://en.wikipedia.org/wiki/Citizens_United_v._FEC

Influence of Money in Politics a Top Concern for Voters. (2015, June 21). *The Wall Street Journal*. Retrieved from http://blogs.wsj.com/washwire/2015/06/21/influence-of-money-in-politics-a-top-concern-for-voters/

Pelmas, S. H. (1998). *America's authors: Creating the citizen in 19th century America*. (Dissertation). University of California, Berkeley, CA.

Peters, J. W., & Shorey, R. (2016, December 9). Trump spent far less than Clinton, but paid his companies well. *New York Times*. Retrieved from www.nytimes.com/2016/12/09/us/politics/campaign-spending-donald-trump-hillary-clinton.html

Prokop, A. (2014, July 30). 40 charts that explain money in politics. *Vox*. Retrieved from www.vox.com/2014/7/30/5949581/money-in-politics-charts-explain

Robinson, J. (2019, May 3). The racist roots of denying incarcerated people their right to vote. *ACLU*. Retrieved from www.aclu.org/blog/voting-rights/racist-roots-denying-incarcerated-people-their-right-vote

Shribman, D. (2020, January 12). Ten years on, citizens united ruling has changed politics—but not in the way many feared. *Los Angeles Times*. Retrieved from www.latimes.com/world-nation/story/2020-01-12/citizens-united-ruling-anniversary-how-it-changed-american-politics

Smith, B. A. (2018). Campaign finance and free speech: Finding the radicalism in citizens united v. Fec. *Harvard Journal of Law & Public Policy*, *4*(1), 139–151.

Turner, K. B., Giacopassi, D., & Vandiver, M. (2006). Ignoring the past: Coverage of slavery and slave patrols in criminal justice texts. *Journal of Criminal Justice Education*, *17*(1), 181–195.

Uggen, C., Larson, R., & Shannon, S. (2016). 6 million lost voters: State-level estimates of felony disenfranchisement, 2016. *The Sentencing Project*. Retrieved from www.sentencingproject.org/publications/6-million-lost-voters-state-level-estimates-felony-disenfranchisement-2016/

7

ECONOMY

Learning Objectives

After reading this chapter, students should be able to:

- Explain the *Phillips v. Martin Marietta* case and decision
- Describe the impact of the Phillips decision on the institution of Economy
- Summarize the concept of double shift
- Detail how child care issues impact the employment of mothers
- Understand the case of *West Coast Hotel Company v. Parrish*
- Generalize the ideological shift in the US Supreme Court pertaining to the issues in *West Coast Hotel Company v. Parrish*
- Explain how theorists like Marx and Weber had different outlooks on work

Key Terms

Gender Gap
gendered
Karl Marx
Max Weber
per curiam decision
Phillips v. Martin Marietta
Second Shift
West Coast Hotel Company v. Parrish

Phillips v. Martin Marietta Corporation Introduction

"Does a refusal to hire women with preschool-age children while hiring men with such children, in the absence of business necessity, violate the Civil Rights Act of 1964?" This was the question that the United States Supreme Court was tasked to answer when they agreed to hear the *Phillips v. Martin Marietta Corporation* case, presented to them in 1970. The Supreme Court delivered a *per curiam* decision in January 1971 (a ruling issued collectively by a group or panel of judges), one month after hearing the case, meaning that the Court itself issued the opinion, as opposed to a specific justice as it was often the case—something that between 1946 and 2012, had only happened in 7 percent of the cases that the Supreme Court had ruled on. The *per curiam* decision had satisfied yet disappointed both the plaintiff and the defendant at the same time.

DOI: 10.4324/9781003021438-8

Four years before the case carrying her name made it to the US Supreme Court, Ida Phillips was earning $45.00 per week working as a waitress for Donut Dinette in Florida. However, she wanted to pursue a different career that would allow her to provide a better quality of life to her seven children whose age range at the time went from three to 15 years. One day, a job advertisement in the newspaper caught her attention. The Martin Marietta Corporation was looking to hire an assembly trainee at their steel plant in Orlando, Florida. The job required the appointed candidate to fit a "steel part into a computer system programmed to produce missiles." The person chosen to work at the plant would earn $2.25 an hour, which would have substantially increased Ida Phillips' income. The prospect was enticing enough that she decided to drive down to the plant and apply for the job.

Once there, however, things did not go as expected. The receptionist working at Martin Marietta Corporation informed Phillips that, given her preschool-aged children, she was not a candidate they would consider because of the assumption that working mothers of young children were not reliable enough as they would probably have to be absent from the job to tend to sick or needy children. When Phillips asked to at least receive an application she could fill out, the receptionist refused, adding that even if she managed for childcare and still make it to work, her mind would be too preoccupied with her children back home to focus exclusively on the job. However, men with preschool-aged children were free—and welcome—to apply.

Ida Phillips received legal representation from a young lawyer, William Robinson, who worked at the Legal Defense and Educational Fund of the National Association for the Advancement of Colored People (NAACP). Even though the NAACP's mission was to focus on the advancement of colored people—and Ida Phillips was a White American woman—they still chose to represent her because of what the impact of the case would bring for minorities as well: "[B]lack mothers were nearly twice as likely to work as White mothers were, so a decision upholding Martin Marietta's rule would be economically disastrous for African American families." A decision in favor of Martin Marietta Corporation also had the potential of threatening Title VII (see Box 7.1) of the Civil Rights Act of 1964, a landmark civil rights law that prohibits discrimination on the basis of race, color, religion, sex, or national origin, and it is enforced by the Equal Employment Opportunity Commission (EEOC). The threat became an additional incentive for the NAACP Legal Defense and Education Fund to take on Philipps' case because they feared that if employers could choose not to hire and discriminate against a woman for simply having preschool-aged children, then they "could re-impose many Jim Crow-era rules: Instead of barring all African Americans from applying, they simply could ban those who, for instance, didn't have a high-school diploma or achieve a certain score on a shoddily-designed aptitude test." When Robinson brought the case to the attention of the lower courts, Fifth Circuit Judge Lewis R. Morgan said that, "discrimination based solely on one of the categories, i.e., in the case of sex; women vis-à-vis men" would have indeed violated Title VII of the Civil Rights Act. However, since Martin Marietta Corporation did not refuse to hire Ida Phillips because she was a woman, but because she was not deemed a reliable candidate due to her preschool-aged children, Judge Morgan sided with Martin Marietta and upheld the bona fide operational qualification (BFOQ) stand that the employer had taken. The BFOQ affords employers the option to not hire or keep employed candidates if their religion, sex, or national origin—race is not included in this list of factors that exempt employers from discrimination liability—would interfere with the normal operation of that specific business.

Phillips, determined to receive justice, filed motions to have her case reconsidered, but they were denied. When Phillips presented the case to the District Court for the Middle District of

Florida at Orlando in October 1969, the petition of rehearing was again denied. However, this time, a judge openly expressed his dissent. Chief Judge John R. Brown stated that,

> The case is simple. A woman with pre-school children may not be employed, a man with pre-school children may. The distinguishing factor seems to be motherhood versus fatherhood. The question then arises: Is this sex-related? To the simple query the answer is just as simple: Nobody—and this includes Judges, Solomonic or life tenured—has yet seen a male mother. A mother, to oversimplify the simplest biology, must then be a woman. It is the fact of the person being a mother—i.e., a woman—not the age of the children, which denies employment opportunity to a woman which is open to a man.

Invigorated by Judge Brown's dissent, Robinson and Phillips brought the case to the US Supreme Court—the first case based on Title VII sex discrimination to do so. However, once the hearing began, Robison soon found out that most justices upheld the same convictions as the defendant's policy. For example, Justice Harry Blackmun said,

> [S]uppose a hospital for years had employed nothing but female registered nurses . . . and then today after the passage of this Act, a male nurse applicant comes along. Do I understand your interpretation of the Act to be that just because they have always had female RNs and like them and got along well, they could not refuse to hire the male nurse?

After Martin Marietta proved that they mostly hired women for the job Ida Phillips had wanted to apply for, and after learning that the job itself did not require any heavy duty, but it was rather intricate work that involved a certain level of attention to detail and precision, Chief Justice Warren Burger stated that, "[W]omen are manually much more adept than men and they do this work better. . . . Just the same reason that most men hire women as their secretaries, because they are better at it than men."

The US Supreme Court didn't take long to issue their per curiam decision, which stated that Martin Marietta Corporation's decision not to hire Ida Phillips went indeed against Title VII because not hiring mothers was just as discriminatory as not hiring women. However, they also sent the case back to lower courts, thus offering Martin Marietta a chance to prove that their reservation on not hiring mothers was funded. Although the corporation had therefore been given the chance to prove that working mothers with preschool-aged children were perhaps more distracted, or took more days off work, they decided to settle the case outside of court. With the modest settlement, Ida Phillips—who had gone back to waitressing while pleading her case—took her preschool-aged child to Walt Disney World in Orlando.

Phillips v. Martin Marietta Corp Decision

PHILLIPS V. MARTIN MARIETTA CORP., 400 U.S. 542 (1971)

Petitioner Mrs. Ida Phillips commenced an action in the United States District Court for the Middle District of Florida under Title VII of the Civil Rights Act of 1964 * alleging that she had been denied employment because of her sex. The District Court granted summary judgment for Martin Marietta Corp. (Martin) on the basis of the following showing: (1) in 1966, Martin informed Mrs. Phillips that it was not accepting job applications from women with pre-school-age children; (2) as of the time of the motion for summary judgment, Martin employed

BOX 7.1 TITLE VII

What if, during a job interview, the employer discriminated against a group of applicants because of the color of their skin? What if a pregnant woman were to be laid off by the employer only because of her pregnancy status? What if, during a job application, the employer dismissed a potential candidate only because their last name sounded too foreign? And what if an employee who identified as being a member of the LGBTQ+ community were to be fired because of their sexual orientation?

The employer could be found non-compliant with Title VII, which protects employees against discrimination in the workplace based on race, color, gender, religion, nation of origin, pregnancy status, and sexual orientation. If the employer were to intentionally discriminate, they would face a jury trial and a legal recompense—which could range between $50,000 if the employer had between five and ten employees, and $300,000 if the employer had over five-hundred employees.

Title VII is a provision of the Civil Rights Act of 1964. Proposed as a bill in 1963 by President John F. Kennedy—who had been persuaded by his many encounters with Civil Rights activists such as A. Philip Randolph and Roy Wilkins, as well as by the constant protests that had been taking place across the country against racial discrimination and Jim Crow laws in the southern states—the bill hit an indefinite halt when presented to the Committee on Rules, a committee of the United States House of Representatives, whose chairman at the time was an outspoken supporter of racial segregation. After the assassination of President Kennedy in late 1963, President Lyndon Johnson pushed to pass the bill—which he perceived as Kennedy's ultimate legacy—as soon as possible. On July 2, 1964, President Johnson signed the bill into law.

Title VII is therefore a federal law that protects employees who work either in the public or private sector and for companies of at least five people—however, it does not protect independent contractors nor federal government employees. The government agency Equal Employment Opportunity Commission (EEOC) enforces Title VII and is allowed to investigate a case of discrimination in the workplace. Even though Title VII was enacted in 1964, its verbiage and meaning continue to be debated by the Supreme Court when there is a case that pushes for more clarification on the umbrella term that is "discrimination."

For example, in the *Bostock v. Clayton County* case, which was argued by the Roberts Court in October 2019, the main question that the nine Justices faced was: Does discrimination on the basis of sex also include sexual orientation? The petitioner, Gerald Bostock had been working as a child welfare services coordinator for Clayton County in Georgia. However, once its employees and employer became aware that Bostock was a gay man, they fired him even though his work performance over the course of a decade had been highly professional and close to impeccable. In a 6–3 majority, the Roberts Court decided that yes, Clayton County had discriminated against Bostock because of his sexual orientation and, as such, it had violated Title VII of the Civil Rights Act.

However, while there are clear classifications of people protected by Title VII, there are also specific jobs protected by the bona fide occupational qualification (BFOQ) that safeguard employers who state a particular requirement for a job. For example, if the employer is looking to cast an actor for the role of President George Washington, the employer might not be violating Title VII if they are looking specifically for candidates who are both White and male.

men with pre-school-age children; (3) at the time Mrs. Phillips applied, 70–75 percent of the applicants for the position she sought were women; 75–80 percent of those hired for the position, assembly trainee, were women, hence no question of bias against women as such was presented.

The Court of Appeals for the Fifth Circuit affirmed, 411 F.2d 1, and denied a rehearing en banc, 416 F.2d.

Section 703(a) of the Civil Rights Act of 1964 requires that persons of like qualifications be given employment opportunities irrespective of their sex. The Court of Appeals therefore erred in reading this section as permitting one hiring policy for women and another for men—each having pre-school-age children. The existence of such conflicting family obligations, if demonstrably more relevant to job performance for a woman than for a man, could arguably be a basis for distinction under § 703(e) of the Act. But that is a matter of evidence tending to show that the condition in question "is a *bona fide* occupational qualification reasonably necessary to the normal operation of that particular business or enterprise." The record before us, however, is not adequate for resolution of these important issues. *See Kennedy v. Silas Mason Co.*, 334 U. S. 249, 334 U. S. 256–257 (1948). Summary judgment was therefore improper, and we remand for fuller development of the record and for further consideration.

Vacated and remanded.

★ Section 703 of the Act, 78 Stat. 255, 42 USC. § 2000e-2, provides as follows:

> "(a) It shall be an unlawful employment practice for an employer—"
>
> "(1) to fail or refuse to hire or to discharge any individual, or otherwise to discriminate against any individual with respect to his compensation, terms, conditions, or privileges of employment, because of such individual's race, color, religion, sex, or national origin. . . ."
>
> "★ ★ ★ ★"
>
> "(e) Notwithstanding any other provision of this title, (1) it shall not be an unlawful employment practice for an employer to hire and employ employees . . . on the basis of . . . religion, sex, or national origin in those certain instances where religion, sex, or national origin is a *bona fide* occupational qualification reasonably necessary to the normal operation of that particular business or enterprise. . . ."

The Impact of *Phillips v. Martin Marietta* on the Institution of the Economy

West Coast Hotel v. Parrish had an impact on the institution of the economy that went beyond its immediate allowance of a minimum wage to be set for women in the state, setting the stage for a federal minimum wage and the ability for states to set minimum wages for both men and women. *Phillips v. Martin Marietta*, a decision that similarly dealt with women's rights in the workplace, likewise had a potential impact that extended beyond the question of whether women can be discriminated against in hiring on the basis of having children. In considering how moving away from legally protecting the stereotyping of women with children affects the economy, we should remember both that women have *always*—in both pre-history and modern history—been major participants and contributors to the economy through their labor (Lindsey, 1997), engaging in economic activities from bartering, cottage industry (producing things for sale in the home), and working for wages outside in a range of skilled jobs (doctors, craftworkers, and pharmacists during colonial times, for example) (Lindsey, 1997). We should also remember the institution of economy is not confined to the formal workplace (sites of production and distribution). It also includes individuals and families at home and leisure, who consume products and services, primarily through spending their wages, and who may produce goods for their own consumption or outside sale. And, as the activists in the Wages for Housework movement have pointed out (see Box 7.2), the family is also the location of the reproduction/production of workers themselves.

Taking this into account, in this final section we look at how the *Phillips v. Martin Marietta* case impacted economy as an institution, focusing on the gender gap in pay, the rise of dual-income household and changes to divisions of labor, and changes in the workplace and society in response to the need for work/life balance.

BOX 7.2 THE WAGES FOR HOUSEWORK MOVEMENT

Should the minimum wage—or indeed *any* wage—be given for labor historically performed in a patriarchal system by women in the home, for her own spouse and family? This work, after all, especially prior to the large-scale entry of women into waged labor outside the home, supported the "outside work," of men (such as cleaning, cooking, doing laundry, shopping), and ensured the reproduction of the future workers of the country—children. This question and how we react to it hinges a lot on what we think of as "real work," which often excludes that performed in the domestic sphere. Such work has been gendered, meaning women are expected to fulfill this role. Beginning in the 19th century in the United States and internationally, feminists have called attention to the importance of domestic work to the continuance of the capitalist economy, and how that work has been devalued. Some notably called for such work to receive a wage.

The Wages for Housework Committee, a feminist organization/movement that originated in Italy but also mobilized in the United States in the 1970s, especially in New York, argued that housework (which they also termed reproductive labor) be compensated by the state in the same way as labor outside of the home is remunerated. Without the "invisible," uncompensated housework of women in the domestic sphere, the work outside of the home would not be possible, they claimed, and capitalism itself would falter. By not having housework compensated, unequal power relations between men and women could be sustained, as society did not even recognize work in the home as work, but as something 'natural' that women just do because they are women as an act of love. The Wages for Housework feminists saw housework as part of the reason why women are oppressed and exploited. They believed that a way towards liberating themselves was by demanding that this labor not be free, thus exposing how much and what types of labor (physical, emotional, even sexual) were provided by women working in the home, and allowing them to reject some of it. The Wages for Housework Movement was ultimately rejected by many feminists. Yet, the question of the value of unwaged work performed in the home continues, as women continue to bear the brunt of the second shift even in the 21st century, and reproductive labor is more and more shunted onto the backs of those lower in the social hierarchy, such as immigrants and working class women (Federici & Austin, 2017).

Source:

Federici, S., & Austin, A. (2017). *The New York wages for housework committee 1972–1977: History, theory and documents*. New York: Autonomedia.

The Dual Income Household and the Double-Shift

Around the same time as the *Phillips* decision, women had begun entering the outside workforce *en masse* following the Civil Rights Act of 1964 (Lease, 2019). By reducing the barriers to employment for these women with children, *Phillips v. Martin Marietta* was another factor in a general societal shifting away from the patriarchal, heteronormative "ideal" of the nuclear family where the working father provided for his wife and their biological children, while the wife tended to the home and children. The dual-earner family is now the US family norm, and two-thirds of mothers with young children in North America are working outside the home (Christopher, 2012). Indeed, mothers who do *not* work outside the home now are non-normative.

The ruling also challenged prevailing cultural stereotypes of women's roles in the economy, such as their being unable to maintain the same rigorous involvement in work life if they have children, or that they are biologically better "suited" for childrearing and keeping the home. Once a mother, according to the cultural logic, "you are likely to be seen as *essentially* a mother" (Becker, 2000, p. 1526), reducible primarily to that role. Career and work, therefore, are secondary. This assumption has not applied in the same way to men who are fathers. Men have traditionally inhabited the position of the "ideal worker," a dedicated employee who is able to spend long hours at work, be flexible to the needs of the employer, and give large amounts of "face-time," largely because of the presence of a spouse able to manage his children and household. Indeed, the lower court rulings in the *Phillips* case indicated that the judges thought mothers should put the needs of family first (Lease, 2019). Thousands of gender discrimination lawsuits since the 1960s, including from mothers alleging discrimination on the basis of being a mother (Lindsey, 1997) show that a single Supreme Court ruling is never sufficient to eradicate deeply entrenched cultural ideas about gender roles and stereotyped ideas of motherhood. Furthermore, essential domestic work continues to be primarily the purview of women, leading to a "second shift," for women.

Renowned sociologist Arlie Hochschild described this **second shift** as the uncompensated "care work," performed for children, spouses, and other dependents like elderly parents that are put in above and beyond paid labor. Hochschild calculated that if we can take their second shifts into account women put in an extra month of work versus men (Becker, 2001, p. 1516), and other scholars note that women do approximately twice the amount of housework and carework. Because this type of labor has traditionally not been thought of *as* work, it often goes unrecognized and taken-for-granted. Although the dramatic entry of women into the workplace in the 20th and 21st century may have occurred, traditional gender role ideas still have an influence. Women expect to have to fulfill this juggling of family and work, as studies of college-age women reveal (Lindsey, 1997), whereas men do not expect to have to negotiate these competing claims on their time.

The Gender Gap

Yet, they have made great gains in their income, especially since the 1970s, and have narrowed the **gender gap**, that is—average difference between the wages and salaries of women and men, across all educational levels. Still, this gap persists, with strong racial effects as well (with White and Asian American women earning more vis-a-vis men than their Black and Latina counterparts), and not only because of policies that can be regulated. Because in the household division of labor in heterosexual relationships women continue to be primarily responsible for childcare and housework, this uncompensated labor can take away from hours dedicated to work (Blau & Kahn, 2017).

Women who continue to work, as Phillips did, earn less money than other workers, even if we take into account the fewer hours that they work, and this depression of wages continues even after childhood. They face what has been described of as a "maternal wall," in their career and pay (Kaminer, 2004). This phenomenon occurs for a number of reasons, including the higher likelihood that a woman will need and take time off from work after giving birth, or drop out entirely if the cost of childcare is so exorbitant that it is more economically rational for her to stay home. The fact that research has shown consistently that increasing childcare subsidies increases the labor supply of mothers hints at this reality (Donovan Fitzpatrick, 2010). Labor supply decisions in heterosexual couples are made in ways that disproportionately impact mothers. For example, women with young children work 2.5 fewer hours per week, and fathers, 2.5 hours more. They are more likely to take family-related leaves of absence and other gaps which are reflected in income, promotions, and other markers of career success (Dunbar & Easton, 2013). Such breaks and gaps may interrupt her "job mobility," or lead to her being seen as a less competitive, a "worker-mom" by her employer (Chamallas, 1999). Women with children may even be considered "riskier hires" to begin with, in a kind of "maternal profiling," and may be turned down for jobs accordingly (Lease, 2019).

Having a child, then, can be considered a cause of "career penalties," that male spouses do not have to contend with (Christopher, 2012). Wage gaps are primarily rooted in these differential family responsibilities differences in education or work (Lease, 2019), but have been narrowing as women have moved into higher-skilled jobs, pursued higher education at rates that have now exceeded men, and have pushed back against stereotypes. Over the past 30 years, the hourly wage of women has increased more quickly than that of men. From 1980 to 2018, the average wage of women increased 45 percent, whereas men's only increased 14 percent. However, women's average wage is still around $22, to men's $26 (Pew, 2020).

Gender Stereotyping and Occupational Segregation

In spite of *Phillips v. Martin Marietta*'s injunction against gender-based stereotyping in hiring decisions, strong social influences are still at work to **de facto** keep occupations gender-typed and segregated, leading to disparate outcomes in income, status attainment, and other cultural benefits. Women either enter into professions associated with lower salaries (such as teaching, social work, nursing, or clerical work), or *because* of their entry into certain fields in large numbers, see their wages drop as the field becomes less male-dominated, thereby losing status. Indeed, occupations with more men are generally better paid, independent of the amount of skill or education required. Some argue occupational segregation can actually impede economic growth broadly. Stereotypes can interfere with workers' entry into jobs for which they are well-suited or jobs in growing industries that might be gender-segregated, and by keeping women's wages lowers, reduce their purchasing power and that of their families (WCEG, 2017). Among the highest paying occupations (financial managers, physicians, surgeons, CEOs, dentists, pilots, architecture and engineering managers, for example), men are overrepresented, whereas women are overrepresented in the lowest-paid occupations (childcare workers, cashiers, fast food workers, personal care aides) (WCEG, 2017).

Yet, large strides have been made by women into "elite" occupations once dominated by men, like becoming doctors, lawyers, or university professors since the 1960s. Now, approximately a third of the U.S's lawyers and doctors are women, and women are now earning approximately half of the medical and law degrees (Cohen, 2012). Additionally, **affirmative action** policies put in place in recognition of the wage gap have bolstered the entry of women into managerial and professional jobs (Lindsey, 1997).

"Work-Life Balance," and the Shifting of Childcare Responsibilities

Whereas *Phillips v. Martin Marietta* presented evidence of how employers considered young mothers to be neglecting their primary duty if they were to be employed, women today show that they consider "work-life balance" to be essential, and that they value outside work in itself highly. Mothers have indicated that even if they would be able to afford staying home with their children, they prefer to also work, for reasons beyond the pay. For example, personal self-esteem, economic independence, and using one's educational credentials were cited as reasons why women would want to work out of home (Christopher, 2012).

Work-life balance is an important determinant in whether women "drop out" of the workforce, which then has an impact on the economy broadly. Men also are disadvantaged in the absence of work-life balance. Rigid work schedules prevent men who are fathers have adequate time to participate meaningfully in child-rearing and housework. Men are also more likely to be stigmatized for taking off from work for parental obligations and less likely to have or take paternity leave (Lease, 2019). Scholars argue that if parents (primarily mothers) are forced out of work to take care of their children, the economy suffers as the nation loses out on tax revenue. Employers who do not have more flexible policies for parents can also be negatively affected as they can experience higher turnover rates and lost productivity when their workers are forced to leave, or experience employee dissatisfaction or lack of commitment. "The failure of the American workplace to meaningfully accommodate working parents has caused harm to individuals, employers, and society" Kaminer argues (2004, p. 311). Indeed, American workers vis-à-vis their European counterparts have longer work hours and fewer vacation days and other days off. They also do not have any mandated paid maternity or paternity leave (Kaminer, 2004). In fact, among the world's richest countries, the United States remains the only one not to nationally mandate some type of paid leave for maternity/paternity. The Family Medical Leave Act (FMLA) provides only some support for working parents, with unpaid leave of up to 12 weeks (Bryant, 2020).

In general, in the US the workforce faces challenges in negotiating the demands of their paid employment and family responsibilities. Almost a third of adults—men and women—experience work-family conflicts during a single work week. Even in the absence of the kind of discrimination seen in the workplace on the basis of gender and maternity status we saw in *Phillips v. Martin Marietta*, in the absence of an economy where paid labor is made compatible with childcare and housework, women will continue to be primarily responsible for resolving those conflicts. Even as the variability in the labor supply of women (known as labor elasticity) has declined over time, meaning women are less likely to drop out of work if they become mothers (Donovan Fitzpatrick, 2010, p. 82), this may mean that *other* women are going to be entrusted with filling that gap in carework. Carework demands have increased with the continued entry of women into the workforce full-time, and almost 90 percent of this work, including childcare work (such as being a nanny), is performed by low-income women without the same resources to consume services. These workers include a growing number of non-US born women and/or women of color (Hartmann, Hayes, Huber, Rolfes-Haase, & Suh, 2018).

Although corporatization in select industries, such as medicine, has helped women with negotiating the kind of work-family conflict that Martin Marietta saw as inimitable to their paid employment, both men and women face intersecting social and economic constraints that impact their decisions about where to work, how to work, and even, whether or not to have children, children who ultimately grow up to become the next generation of producers and consumers.

West Coast Hotel Company v. Parrish Introduction

"The switch in time that saved nine" (Goldman, 2012). A play on the old adage that professes the importance of fixing an issue right away to avoid bigger problems in the future, this aphorism refers to Justice Owen J. Roberts whose vote on the 1937 case of *West Coast Hotel Company v. Elsie Parrish* symbolized the stark shift in doctrine and ideology of the justice who upheld the minimum wage law of the state of Washington. Justice Roberts's previously conservative decision to strike down federal minimum wage laws—labeled as unconstitutional—in the 1923 case of *Adkins v. Children's Hospital* (5–3 vote) and in the 1936 case of *Morehead v. New York ex rel. Tipaldo* (5–4 vote) was still fresh in everybody's mind, thus making his ideological shift that much more unexpected as it formally ended the *Lochner* era (5–4 vote). Remembered as a period (1890–1937) in which the Supreme Court, "using a broad interpretation of due process that protected economic rights, tended to strike down economic regulations of working conditions, wages or hours in favor of laissez-faire economic policy," the name derives from the 1905 case of *Lochner v. New York* in which the Court stated that a New York statute—which prohibited employees from working over 60 hours a week, 10 hours a day, in a bakery—was invalid as it interfered with the right of contract between employers and employees.

There are two schools of thought when it comes to Justice Roberts's sudden shift. One believes that his switch from his previously conservative stance on the matter was strategic and aimed at protecting the Supreme Court's integrity against President Franklin Roosevelt's court-reform bill—also referred to as the court-packing plan. The Court had been striking down many pieces of legislation presented by the president in his New Deal plan to save the US economy during the Great Depression. Frustrated that he was experiencing such difficulty with the Court, the president introduced the Judicial Procedures Reform Bill (1937), a legislative initiative that aimed at adding up to six more justices to the Supreme Court—thus raising the

FIGURE 7.1 "Fast food strike and protest for $15 minimum wage at University of Minnesota"

number to a total of 15 justices—for every justice who was over 70 years of age and had served for more than ten years. The other school of thought believes that Justice Roberts simply had a change of heart.

Regardless of what prompted him to make the famous ideological shift, *West Coast Hotel Company v. Parrish* became a landmark case that would impact millions of Americans and it had all started with an Elsie Parrish, a woman who lived in Washington and worked as a chambermaid for the Wenatchee's West Coast Hotel. Washington had been one of the first states to enact minimum wage laws—Massachusetts was the first in 1912—and it required that a woman be paid $14.50 for a 48-hour work week. But in the spring of 1935, Elsie found out that her employer had failed to pay her what the state mandated, and she was still owed $216.19—which, in the time of the Great Depression was even more valuable. Not one to shy away from an uphill battle, Parrish took legal action.

Elsie Parrish (née Murray) was born in 1899 in Penalosa, Kansas, one of six children. Of Irish heritage—her ancestors had come to the United States in the 1700s and soon moved as far west as they could reach—she experienced tragedy at a very early age. She was a little over one year old), when her father Ed, who was highly respected in the community, suffered a farming accident that made the news in the *Hutchinson Daily News* and called, "one of the more deplorable and horrible accidents which ever has occurred in the county." According to the newspaper, Ed Murray was barely 40 years old when he

> walked across the top of the thresher. The cap over the cylinder had been removed by someone, a fact of which Mr. Murray was ignorant. The top of the machine was covered with straw and believing that the cylinder was covered the owner of the thresher stepped directly into the cylinder while the machine was in motion. Instantly his leg was nearly torn from his body.

Although he managed to pull himself out of the thresher, Murray died soon after the accident, leaving his six children in the sole care of his wife, who also found herself in charge of a 160-acre farm. A year later after the tragedy, another one occurred when Elsie Murray's oldest brother died. At the age of 15, Elsie Murray married Roy Lee, nine years her senior, and a year later she gave birth to the first of seven children. Soon after moving to Washington, however, Murray divorced Lee due to his alcohol addiction—the couple had lost an eight-years-old-child in the years prior to their move. In 1933, she began working as a chambermaid at the West Coast Hotel, where she earned around 23 cents an hour. Dedicated and committed to her job, she worked a full shift even on her wedding day—she remarried in 1934 to Ernest Parrish.

In 1918, Washington Governor Ernest Lister approved the request to increase minimum wage from $13.20 in all industries to $14.50. This decision—along with Lister's choice of appointing three women to his commission tasked with surveying wages across the state—had been highly acclaimed especially by Florence Kelley, an American social reformer and political activist who fought for social welfare legislation, helped form the National Association for the Advancement of Colored People (NAACP) in 1909, and served as vice president of the National American Woman Suffrage of Association. Parrish took notice of the increase and, when she did the math and saw that she was still owed, her husband filed a lawsuit on her behalf—at the time, married women were not allowed to file a lawsuit under Washington's community property law.

Even though she didn't have enough money to pay him, lawyer Charles B. Conner agreed to represent Parrish and in June 1935, he filed *Ernest Parrish and Elsie Parrish, his wife, v. West Coast Hotel Company* at the county courthouse. "I would be false to myself did I think of compensation from this case as is measured by money," he stated. "Working women are receiving better wages, children have more food and better clothes. May I not have a reason to hope that I have served my country and in this thought receive a very handsome remuneration indeed?"

The judge sided with the West Coast Hotel Company, citing the *Adkins* case and claiming that the state's minimum wage law was unconstitutional. Conner appealed to the state supreme court, claiming that this issue "reaches into every home where the woman does or may have to perform labor for the purpose of feeding herself and children." The Washington Supreme Court turned the case on its head by siding with Parrish. However, the hotel company decided not to back down and took the case to the United States Supreme Court, which agreed to hear the arguments in December 1936. The main question presented to the justices was: "Does a minimum wage law for women violate the Due Process Clause of the Fifth Amendment, as applied to the states by the Fourteenth Amendment?"

And that's when the famous switch occurred with Justice Owen Roberts siding with the liberals. In the opinion, Chief Justice Hughes asked:

> What can be closer to the public interest than the health of women and their protection from unscrupulous and overreaching employers? And if the protection of women is a legitimate end of the exercise of state power, how can it be said that the requirement of the payment of a minimum wage fairly fixed in order to meet the very necessities of existence is not an admissible means to that end?

The Supreme Court overturned the *Adkins* decision and awarded Parrish the $216.19 the West Coast Hotel still owed her. After the landmark decision, Elsie Parrish and her husband moved to California and enjoyed the company of their many grandchildren.

West Coast Hotel Co. v. Parrish Decision

WEST COAST HOTEL CO. V. PARRISH, 300 U.S. 379 (1937)

MR. CHIEF JUSTICE HUGHES delivered the opinion of the Court.

This case presents the question of the constitutional validity of the minimum wage law of the State of Washington.

The Act, entitled "Minimum Wages for Women," authorizes the fixing of minimum wages for women and minors. Laws of 1913 (Washington) chap. 174; Remington's Rev. Stat. (1932), § 7623 *et seq.* It provides:

> SECTION 1. The welfare of the State of Washington demands that women and minors be protected from conditions of labor which have a pernicious effect on their health and morals. The State of Washington, therefore, exercising herein its police and sovereign power declares that inadequate wages and unsanitary conditions of labor exert such pernicious effect.
>
> SEC. 2. It shall be unlawful to employ women or minors in any industry or occupation within the State of Washington under conditions of labor detrimental to their health or morals, and it shall be unlawful to employ women workers in any industry within the State of Washington at wages which are not adequate for their maintenance.
>
> SEC. 3. There is hereby created a commission to be known as the "Industrial Welfare Commission" for the State of Washington, to establish such standards of wages and conditions of labor for women and minors employed within the State of Washington as shall

> be held hereunder to be reasonable and not detrimental to health and morals, and which shall be sufficient for the decent maintenance of women.

Further provisions required the Commission to ascertain the wages and conditions of labor of women and minors within the State. Public hearings were to be held. If, after investigation, the Commission found that, in any occupation, trade or industry, the wages paid to women were "inadequate to supply them necessary cost of living and to maintain the workers in health," the Commission was empowered to call a conference of representatives of employers and employees together with disinterested persons representing the public. The conference was to recommend to the Commission, on its request, an estimate of a minimum wage adequate for the purpose above stated, and, on the approval of such a recommendation, it became the duty of the Commission to issue an obligatory order fixing minimum wages. Any such order might be reopened, and the question reconsidered with the aid of the former conference or a new one. Special licenses were authorized for the employment of women who were "physically defective or crippled by age or otherwise," and also for apprentices, at less than the prescribed minimum wage.

By a later Act, the Industrial Welfare Commission was abolished, and its duties were assigned to the Industrial Welfare Committee, consisting of the Director of Labor and Industries, the Supervisor of Industrial Insurance,

> the Supervisor of Industrial Relations, the Industrial Statistician, and the Supervisor of Women in Industry. Laws of 1921 (Washington) c. 7; Remington's Rev. Stat. (1932), §§ 10840, 10893.

The appellant conducts a hotel. The appellee, Elsie Parrish, was employed as a chambermaid and (with her husband) brought this suit to recover the difference between the wages paid her and the minimum wage fixed pursuant to the state law. The minimum wage was $14.50 per week of 48 hours. The appellant challenged the act as repugnant to the due process clause of the Fourteenth Amendment of the Constitution of the United States. The Supreme Court of the State, reversing the trial court, sustained the statute and directed judgment for the plaintiffs. *Parrish v. West Coast Hotel Co.* The case is here on appeal.

The appellant relies upon the decision of this Court in *Adkins v. Children's Hospital*, which held invalid the District of Columbia Minimum Wage Act, which was attacked under the due process clause of the Fifth Amendment. On the argument at bar, counsel for the appellees attempted to distinguish the *Adkins* case upon the ground that the appellee was employed in a hotel, and that the business of an innkeeper was affected with a public interest. That effort at distinction is obviously futile, as it appears that, in one of the cases ruled by the *Adkins* opinion, the employee was a woman employed as an elevator operator in a hotel. *Adkins v. Lyons.*

The recent case of *Morehead v. New York ex rel. Tipaldo*, came here on certiorari to the New York court, which had held the New York minimum wage act for women to be invalid. A minority of this Court thought that the New York statute was distinguishable in a material feature from that involved in the *Adkins* case, and, that for that and other reasons, the New York statute should be sustained. But the Court of Appeals of New York had said that it found no material difference between the two statutes, and this Court held that the "meaning of the statute" as fixed by the decision of the state court "must be accepted here as if the meaning had been specifically expressed in the enactment." That view led the affirmance by this Court of the judgment in the *Morehead* case, as the Court considered that the only question before it was whether the *Adkins* case was distinguishable, and that reconsideration of that decision had not been sought. Upon that point, the Court said:

> The petition for the writ sought review upon the ground that this case [*Morehead*] is distinguishable from that one [*Adkins*]. No application has been made for reconsideration of the constitutional question there decided. The validity of the principles upon which that decision rests is not challenged. This court confines itself to the ground upon which the writ was asked or granted. . . . Here, the review granted was no broader than that sought by the petitioner. . . . He is not entitled, and does not ask, to be heard upon the question whether the *Adkins* case should be overruled. He maintains that it may be distinguished on the ground that the statutes are vitally dissimilar.

We think that the question which was not deemed to be open in the *Morehead* case is open and is necessarily presented here. The Supreme Court of Washington has upheld the minimum wage statute of that State. It has decided that the statute is a reasonable exercise of the police power of the State. In reaching that conclusion, the state court has invoked principles long established by this Court in the application of the Fourteenth Amendment. The state court has refused to regard the decision in the *Adkins* case as determinative, and has pointed to our decisions both before and since that case as justifying its position. We are of the opinion that this ruling of the state court demands on our part a reexamination of the *Adkins* case. The importance of the question, in which many States having similar laws are concerned, the close division by which the decision in the *Adkins* case was reached, and the economic conditions which have supervened, and in the light of which the reasonableness of the exercise of the protective power of the State must be considered, make it not only appropriate, but we think imperative, that, in deciding the present case, the subject should receive fresh consideration.

The history of the litigation of this question may be briefly stated. The minimum wage statute of Washington was enacted over twenty-three years ago. Prior to the decision in the instant case, it had twice been held valid by the Supreme Court of the State. *Larsen v. Rice*; *Spokane Hotel Co. v. Younger*. The Washington statute is essentially the same as that enacted in Oregon in the same year. Laws of 1913 (Oregon) chap. 62. The validity of the latter act was sustained by the Supreme Court of Oregon in *Stettler v. O'Hara*, and *Simpson v. O'Hara*. These cases, after reargument, were affirmed here by an equally divided court, in 1917. The law of Oregon thus continued in effect. The District of Columbia Minimum Wage Law was enacted in 1918. The statute was sustained by the Supreme Court of the District in the *Adkins* case. Upon appeal, the Court of Appeals of the District first affirmed that ruling, but, on rehearing, reversed it, and the case came before this Court in 1923. The judgment of the Court of Appeals holding the Act invalid was affirmed, but with Chief Justice Taft, Mr. Justice Holmes and Mr. Justice Sanford dissenting, and Mr. Justice Brandeis taking no part. The dissenting opinions took the ground that the decision was at variance with the principles which this Court had frequently announced and applied. In 1925 and 1927, the similar minimum wage statutes of Arizona and Arkansas were held invalid upon the authority of the *Adkins* case. The Justices who had dissented in that case bowed to the ruling, and Mr. Justice Brandeis dissented. *Murphy v. Sardell*; *Donham v. West-Nelson Co*. The question did not come before us again until the last term in the *Morehead* case, as already noted. In that case, briefs supporting the New York statute were submitted by the States of Ohio, Connecticut, Illinois, Massachusetts, New Hampshire, New Jersey and Rhode Island. Throughout this entire period, the Washington statute now under consideration has been in force.

The principle which must control our decision is not in doubt. The constitutional provision invoked is the due process clause of the Fourteenth Amendment, governing the States, as the due process clause invoked in the *Adkins* case governed Congress. In each case, the violation alleged by those attacking minimum wage regulation for women is deprivation of freedom of contract. What is this freedom? The Constitution does not speak of freedom of contract. It speaks of liberty and prohibits the deprivation of liberty without due process of law. In prohibiting that deprivation, the Constitution does not recognize an absolute and uncontrollable liberty. Liberty in each of its phases has its history and connotation. But the liberty safeguarded is liberty in a social organization which requires the protection of law against the evils which menace the health, safety, morals and welfare of the people. Liberty under the Constitution is thus necessarily subject to the restraints of due process, and regulation which is reasonable in relation to its subject and is adopted in the interests of the community is due process.

This essential limitation of liberty in general governs freedom of contract in particular. More than twenty-five years ago, we set forth the applicable principle in these words, after referring to the cases where the liberty guaranteed by the Fourteenth Amendment had been broadly described:

> But it was recognized in the cases cited, as in many others, that freedom of contract is a qualified, and not an absolute, right. There is no absolute freedom to do as one wills or to contract as one chooses. The guaranty of liberty does not withdraw from legislative supervision that wide department of activity which consists of the making of contracts, or deny to government the power to provide restrictive safeguards. Liberty implies the absence of arbitrary restraint, not immunity from reasonable regulations and prohibitions imposed in the interests of the community.

This power under the Constitution to restrict freedom of contract has had many illustrations. That it may be exercised in the public interest with respect to contracts between employer and employee is undeniable. Thus, statutes have been sustained limiting employment in underground mines and smelters to eight hours a day; in requiring redemption in cash of store orders or other evidences of indebtedness issued in the payment of wages; in forbidding the payment of seamen's wages in advance; in making it unlawful to contract to pay miners employed at quantity rates upon the basis of screened coal instead of the weight of the coal as originally produced in the mine; in prohibiting contracts limiting liability for injuries to employees; in limiting hours of work of employees in manufacturing establishments, and in maintaining workmen's compensation laws. In dealing with the relation of employer and employed, the legislature has necessarily a wide field of discretion in order that there may be suitable protection of health and safety, and that peace and good order may be promoted through regulations designed to insure wholesome conditions of work and freedom from oppression.

The point that has been strongly stressed that adult employees should be deemed competent to make their own contracts was decisively met nearly forty years ago in *Holden v. Hardy, supra*, where we pointed out the inequality in the footing of the parties. We said:

> The legislature has also recognized the fact, which the experience of legislators in many States has corroborated, that the proprietors of these establishments and their operatives do not stand upon an equality, and that their interests are, to a certain extent, conflicting. The former naturally desire to obtain as much labor as possible from their employees, while the latter are often induced by the fear of discharge to conform to regulations which their judgment, fairly exercised, would pronounce to be detrimental to their health or

> strength. In other words, the proprietors lay down the rules and the laborers are practically constrained to obey them. In such cases, self-interest is often an unsafe guide, and the legislature may properly interpose its authority.

And we added that the fact

> "that both parties are of full age and competent to contract does not necessarily deprive the State of the power to interfere where the parties do not stand upon an equality, or where the public health demands that one party to the contract shall be protected against himself."
>
> "The State still retains an interest in his welfare, however reckless he may be. The whole is no greater than the sum of all the parts, and when the individual health, safety and welfare are sacrificed or neglected, the State must suffer."

It is manifest that this established principle is peculiarly applicable in relation to the employment of women, in whose protection the State has a special interest. That phase of the subject received elaborate consideration in *Muller v. Oregon*, where the constitutional authority of the State to limit the working hours of women was sustained. We emphasized the consideration that "woman's physical structure and the performance of maternal functions place her at a disadvantage in the struggle for subsistence," and that her physical wellbeing "becomes an object of public interest and care in order to preserve the strength and vigor of the race." We emphasized the need of protecting women against oppression despite her possession of contractual rights. We said that,

> though limitations upon personal and contractual rights may be removed by legislation, there is that in her disposition and habits of life which will operate against a full assertion of those rights. She will still be where some legislation to protect her seems necessary to secure a real equality of right.

Hence, she was "properly placed in a class by herself, and legislation designed for her protection may be sustained even when like legislation is not necessary for men and could not be sustained."

We concluded that the limitations which the statute there in question "placed upon her contractual powers, upon her right to agree with her employer as to the time she shall labor," were "not imposed solely for her benefit, but also largely for the benefit of all." Again, in *Quong Wing v. Kirkenda* in referring to a differentiation with respect to the employment of women, we said that the Fourteenth Amendment did not interfere with state power by creating a "fictitious equality." We referred to recognized classifications on the basis of sex with regard to hours of work and in other matters, and we observed that the particular points at which that difference shall be enforced by legislation were largely in the power of the State. In later rulings, this Court sustained the regulation of hours of work of women employees.

This array of precedents and the principles they applied were thought by the dissenting Justices in the *Adkins* case to demand that the minimum wage statute be sustained. The validity of the distinction made by the Court between a minimum wage and a maximum of hours in limiting liberty of contract was especially challenged. That challenge persists, and is without any satisfactory answer. As Chief Justice Taft observed:

> In absolute freedom of contract, the one term is as important as the other, for both enter equally into the consideration given and received, a restriction as to the one is not greater,

> in essence, than the other, and is of the same kind. One is the multiplier, and the other the multiplicand.

And Mr. Justice Holmes, while recognizing that "the distinctions of the law are distinctions of degree," could

> perceive no difference in the kind or degree of interference with liberty, the only matter with which we have any concern, between the one case and the other. The bargain is equally affected whichever half you regulate.

One of the points which was pressed by the Court in supporting its ruling in the *Adkins* case was that the standard set up by the District of Columbia Act did not take appropriate account of the value of the services rendered. In the *Morehead* case, the minority thought that the New York statute had met that point in its definition of a "fair wage," and that it accordingly presented a distinguishable feature which the Court could recognize within the limits which the *Morehead* petition for certiorari was deemed to present. The Court, however, did not take that view, and the New York Act was held to be essentially the same as that for the District of Columbia. The statute now before us is like the latter, but we are unable to conclude that, in its minimum wage requirement, the State has passed beyond the boundary of its broad protective power.

The minimum wage to be paid under the Washington statute is fixed after full consideration by representatives of employers, employees and the public. It may be assumed that the minimum wage is fixed in consideration of the services that are performed in the particular occupations under normal conditions. Provision is made for special licenses at less wages in the case of women who are incapable of full service. The statement of Mr. Justice Holmes in the *Adkins* case is pertinent:

> This statute does not compel anybody to pay anything. It simply forbids employment at rates below those fixed as the minimum requirement of health and right living. It is safe to assume that women will not be employed at even the lowest wages allowed unless they earn them, or unless the employer's business can sustain the burden. In short the law, in its character and operation, is like hundreds of so-called police laws that have been upheld.

And Chief Justice Taft forcibly pointed out the consideration which is basic in a statute of this character:

> Legislatures which adopt a requirement of maximum hours or minimum wages may be presumed to believe that, when sweating employers are prevented from paying unduly low wages by positive law, they will continue their business, abating that part of their profits which were wrung from the necessities of their employees, and will concede the better terms required by the law, and that, while in individual cases hardship may result, the restriction will enure to the benefit of the general class of employees in whose interest the law is passed, and so to that of the community at large.

We think that the views thus expressed are sound, and that the decision in the *Adkins* case was a departure from the true application of the principles governing the regulation by the State of the relation of employer and employed. Those principles have been reenforced by our subsequent decisions. Thus, in *Radice v. New York*, we sustained the New York statute which restricted the employment of women in restaurants at night. In *O'Gorman & Young v. Hartford Fire Insurance*

Co., which upheld an act regulating the commissions of insurance agents, we pointed to the presumption of the constitutionality of a statute dealing with a subject within the scope of the police power and to the absence of any factual foundation of record for deciding that the limits of power had been transcended. In *Nebbia v. New York*, dealing with the New York statute providing for minimum prices for milk, the general subject of the regulation of the use of private property and of the making of private contracts received an exhaustive examination, and we again declared that, if such laws

> have a reasonable relation to a proper legislative purpose, and are neither arbitrary nor discriminatory, the requirements of due process are satisfied;

that

> with the wisdom of the policy adopted, with the adequacy or practicability of the law enacted to forward it, the courts are both incompetent and unauthorized to deal;

that

> times without number, we have said that the legislature is primarily the judge of the necessity of such an enactment, that every possible presumption is in favor of its validity, and that, though the court may hold views inconsistent with the wisdom of the law, it may not be annulled unless palpably in excess of legislative power.

With full recognition of the earnestness and vigor which characterize the prevailing opinion in the *Adkins* case, we find it impossible to reconcile that ruling with these well considered declarations. What can be closer to the public interest than the health of women and their protection from unscrupulous and overreaching employers? And if the protection of women is a legitimate end of the exercise of state power, how can it be said that the requirement of the payment of a minimum wage fairly fixed in order to meet the very necessities of existence is not an admissible means to that end? The legislature of the State was clearly entitled to consider the situation of women in employment, the fact that they are in the class receiving the least pay, that their bargaining power is relatively weak, and that they are the ready victims of those who would take advantage of their necessitous circumstances. The legislature was entitled to adopt measures to reduce the evils of the "sweating system," the exploiting of workers at wages so low as to be insufficient to meet the bare cost of living, thus making their very helplessness the occasion of a most injurious competition. The legislature had the right to consider that its minimum wage requirements would be an important aid in carrying out its policy of protection. The adoption of similar requirements by many States evidences a deep-seated conviction both as to the presence of the evil and as to the means adapted to check it. Legislative response to that conviction cannot be regarded as arbitrary or capricious, and that is all we have to decide. Even if the wisdom of the policy be regarded as debatable and its effects uncertain, still the legislature is entitled to its judgment.

There is an additional and compelling consideration which recent economic experience has brought into a strong light. The exploitation of a class of workers who are in an unequal position with respect to bargaining power, and are thus relatively defenceless against the denial of a living wage, is not only detrimental to their health and wellbeing, but casts a direct burden for their support upon the community. What these workers lose in wages, the taxpayers are called upon to pay. The bare cost of living must be met. We may take judicial notice of the unparalleled demands for relief which arose during the recent period of depression and still continue to an alarming extent despite the degree of economic recovery which has been achieved. It is unnecessary to cite official statistics to establish what is of common knowledge through the length and breadth of the land. While, in the instant case, no factual brief has been presented, there is no reason to doubt that the State of Washington has encountered the same social problem that is present elsewhere. The community is not bound to provide what is, in effect, a subsidy for unconscionable employers. The community may direct its lawmaking power to correct the abuse which springs from their selfish disregard of the public interest. The argument that the legislation in question constitutes an arbitrary discrimination, because it does not extend to men, is unavailing. This Court has frequently held that the legislative authority, acting within its proper field, is not bound to extend its regulation to all cases which it might possibly reach. The legislature "is free to recognize degrees of harm and it may confine its restrictions to those classes of cases where the need is deemed to be clearest." If "the law presumably hits the evil where it is most felt, it is not to be overthrown because there are other instances to which it might have been applied."

There is no "doctrinaire requirement" that the legislation should be couched in all embracing terms. This familiar principle has repeatedly been applied to legislation which singles out women, and particular classes of women, in the exercise of the State's protective power. Their relative need in the presence of the evil, no less than the existence of the evil itself, is a matter for the legislative judgment.

Our conclusion is that the case of *Adkins v. Children's Hospital, supra*, should be, and it is, overruled. The judgment of the Supreme Court of the State of Washington is *Affirmed*.

The Impact of *West Coast Hotel v. Parrish* on the Institution of Economy in the United States

There is strong agreement that there was a dramatic shift in the Supreme Court's position on matters dealing with the economy of the United States in the mid to late 1930s with the *West Coast Hotel v. Parrish* decision being the first among those auguring in the substantial shift (Waltman, 2006). Economy, as we saw in Chapter 2, is the social institution responsible for the production, distribution, and consumption of goods and services. The United States' economy is largely capitalist, which means property and the means of production are privately owned, and prices are set by supply and demand among consumers in a competitive marketplace which operates without government interference, under a *laissez faire* (hands off) policy. However, the US economy in practice is mixed, meaning free market practices exist side-by-side with government interventions. How, then, did the Supreme Court's declaring state minimum wage laws for women impact the institution of the economy in the United States?

Since human labor is involved in production, distribution, and consumption—and is *in itself* a "good" and "service," it was a very large impact. It was a stark departure from other Supreme Court decisions in the 20th century, which had for the most part upheld the more *laissez faire* approach to capitalism where there is little state intervention in the workplace which was prevalent in the 19th century. In that era, the law was supportive of the notion that the exchange of one's labor for a wage was a private matter between the employee and the employers, the buyer and seller of goods (Van Wezel, 1981). Right up until *West Coast Hotel v. Parrish*, the Supreme Court abided by a very expansive view of the Due Process Clause of the Fourteenth Amendment to strike down most regulation of state economies (Waltman, 2006). In fact, the Court was "one of the major obstacles to wage-hour and child labor laws" (Grossman, 2020). It even ruled in 1936 in a notorious and unpopular decision (*Morehead v. Tipaldo)*, that laundry women in New York paid only 10 dollars a week in violation of New York's minimum wage law by their boss were not entitled constitutional protection. The case created so much uproar it was labeled 'The new Dred Scott' (Grossman, 2020).

Following the *West Coast Hotel v. Parrish* ruling, it became clear the Supreme Court justices now were open to the view that wages were not only a private matter, but one of public concern (Van Wezel, 1981), and states were justified in using their police powers in those matters (Oyez, 2020). That this consensus emerged out of the Great Depression, amid President Franklin Roosevelt's successful reelection campaign and enormously popular "New Deal," to get the United States' economy roaring again, shows how the Supreme Court is embedded deeply in social, economic, and political history. Indeed, only a few weeks after *West Coast Hotel v. Parrish*, other major Supreme Court cases with impacts on the economy of the United States showed the willingness of the court to allow government regulation, allowing for the constitutionality of the Social Security Act, the Wagner Labor Act (Alexander, 2013). A year later, the Fair Labor Standard Act of 1938 set the minimum hourly wage at 25 cents an hour, and ended "oppressive" child labor, among other interventions and reforms (Grossman, 2020). In the following paragraphs, we discuss first briefly, how two of the most influential classical sociological theorists—Karl Marx and Max Weber—have interpreted the minimum wage, before looking at the impact of the Supreme Court's ruling on the economy both broadly and for specific subsets of the population.

Two Sociologists' Viewpoints on Minimum Wage: Max Weber and Karl Marx

As we learned in Chapter 2, Karl Marx was a 19th century German-born philosopher and sociologist, argued that class warfare is endemic to capitalist systems. Capitalism is set up to pit the interests of the workers against those who owned the means of producing goods and services, the capitalists, whose motive is to extract as much profit as possible from the worker's labor, regardless of the human costs. Consequently, he rejects the idea that workers and capitalists meet in a marketplace and have a "fair" exchange of a wage in exchange for labor—even if that wage offered is above what is minimally necessary for survival. Wages for labor only partially pay for the full value of what the worker has produced—in other words, the worker is exploited. If this were not the case, if the capitalist did pay the worker for all of the value she produced, profits would disappear. There always must be more value added by the worker than that which existed beforehand because human labor, for Marx, is the value of any good or service. The more profit the workers produce in relation to how much they are compensated, the more they are exploited by the capitalist.

In relation to the minimum wage, Marx's writings make clear he does not think that workers should unite merely for a "fair" wage, but to abolish the entire system of wages entirely (Marx, 1865) in favor of a different economic system, e.g. socialism. He argues that the "general level of wages," for workers are not just a freely set number determined between two parties, reliant on supply and demand. They also are generally determined by the minimum amount of payment that would be necessary to make sure the worker is able to survive and keep doing his or her work, and reproduce more workers. He claims that the wage also depends on the relative strength of the "two adversaries" in the struggle (e.g. workers and capitalists). If the workers gain more power, they have the ability to increase the wage, but the more power the capitalist exerts, the more that wage can be limited (Garcia Abalos, 1997, p. 98). The sheer vast number of workers, the 'reserve army of the unemployed,' means though that it is easy for capitalists to keep wages extremely low, as there are always more low-skilled employees.

In the *West Coast Hotel v. Parrish* decision, faced with the kind of harsh industrial exploitation of the working class that Marx had described, where employers'

> abuses of their employees came at a significant cost to society . . . the [Supreme] Court had found itself unable to respond to the harsh realities of capitalism and the modern economy . . . they couldn't be neutral when there was such a huge power imbalance.
>
> *(Martens, 2007, pp. 99–100)*

Capitalism, then, was not allowed to run completely unfettered, but was brought back to an ideal of human rights and fundamental fairness.

Unlike Marx, Max Weber, also a German philosopher and sociologist born in the 19th century, did not see class struggle as the unilateral driver of societal change, and had his own thought about the minimum wage. He did agree with Marx that a 'surplus population,' of cheap workers were necessary for capitalism to develop. He pointed out problems with having wages so low that they could not sustain a worker that went beyond exploitation, mentioning that

> the efficiency of labor decreases with a wage that is physiologically unfit . . . low wages fail even from a purely business point of view wherever it is a question of producing goods which require skills, expensive machinery, attention or initiative . . . here low wages do not pay and the effect is the opposite of that which is intended.

To have efficient and effective capitalism, workers must be able to physically and mentally perform the task well, and that requires a reasonable wage. Even if wages are poor, though, Weber says that a capitalist society has so conditioned us to see work as noble in itself—an almost religious calling—that there is rarely any difficulty for the capitalist in recruiting a labor force (Weber, 1905).

Patriarchy, the Minimum Wage for Women, and the Continued Wage Gap

Important to remember about *West Coast Hotel v. Parrish* and its impact on the US economy was that it specifically dealt with the minimum wage for women in states, although it did pave the way for also upholding the minimum wage for men in the *United States v. Darby* decision. The FLSA, as mentioned, established a federal minimum wage and set a limit on the maximum of hours that could be worked by men *and* women.

The decision's text points out that women are different than men, and therefore the state has a "special" interest in their protection. However well-intended, the language reinforced patriarchy and the paternalism of the state toward women. According to the justices, the reason why women would "need" the protections afforded by minimum wages is that they are more vulnerable: They are more likely to be exploited, their health is "related to the vigor of the race," in other words, because women are capable of reproducing, their health impacts that also of children. Also, the Court stated that if women are denied a living wage it not only affects their health, but necessitates their "support" by others in the community. State attempts to carve out regulations became "gendered exceptions" (as was the *West Coast Hotel* decision) with a kind of maternalistic rationale to protect them based on sexist conceptions of women and their roles (Martens, 2007).

The gendered exception which the Supreme Court approved in *West Coast Hotel v. Parrish* did not come about without a strong women's movement with constitutional activism.

However, this exception was not only promoted to help women at first, but perversely, to keep them from having wages so low that they could take jobs away from men. Labor movements in the early 20th century saw women's entry into the workforce as competing with—and undercutting—men's work. By 1910, women were 21 percent of the workforce in the US, and so "Labor reformers wanted to protect employment *from* women as much as they wanted to protect women from employment. Reformers who led the campaign for minimum wages accused them of undercutting male breadwinners entitled to a 'family wage'" (Leonard, 20 1 6).

Since *West Coast Hotel v. Parrish*'s intervention on behalf of female workers, other interventions have been made to ensure that women are not being exploited. In 1963 President John Kennedy signed into law the Equal Pay Act, which mandated that the federal minimum wage had to be paid the same, for the same work, regardless of gender. Currently, women, who make up 47 percent of the workforce (DeWolf, 2017) are still overrepresented among the low-wage workforce and among minimum wage workers, even as they are more likely than they were in the time of *West Coast Hotel v. Parrish* to be heads of households with children. Yet, they have made great gains in their income, especially since the 1970s, and have narrowed the **gender gap**, that is—average difference between the wages and salaries of women and men, across all educational levels. Still, this gap persists, and not only because of policies that can be regulated. Because in the household division of labor in heterosexual relationships women continue to be primarily responsible for childcare and housework, this uncompensated labor can take away from hours dedicated to work (Blau & Kahn, 2017).

Socio-Economic Impact of Minimum Wage Laws

State minimum wages that were constitutionally viable after *West Coast Hotel v. Parrish* adopted rates that were above the federal minimum and vary state-by-state. Key arguments in favor of these laws were improving the general economic circumstances of individuals, families, and communities, and the US economy as whole. The logic here is that if people have higher wages, and are healthier economically and physically, they also have more power to purchase and consume other goods and services, and do not need to be dependent on government subsidies made possible through taxes. However, sociologists and other social scientists have found that the impact of these laws has been mixed, both in terms of economic outcomes and broad social outcomes, like physical and mental well-being.

Wage inequalities since the 1970s have been linked to socioeconomic disparities in health. As we might predict, lower income individuals have shorter average life expectancies and more chronic diseases than their wealthier counterparts. Higher minimum wages have been associated in some studies with positive health outcomes, such as reduced mortality rates by suicide and certain illnesses such as diabetes or cardiovascular disease. However, other studies have shown that for certain subsets of the population, they may have the opposite effect. For example, positive associations (e.g. increases) were found between the minimum wage, obesity and Body Mass Index (BMI) in working-age male adults under 35 years of age who were non-White. Yet, the same study showed the minimum wage was associated with lower hypertension among working-age men. Overall, the consequences of these minimum wage laws differ according to a range of factors, from gender, race, and age to the types of additional labor regulations found within the state (Buszkiewicz, Dill, & Otten, 2020).

Much debate exists over the more direct economic impact of the minimum wage on workers. Do prices increase when the minimum wage increases? Do some people lose jobs if employers hire fewer people, as standard economic theory predicts? Again, there are heterogenous results from social scientists which means that easy conclusions are hard to make. Some studies have shown no negative repercussions like significantly higher prices or lowered employment associated with increasing the minimum wage. Yet, others have pointed to some unintended outcomes. For example, while some workers may benefit from higher wages, others may lose their jobs due to it, or have their hours cut (Ford, Minor, & Owens, 2012). In New York, minimum wage increases have led to adverse consequences for low-skilled employment (Sabia, Burkhauser, & Hansen, 2016). Higher minimum wages can lure teenagers away from school, lowering enrollment, and leading to lower lifelong earnings (Ford et al., 2012). "The overall body of recent evidence suggests that the most credible conclusion is a higher minimum wage results in some job loss for the least-skilled workers" (Neumark, 2015).

Current Minimum Wage Laws and Attitudes in the United States

Since Massachusetts enacted the first minimum wage law in 1912, 110 years later, the expansion of such laws and the federal minimum wage have meant that the economy of the United States largely assumes their continuance, even if debate exists about how much the hourly wage should be. Employers have to abide under penalty by regulation that sets the minimum floor for the price of labor. In fact, every employer subject to the FLSA has to keep a notice of workers' rights in a readily visible place so employees can read it. So, while the price of labor may fluctuate depending on a host of factors such as education, qualifications, and training, it is not like other goods in being able to hypothetically have a "price" that is entirely set by demand or willingness to pay. Even if someone is willing to work for below minimum wage, an employer covered by the FLSA cannot accept this bargain. Furthermore, within the confines of the United States' federalist system, states have decided to require that minimum hourly wages are even higher than that set by the federal government. As of 2019, 29 states—more than half—plus Washington D.C. have minimum wage laws (made constitutionally viable due to *West Coast Hotel v. Parrish*) that exceed the federal standard, which covers about 61 percent of the working age population. Some have even pegged this wage to the cost of living in those areas. As federal minimum wage cycles can last for long periods of time without an increase (for example, one cycle lasted from 1997–2006), states' politicians may feel pressured to act more quickly (Ford et al., 2012).

Most US workers are hourly workers—approximately 60 percent (BLS, 2018). Nearly half (42.4 percent) of working Americans make less than $15 per hour (TCF, 2019). Since almost 21 million people work for close to their respective states' minimum wage—30 percent of all hourly workers over 18 who are not self-employed—it is an issue that affects large swaths of the US population, but is especially salient for certain demographics. Minimum wage workers tend to be young, with a higher percentage of women, those without a high school diploma, the never-married, and those who reside in southern states, making wages at or below the federal minimum (BLS, 2018). Cashiers, retail salespeople, waitstaff, and janitors are all common occupations for which minimum wages are offered. About 2.2 million working people are paid the federal minimum wage of $7.25 an hour or less. Overall, US voters are supportive of minimum wage increases. In looking at the federal minimum wage, 52 percent of people favored increasing the federal minimum to $15 an hour, with support falling heavily along racial lines. Hispanics and Blacks support the measure by large majorities, whereas a majority of White voters (54 percent) oppose it (Desilver, 2017).

Review Questions

1. How did the court rule in the *Phillips* case? What reasoning did the court use?
2. How did the *West Coast Hotel* case impact the US economy?

3. How did Karl Marx's view on the minimum wage differ from Max Weber's view?
4. What aspects of gender inequality in occupations persist in spite of *Phillips v. Martin Marietta*?
5. Describe the socio-economic impact of minimum wage laws in the US.

References

Alexander, G. L. (2013). Parrish v. West Coast hotel company: A Chelan County chambermaid makes history. *Columbia: The Magazine of Northwest History*, 1–4.

Becker, M. (2000). Caring the Children and Caretakers. Chi.-Kent L. Rev., 76, 1495-1539.

Blau, F. D., & Kahn, L. M. (2017). The gender wage gap: Extent, trends, and explanations. *Journal of Economic Literature*, *55*(3), 789–865.

Bryant, M. (2020, January 27). Maternity leave: US policy is worst on the list of the world's richest countries. *The Guardian*.

Bureau of Labor Statistics (BLS). (2018). *Characteristics of minimum wage workers, 2017*. Retrieved from www.bls.gov/opub/reports/minimum-wage/2017/home.htm

Buszkiewicz, J. H., Dill, H. D., & Otten, J. J. (2020). Association of state minimum wage rates and health in working age adults using the national health interview survey. *American Journal of Epidemiology*, advance access publication.

The Century Foundation (TCF). (2019). *Making the economic case for $15 an hour*. Retrieved from https://tcf.org/content/commentary/making-economic-case-15-minimum-wage/?agreed=1

Chamallas, M. (1999). Mothers and disparate treatment: The ghost of Martin Marietta. *Villanova Law Review*, *44*(3), 337–355.

Christopher, K. (2012). Employed mothers' construction of the good mother. *Gender and Society*, *26*(1), 73–96.

Cohen, P. (2012, December 11). More women are doctors and lawyers than ever—but progress is stalling. *The Atlantic*.

Desilver, D. (2017). *5 facts about the minimum wage*. Pew Research Center. Retrieved from www.pewresearch.org/fact-tank/2017/01/04/5-facts-about-the-minimum-wage/corrected in text

DeWolf, M. (2017). *Twelve stats about working women*. Blog post, Retrieved from https://blog. dol.gov/2017/03/01/12-stats-about-working-women

Donovan Fitzpatrick, M. (2010). Preschoolers enrolled and mothers at work? The effects of universal pre-kindergarten. *Journal of Labor Economics*, *28*(1), 51–85.

Dunbar, G. R., & Easton, S. T. (2013). Working parents and total factor productivity growth. *Journal of Popular Economics*, *26*, 1431–1456.

Ford, W. F., Minor, T., & Owens, M. F. (2012). State minimum wage differences: Economic factors or political inclinations. *Business Economics*, *47*, 57–67.

Garcia Abalos, J. M. (1997). The distribution of national income: Theory and practice of Marxist analysis. *International Journal of Political Economy*, *27*(4), 96–114.

Goldman, B. (2012, January 1). *The switch in time that saved nine: A study of justice Owen Roberts's vote in West Coast hotel Co. v. Parrish*. College Undergraduate Research Electronic Journal. Philadelphia: University of Pennsylvania.

Grossman, J. (2020). *Fair labor standards act of 1938: Maximum struggle for a minimum wage*. US Department of Labor. Retrieved from www.dol.gov/general/aboutdol/history/flsa1938

Hartmann, H., Hayes, J., Huber, R., Rolfes-Haase, K., & Suh, J. (2018). *The shifting supply and demand of care work: The growing role of people of color and immigrants*. The Institute for Women's Policy Research. Retrieved from https://iwpr.org/publications/supply-demand-care-work-immigrants-people-of-color/

Kaminer, D. N. (2004). The work-family conflict: Developing a model of parental accommodation in the workplace. *American University Law Review*, *54*(2), 305–360.

Lease, K. (2019). A reasonable solution for working parents. *William & Mary Journal of Race, Gender, and Social Justice*, *25*, 209–735.

Leonard, T. C. (2016). Minimum wages were first designed to keep women and minorities out of jobs. *The Los Angeles Times*.

Lindsey, L. (1997). *Gender roles: A sociological perspective*. Upper Saddle River, NJ: Prentice Hall.

Martens, A. M. (2007). *A movement of one's own? American social movements and constitutional development in the twentieth century* (PhD Dissertation). The University of Texas, Austin.
Marx, K. (1865). *The struggle between capital and labor and its results.* Retrieved from www.marxists.org/archive/marx/works/1865/value-price-profit/ch03.htm
Neumark, D. (2015). The effects of minimum wages on employment. *Federal Research Bank of San Francisco Economic Letter.* Retrieved from www.frbsf.org/economic-research/publications/economic-letter/2015/december/effects-of-minimum-wage-on-employment/
Pew. (2020). *Women make gains in workplace amid rising demand for skilled workers.* Retrieved from www.pewsocialtrends.org
Sabia, J. J., Burkhauser, R. V., & Hansen, B. (2016). Are the effects of minimum wage increases always small? New evidence from a case study of New York State. *HR Review, 69*(2), 312–319.
van Wezel Stone, K. (1981). The post-war paradigm in American labor law. *The Yale Law Journal, 90*(7), 1509–1508.
Waltman, J. (2006). Supreme court activism in economic policy in the warning days of the new deal: Interpreting the fair labor standards act 1941–1946. *Journal of Supreme Court History, 31,* 58–80.
Washington Center for Equitable Growth (WCEG). (2017). *Occupational segregation in the United States.* Retrieved from https://equitablegrowth.org/fact-sheet-occupational-segregation-in-the-united-states/
Weber, M. (1905). *The protestant ethic and the spirit of capitalism* (Chapter 2). Retrieved from www.marxists.org/reference/archive/weber/protestant-ethic/ch02.htm
West Coast Hotel Company v. Parrish. (n.d.). *Oyez.* Retrieved July 21, 2020, from www.oyez.org/cases/1900-1940/300us379

INDEX

Page numbers in *italics* indicate a figure on the corresponding page.

For Product Safety Concerns and Information please contact our EU representative GPSR@taylorandfrancis.com
Taylor & Francis Verlag GmbH, Kaufingerstraße 24, 80331 München, Germany

www.ingramcontent.com/pod-product-compliance
Ingram Content Group UK Ltd.
Pitfield, Milton Keynes, MK11 3LW, UK
UKHW050234200926
475702UK00020B/3035
9780367898489